Praise for *Math Games for Independent Practice . . .*

This resource is my number one go-to resource for planning my mathematics workshop! Having taught elementary-age students for seventeen years, it is my experience that the best way to get students involved with mathematics—to really examine the operations they are practicing and strategies that will improve their facility with number—is through games. The games in *Math Games for Independent Practice* are meaningful, fun, and filled with great ideas for extensions and alternative ways to play. I love that I can find a game to meet the needs of all learners in my classroom with one resource. The organization, practicality of use, and insights into how children learn are invaluable. It is evident that Jamee has practiced and applied these games; she writes with a true practitioner's point of view. I am equally excited to use this resource with my elementary-age students and to get it into the hands of my colleagues.

—*Kristin Cayo, fifth-grade teacher, Forest Hills Elementary, Eden Prairie, Minnesota*

Gamelike activities develop intuitive attention and engagement in the classroom. Hattie (2009) reported strong percentile gains (13%–18%) in student achievement as noted in his meta-analysis. This compilation of classroom games is wonderful! It clearly shares the connected CCSS, the materials needed, a thorough synopsis of each game, along with recommended grades and time frames. Jamee has captured academic games as a great way for teachers to help students deepen their understanding of key concepts.

—*Dr. Tammy Heflebower, Vice President, Marzano Research Laboratory*

Jamee Petersen has created a fantastic resource of math games. These super-engaging games invite opportunities for deep thinking and ongoing practice. They are an ideal addition to the math workshop. Teachers will love this book because it is so useful and mathematically rich; students will love the games because they are fun!

—*Maggie Siena, author,* From Reading to Math: How Best Practices in Literacy Can Make You a Better Math Teacher, Grades K–5

This is an excellent resource to extend and reinforce critical concepts in elementary math. The games are incredibly engaging for students and are well thought out for teachers to introduce quickly and use. The teaching tips, ideas for differentiation, and ready-made reproducibles make this resource an invaluable addition to every elementary math classroom.

—*Emily Puetz, Chief Academic Officer, Minneapolis Public Schools*

Jamee is a classroom teacher who clearly understands what is needed in a math resource. The games are structured for high engagement of the learners and grounded in essential mathematical concepts. The teacher-friendly format offers technology tips, Common Core connections, key questions to ask students, connections to writing, time-saving ideas, assessment suggestions, and ways to address the needs of all learners in a classroom. The resource is a "must have" for classroom teachers wanting to increase active engagement in their math lessons.

—*Sue Feigal-Hitch, district coordinator of gifted programs, Eden Prairie School District, Eden Prairie, Minnesota*

MATH GAMES
for Independent Practice

MATH GAMES
for Independent Practice

Games to Support
Math Workshops
and More

Math Solutions
Sausalito, California, USA

JAMEE PETERSEN

Math Solutions
One Harbor Drive, Suite 101
Sausalito, California, USA 94965
www.mathsolutions.com

ISBN-13: 978-1-935099-43-7
ISBN-10: 1-935099-43-4

Editor: Jamie Ann Cross
Production: Denise A. Botelho
Cover and interior design: Susan Barclay, Barclay Design
Cover photos: iStockphoto
Composition: Susan Barclay, Barclay Design

3   4   5   6   7   8   9   10   31   22   21   20   19   18   17   16   15   14

A Message from Math Solutions

We at Math Solutions believe that teaching math well calls for increasing our understanding of the math we teach, seeking deeper insights into how students learn mathematics, and refining our lessons to best promote students' learning.

Math Solutions shares classroom-tested lessons and teaching expertise from our faculty of professional development consultants as well as from other respected math educators. Our publications are part of the nationwide effort we've made since 1984 that now includes

- more than five hundred face-to-face professional development programs each year for teachers and administrators in districts across the country;
- professional development books that span all math topics taught in kindergarten through high school;
- videos for teachers and for parents that show math lessons taught in actual classrooms;
- on-site visits to schools to help refine teaching strategies and assess student learning; and
- free online support, including grade-level lessons, book reviews, inservice information, and district feedback, all in our Math Solutions Online Newsletter.

For information about all of the products and services we have available, please visit our website at *www.mathsolutions.com.* You can also contact us to discuss math professional development needs by calling (800) 868-9092 or by sending an email to *info@mathsolutions.com.*

We're always eager for your feedback and interested in learning about your particular needs. We look forward to hearing from you.

FOUNDED BY MARILYN BURNS

To Blake
May you always love learning.

Contents

How to Use This Resource

*What we want from children who play games is for them to construct insights into the games, create mathematical strategies for winning the games, explain those insights and strategies to others in their own words, have good reasons for believing in their insights and that their strategies work, and respond appropriately to challenges to the adequacy of those reasons and strategies. **These are important skills to acquire not only for mathematics but also in life in general.***

—Michael S. Schiro, Associate Professor,
Boston College and author of numerous games articles

Why These Games?
The Selection Process

The games in this resource have been selected carefully through a three-step process:

1. First, each game was chosen for its success, time and time again, in helping students build their number sense. In *Math Games for Independent Practice,* you will find all-time favorites such as *Circles and Stars, Leftovers, Cross Out Singles,* and *Tens Go Fish.* You will also find games that you've likely not encountered before, as well as twists on some of your personal favorites!

2. Second, the list of games was narrowed to those games that can be played successfully by learners on their own, in math workshops, or at workstations.

3. Third, every game was considered carefully within the context of the Common Core State Standards, resulting in those that strongly support teaching with the Common Core (see the connections on pages xv–xxi).

My Story

When I first began teaching, I was constantly looking for resources to support my students' learning in the area of number. My search often led me to Math Solutions' publications. In later years, I became a consultant for Math Solutions. As I led professional development courses across the nation, I found that much of my time was dedicated to developing capacity and depth in the area of number. Teachers near and far wanted ways to support their learning as well as their learners in number sense.

Most recently, in my district I facilitated professional development for implementing math workshops. One component of a math workshop is games that support students' learning in number. I pulled some games from my library of resources and shared them enthusiastically with the workshop participants, who looked like children in a candy store! However, their excitement quickly turned to exasperation when they realized how much time it would take them to sift through their own resources to find more games. I went home that evening and

> I pulled some games from my library of resources and shared them enthusiastically with the workshop participants, who looked like children in a candy store! However, their excitement quickly turned to exasperation when they realized how much time it would take them to sift through their own resources to find more games . . . hence *Math Games for Independent Practice* was born.

mused over my stacks and stacks of books—some for certain grade bands; others for measurement, geometry, data, and number; and still others with a month-by-month approach. So many books to sift through, yet so little time to do it! I understood completely the exasperation of the workshop participants.

This was my cue. I needed to create a resource that offered a collection of games that focus on supporting number sense—a collection drawn from my more than twenty years of teaching experience. Hence, *Math Games for Independent Practice* was born.

Do I Have Time for These Games?

The instruction of each game takes approximately one math lesson or 60 minutes (some are slightly less than an hour and others are slightly more). The independent play of each game takes twenty to thirty minutes on average. It's important to note that every game is designed so students can ultimately play them independently, freeing you for time to do small-group instruction and more.

Do These Games Support My Curriculum?

The games offered within this resource support and sustain a math workshop model while complementing any math curriculum. The games support standards, with an emphasis on the Common Core State Standards.

How Is This Resource Organized?

Step-by-Step Instructions

The format of this resource is intended to be friendly and accessible for you, the teaching professional. Each game features step-by-step instructions, organized in four steps:

Part I: The Connection: Relate the game to students' ongoing work.

Part II: The Teaching: Introduce and model the game to students.

Part III: Active Engagement: Engage students to ensure they understand how to play the game.

Part IV: The Link: Students play the game independently.

These steps are adapted from the Math Solutions resource *From Reading to Math: How Best Practices in Literacy Can Make You a Better Math Teacher* by Maggie Siena (2009).

Tips

Various tips are included in the margins of each game for quick reference; these tips are intended to facilitate the teaching of the game, and give insights into managing game materials, how students might experience the game, how technology might assist when modeling the game, and more.

Key Questions

Every game includes key questions to ask students as you observe them playing. Asking these questions assists you in understanding how or whether students are developing strategies. By asking questions, students are given the opportunity to hear each other's thinking and to develop their own understanding of the content even further.

Differentiating Your Instruction and Assessments

Every game includes insights on how it can be modified according to the levels and needs of your students. Differentiation occurs when you alter content, process or product. In some cases, assessments are also included.

Reproducibles

As often as possible, game materials—especially game boards and recording sheets—are provided in reproducible format at the end of this book. As you might imagine, recording sheets encourage students to record their thinking; it is important for students to be able to articulate how they compute. It is equally valuable for other students to see how their partner is computing. Numeral cards and hundreds chart reproducibles are also included.

Game Directions

At the end of the resource, you will find a condensed page of each game's directions written for students (these reproducibles are numbered starting with the letter G). These directions can be reproduced and handed out as needed to facilitate the game, especially during math workshops. The directions support students' success in playing each game.

Get Started!

The games can be accessed in any order. To help you find the game you want as quickly as possible, three contents lists are provided:

This resource is written for professionals who wish to support students' understanding in learning about how numbers work. It's written to help students explore numbers by using materials, interacting with peers, talking about numbers, and deepening their understanding. This resource is written for us—the teachers and teaching professionals who want their students to succeed in mathematics. It is written with a love for learning, compassion for colleagues, and dedication to students past, present, and future. My hope is that *Math Games for Independent Practice* enriches the understanding of your students while minimizing your planning and preparation time. It's all here, so roll the dice!

Alphabetical List: Games Ordered Alphabetically by Title with Grade-Level Indication

Game	Recommended Grade Level						Page
	K	1	2	3	4	5	
1. A "Mazing" 100		X	X	X			1
2. Addition Table Trail		X	X	X			6
Variation: Multiplication Table Trail				X	X	X	
3. Addition Tic-Tac-Toe		X	X	X			12
4. Anything but Ten!	X	X	X				17
5. Build Ten	X	X	X				22
6. Circles and Stars			X	X			26
7. Close to 100				X	X	X	32
Variation: Close to 0					X	X	
Variation: Close to 20		X	X	X			
Variation: Close to 1,000				X	X	X	
8. Compare (Shake and Spill)	X	X					40
9. Cross Out Singles			X	X	X		45
10. Cross Out Sums		X	X				51
11. Digit Place (A Secret Number Quest)				X	X	X	56
12. Equation Building				X	X	X	61
13. Fifteen-Number Cross-Out			X	X	X		66
14. Finding Factors				X	X	X	72
15. Greater Than, Less Than, Equal To	X	X	X	X	X		78
16. Hit the Target (Mental Multiplication)					X	X	86
17. How Close to 0?				X	X	X	92
18. Leftovers with 15				X	X	X	98
Variation: Leftovers with 100					X	X	

continued

Alphabetical List: Games Ordered Alphabetically by Title with Grade-Level Indication, continued

Game	Recommended Grade Level						Page
	K	1	2	3	4	5	
19. Making Moves on the Hundreds Chart		X	X				103
20. Missing Addend or Factor (Salute!)			X	X	X	X	108
21. More!	X	X					113
22. Odd or Even?	X	X	X				119
23. Oh No! 20!		X	X	X			124
24. Order Up 21!						X	132
25. Pathways (Products Tic-Tac-Toe)					X	X	137
Variation: Times Ten					X	X	
26. Roll 6 for 100				X	X	X	141
27. Roll for $1.00			X	X	X	X	147
Variation: Roll for 1			X	X	X	X	
28. Spinning Sums and Differences			X	X	X	X	152
29. Take Five, Make Ten!				X	X	X	158
30. Target 300 (A Multiplication Game)				X	X	X	163
31. Target "Pick Your Sum"		X	X	X			170
32. Tens Go Fish	X	X	X				176
33. Wipeout (Fractional Relationships)					X	X	181

Connections Lists: Teaching with the Common Core State Standards for Mathematics

Kindergarten Connections

Kindergarten Common Core Standards	4. Anything but Ten!	5. Build Ten	8. Compare (Shake and Spill)	15. Greater Than, Less Than, Equal To	21. More!	22. Odd or Even?	32. Tens Go Fish
Counting and Cardinality							
Know number names and the count sequence.	X	X	X	X	X	X	X
Count to tell the number of objects.	X	X	X	X	X		X
Compare numbers.			X	X	X	X	
Operations and Algebraic Thinking							
Understand addition as putting together and adding to, and understand subtraction as taking apart and taking from.	X	X		X		X	X
Number and Operations in Base Ten							
Work with numbers 11–19 to gain foundations for place value.	X	X			X		

Connections Lists: Teaching with the Common Core State Standards for Mathematics

Grade 1 Connections

Grade 1 Common Core Standards	1. A "Mazing" 100	2. Addition Table Trail	3. Addition Tic-Tac-Toe	4. Anything But Ten!	5. Build Ten	7. Variation: Close to 20	8. Compare (Shake and Spill)	10. Cross Out Sums	15. Greater Than, Less Than, Equal To	19. Making Moves on the Hundreds Chart	21. More!	22. Odd or Even?	23. Oh No! 20!	31. Target "Pick Your Sum"	32. Tens Go Fish
Operations and Algebraic Thinking															
Understand and apply properties and the relationship between addition and subtraction.	X	X	X	X	X	X	X	X		X	X	X	X	X	X
Add and subtract within 20.	X	X	X	X	X	X		X		X		X	X	X	X
Work with addition and subtraction.	X	X	X	X	X	X		X	X	X		X	X	X	X
Number and Operations in Base Ten															
Extend the counting sequence.	X		X	X						X					
Understand place value.	X		X	X	X	X			X	X			X	X	
Use place value understanding and properties of operations to add and subtract.	X		X	X	X	X		X		X			X	X	

Connections Lists: Teaching with the Common Core State Standards for Mathematics

Grade 2 Connections

Grade 2 Common Core Standards	1. A "Mazing" 100	2. Addition Table Trail	3. Addition Tic-Tac-Toe	4. Anything But Ten!	5. Build Ten	6. Circles and Stars	7. Variation: Close to 20	9. Cross Out Singles	10. Cross Out Sums	13. Fifteen-Number Cross-Out	15. Greater Than, Less Than, Equal To	17. How Close to 0?	19. Making Moves on the Hundreds Chart	20. Missing Addend or Factor (Salute!)	22. Odd or Even?	23. Oh No! 20!	27. Roll for $1.00 and Variation: Roll for 1	31. Target "Pick Your Sum"	32. Tens Go Fish
Operations and Algebraic Thinking																			
Add and subtract within 20.	X	X	X	X	X	X	X	X	X	X	X	X	X	X	X	X	X	X	X
Work with equal groups of objects to gain foundations for multiplication.						X				X					X				
Number and Operations in Base Ten																			
Understand place value.	X			X			X				X	X	X			X	X		
Use place value understanding and properties to add and subtract.	X		X	X			X	X	X	X		X	X				X	X	

Connections Lists: Teaching with the Common Core State Standards for Mathematics

Grade 3 Connections

Grade 3 Common Core Standards	1. A "Mazing" 100	2. Addition Table Trail	2. Variation: Multiplication Table Trail	3. Addition Tic-Tac-Toe	6. Circles and Stars	7. Close to 100 and Variations: Close to 20 and Close to 1,000	9. Cross Out Singles	11. Digit Place (A Secret Number Quest)	12. Equation Building	13. Fifteen-Number Cross Out	14. Finding Factors	15. Greater Than, Less Than, Equal To	17. How Close to 0?	18. Leftovers with 15	20. Missing Addend or Factor (Salute!)	23. Oh No! 20!	25. Pathways and Variation: Times Ten	26. Roll 6 for 100	27. Roll for $1.00 and Variation: Roll for 1	29. Take Five, Make Ten!	30. Target 300 (A Multiplication Game)	31. Target "Pick Your Sum"
Operations and Algebraic Thinking																						
Understand properties of multiplication and the relationship between multiplication and division.			X		X						X			X			X			X	X	
Multiply and divide within 100.			X		X							X		X	X		X	X		X	X	
Solve problems involving the four operations and identify and explain patterns in arithmetic.		X	X			X	X		X	X			X			X				X		X
Number and Operations in Base Ten																						
Use place value understanding and properties of operations to perform multidigit arithmetic.	X	X		X	X	X	X	X	X	X		X	X	X	X	X	X	X	X	X		X
Number and Operations—Fractions																						
Develop understanding of fractions as numbers.																						

Connections Lists: Teaching with the Common Core State Standards for Mathematics

Grade 4 Connections

Grade 4 Common Core Standards	2. Variation: Multiplication Table Trail	7. Close to 100 and Variations: Close to 0 and Close to 1,000	9. Cross Out Singles	11. Digit Place (A Secret Number Quest)	12. Equation Building	13. Fifteen-Number Cross-Out	14. Finding Factors	15. Greater Than, Less Than, Equal To	16. Hit the Target (Mental Multiplication)	17. How Close to 0?	18. Leftovers with 15 and Variation: Leftovers with 100	20. Missing Addend or Factor (Salute!)	25. Pathways (Products Tic-Tac-Toe) and Variation: Times Ten	26. Roll 6 for 100	27. Roll for $1.00 and Variation: Roll for 1	29. Take Five, Make Ten!	30. Target 300 (A Multiplication Game)	33. Wipeout (Frational Relationships)
Operations and Algebraic Thinking																		
Use the four operations with whole numbers to solve problems.	X	X			X		X		X	X			X	X	X	X	X	
Gain familiarity with factors and multiples.	X						X					X	X				X	
Generate and analyze patterns.		X	X		X	X			X		X		X					
Number and Operations in Base Ten																		
Generalize place value understanding for multidigit whole numbers.				X	X			X	X		X	X	X	X			X	
Use place value understanding and properties of operations to perform multidigit arithmetic.		X	X	X	X	X					X	X		X	X	X		

continued

Connections Lists: Teaching with the Common Core State Standards for Mathematics

Grade 4 Connections, continued

Grade 4 Common Core Standards	2. Variation: Multiplication Table Trail	7. Close to 100 and Variations: Close to 0 and Close to 1,000	9. Cross Out Singles	11. Digit Place (A Secret Number Quest)	12. Equation Building	13. Fifteen-Number Cross-Out	14. Finding Factors	15. Greater Than, Less Than, Equal To	16. Hit the Target (Mental Multiplication)	17. How Close to 0?	18. Leftovers with 15 and Variation: Leftovers with 100	20. Missing Addend or Factor (Salute!)	25. Pathways (Products Tic-Tac-Toe) and Variation: Times Ten	26. Roll 6 for 100	27. Roll for $1.00 and Variation: Roll for 1	29. Take Five, Make Ten!	30. Target 300 (A Multiplication Game)	33. Wipeout (Fractional Relationships)
Number and Operations—Fractions																		
Develop understanding of fractions as numbers.					X					X						X		X
Build fractions from unit fractions by applying and extending previous understandings of operations on whole numbers.																		X
Understand decimal notation for fractions and compare decimal fractions.										X								X

Connections Lists: Teaching with the Common Core State Standards for Mathematics

Grade 5 Connections

Grade 5 Common Core Standards	7. Close to 100 and Variations: Close to 0 and Close to 1,000	11. Digit Place (A Secret Number Quest)	12. Equation Building	14. Finding Factors	16. Hit the Target (Mental Multiplication)	18. Leftovers with 15 and Variation: Leftovers with 100	20. Missing Addend or Factor (Salute!)	24. Order Up 21!	25. Pathways (Products Tic-Tac-Toe) and Variation: Times Ten	26. Roll 6 for 100	27. Roll for $1.00 and Variation: Roll for 1	28. Spinning Sums and Differences	29. Take Five, Make Ten!	30. Target 300 (A Multiplication Game)	33. Wipeout (Fractional Relationships)
Operations and Algebraic Thinking															
Write and interpret numerical expressions.			X					X		X			X	X	
Analyze patterns and relationships.	X			X	X	X	X		X						
Number and Operations in Base Ten															
Understand the place value system.	X	X	X	X	X			X	X		X	X	X	X	X
Perform operations with multidigit whole numbers and with decimals to hundredths.	X		X	X	X	X		X		X	X		X	X	
Number and Operations, Fractions															
Use equivalent fractions as a strategy to add and subtract fractions.			X					X			X	X			X
Apply and extend previous understandings of multiplication and division to multiply and divide fractions.			X					X				X			X

Materials List: List of Games by Materials Used

Base Ten Rods and Cubes

Counters (tiles, interlocking cubes, and so forth)

Die or Dice

Game Boards

Hundreds Chart (REPRODUCIBLE A)

Numeral Cards (REPRODUCIBLE B)

Pattern Blocks

continued

Materials List: List of Games by Materials Used, continued

Playing Cards (Deck)

Paper and Pencil Only

A "Mazing" 100

Overview

In this game, the hundreds chart becomes the game board. Students are encouraged to think about the base ten number system as they move their pieces both horizontally (by ones) and vertically (by tens). The goal of this game is to create a maze through the hundreds chart; students roll a die to determine their moves, assigning either a value of 1 or 10 to each number rolled. After students have completed their maze, they have the option to record equations for one hundred.

Materials

- hundreds chart, enlarged for classroom use
- Hundreds Chart (REPRODUCIBLE A), 1 per pair of students
- marker, crayon, or colored pencil, 1 per pair of students
- die (labeled *1–6*), 1 per pair of students
- A "Mazing" 100 Game Directions (REPRODUCIBLE G-1), 1 per pair of students

Related Game

Game 27: Roll for $1.00

Key Questions

- Why did you decide to take this path?
- Tell me about the path you took to one hundred.

Recommended Grades 1–3

Time   Instruction: 45–60 minutes
Independent Play: 15–20 minutes

TIME SAVER
Reusable Game Boards
Instead of making consumable copies of the hundreds chart, consider laminating a set or placing copies in plastic sleeves and providing dry erase pens.

See the Connections to the Common Core State Standards for Mathematics, page xv.

Teaching Directions

Part I: The Connection

Relate the game to students' ongoing work.

Build background with students by showing them a book of mazes. Ask, "Who has completed a maze before?" You may want to point out that children's menus or placemats at restaurants often offer a maze to complete while they're waiting for their food.

Discuss the various paths a maze can take to get from the starting point to the ending point. Review key vocabulary: *horizontal* and *vertical*.

Students will also need familiarity with the structure of a hundreds chart, counting by both ones and tens. Keep in mind that students can often count by tens when starting *on 10*. In this game; however, students need to count by tens from numbers *other than ten* in order to complete their mazes.

Part II: The Teaching

Introduce and model the game to students.

1. Tell students they will be playing the game *A "Mazing" 100* with a partner. To model the game, display an enlarged, laminated hundreds chart where everyone can see it. Tell students they will be using individual versions of the hundreds chart (REPRODUCIBLE A) to create their mazes.

2. Ask students, "What do you know about how the hundreds chart is organized?" Elicit information, specifically counting by ones when moving in a row and counting by tens when moving down the columns. Practice counting by ones and tens from any number on the hundreds chart. Note that for this particular game, students will only be counting on, not back.

3. Show students where zero would be on the hundreds chart. Tell them this is the start point. They should write *Start* in the margin

TECHNOLOGY TIP
The Hundreds Chart
An interactive whiteboard can be used to display the hundreds chart; this chart is available in the tool kit of most interactive whiteboards. Usually there are two hundreds charts available—one is interactive and one is not. Either will serve as a useful tool for introducing this game.

next to the number 1 square on their charts. Model this on the enlarged hundreds chart.

4. Tell students that the end point is one hundred. Write the word *End* in the margin after the number 100 square on the enlarged chart.

5. Tell students they will be using a die to determine the path their maze takes. Roll the die. Now point out how students have a choice to count by ones or tens. Demonstrate what it would look like to move by either choice. For example, if you are on the number 2 square and roll a 4:

   - You may choose to count by ones, "three, four, five, six," moving to the right of the chart;

     or

   - You may choose to count by tens, "twelve, twenty-two, thirty-two, forty-two," moving down the chart. (See Figure 1.1.)

6. Clearly draw the path (maze) with a crayon, marker, or colored pencil.

7. Continue rolling the die and modeling movements to the corresponding squares, both by ones or tens. Have students help determine whether the number rolled should represent a ten or a one. Some will have a rationale to offer. For example, two students might be on number 25 and roll a 5:

   Player 1: We should value the five as ones, then we will land on thirty. Then we can just move down to one hundred.

   Teacher: What do you mean, "down to one hundred?"

   Player 1: We could just count by tens until we get to one hundred.

   Player 2: I have another idea! I think we should use the five as a ten and count fifty more. If we count fifty more we would be at [student points with her finger to the space labeled 25 and begins

Start

1	2	3	4	5	6	7	8	9	10
11	12	13	14	15	16	17	18	19	20
21	22	23	24	25	26	27	28	29	30
31	32	33	34	35	36	37	38	39	40
41	42	43	44	45	46	47	48	49	50
51	52	53	54	55	56	57	58	59	60
61	62	63	64	65	66	67	68	69	70
71	72	73	74	75	76	77	78	79	80
81	82	83	84	85	86	87	88	89	90
91	92	93	94	95	96	97	98	99	100

End

Figure 1.1 A hundreds chart showing the two paths possible if a student rolls the number 4.

TEACHING TIP
Reaching the End of the Maze (100)
As the teacher, decide whether students need to roll exactly to 100 to end the game or if they may roll beyond 100:

Option 1: Rolling Exactly to 100
Rolling an exact number to get to 100 requires no additional directions.

Option 2: Rolling Beyond 100
Allowing students to roll beyond 100 necessitates one more rule. Tell students they may only roll beyond 100 if they are on square 95 and beyond. Students may want to shade the squares with numbers 95, 96, 97, 98, and 99 as a reminder. The reasoning behind this rule is to ensure students don't stop playing the game when on number 41 or greater (if this was the case, and a student was on number 41, rolled a 6, assigned it the value of 10, and moved to 101, the game would be over).

TEACHING TIP
Emphasize Collaboration
Explain that students will be playing in teams of two with their partner, not against him or her. The goal is for students to work together in understanding how to play the game and the math involved.

TEACHING TIP
Pairing Students
When pairing students for this game, consider placing students of similar abilities together to ensure both students are engaged in the mathematics. One student, for example, wouldn't be making all the decisions for the game because of her strength in number sense and computation, while the other becomes a bystander. However, after students have had experience in playing the game numerous times on numerous occasions, partnering them with someone who has *different* thinking provides students with an opportunity to grow in their mathematical understandings.

counting by tens, moving vertically down the chart] ten, twenty, thirty, forty, fifty. We'd be on space seventy-five.

Teacher: Tell me, why do you think this is a better move?

Player 2: Because seventy-five is much closer to one hundred than thirty!

8. Finish modeling the game when you've arrived at the end of drawing your maze (the number 100).

Part III: Active Engagement

Engage students to ensure they understand how to play the game.

9. Have students play the game in pairs as you circulate and support as needed. Remind students that they are playing as a team of two, making decisions *together* about how to move through the hundreds chart.

10. Monitor students. Look for those who are comfortable and move fluently toward 100. Note those students who are hesitant. Try to gauge if this is because of strategizing or skill. This will help determine how to differentiate your instruction for students. Some students may need more challenge, others more practice, and still others guided practice.

DIFFERENTIATING YOUR INSTRUCTION
Guided Small-Group Support/Strategy
For students who need more of a challenge, first give them guided instruction by grouping them together and showing how they can document their moves into an equation (refer to Figure 1.2). For students who are only counting by ones, even when adding ten or more, guide them through a lesson around counting by tens from any number using the hundreds chart. Key questions include:

- Tell me about the path you took to 100.

- How many more until _____ [insert the next nearest multiple of ten here]? How do you know?

- Show me how you are counting.

$$3 + 40 + 6 + 20 + 1 + 30 = 100$$

Figure 1.2 An example of a complete hundreds chart; the maze (the path) corresponds to the numbers rolled on the die (and the decisions students made to assign a ones or tens value to each number rolled).

Part IV: The Link

Students play the game independently.

11. Set students up for independent practice with the game. Each pair of students should have a hundreds chart (REPRODUCIBLE A); a marker, crayon, or colored pencil; and a die. Also distribute the directions (REPRODUCIBLE G-1) as needed.

12. Give students time to play at least three to four rounds over the next few class periods. When observing and talking with students as they play, ask key questions such as "Why did you decide to take this path?" or "Tell me about your path to one hundred."

MATH WORKSHOP AND SUMMARIZING THE EXPERIENCE

Teach this game at the beginning of the week to the whole class, then make it an integral part of your math workshop (for more on math workshops, see Chapter 5 in *From Reading to Math* by Maggie Siena). Build in time to observe students playing the game. Note their individual skill level and the strategies being utilized; come together later in the week and hold a discussion about the mathematics involved in the game. Refer to your notes during the discussion. Ask students, "Where is the math in *A 'Mazing' 100*?" Students may need help arriving at what mathematical concepts are needed, developed, and practiced; be prepared to help build their vocabulary and guide their thinking with:

· counting by ones

· counting by tens

· counting on from a number

· adding

· understanding how a hundreds chart is organized

· understanding of place value of a one and a ten

· understanding the power of ten

DIFFERENTIATING YOUR INSTRUCTION

There are several ways to modify this game according to the levels and needs of your students.

Recording Moves into Equations

Have students note their moves in an equation. For example: $3 + 40 + 6 + 20 + 1 + 30 = 100$. Refer back to the maze and corresponding equation in **Figure 1.2**. When adding this extension, it is important to emphasize that students need to record their move *after* each roll.

Gallery of "Sums of 100"

Have students create a gallery of "sums of 100" by posting their mazes and equations in the classroom for everyone to see. Refer to these postings later (see "Math Workshop and Summarizing the Experience").

Mandatory Vertical Moves

Add a constraint of having to use at least one vertical move (this works especially well for students reluctant to count by tens).

A "Mazing" 300

Substitute a 300-chart for the 100-chart.

Reverse the Maze

Have students begin at 100 and end at zero (reversing the direction of the maze).

Addition Table Trail
Variation: Multiplication Table Trail

Recommended Grades 1–5

Time Instruction: 45–60 minutes
Independent Play: 20–30 minutes

TEACHING TIPS
Transparent Counters
Use transparent counters. This way, the number is still visible on the game board when a counter is placed on it. This is especially helpful for students who struggle with number patterns.

Addition and Multiplication Tables
Be sure to give students addition or multiplications tables that are large enough for the game counters to cover a space without overlapping into the next space. **REPRODUCIBLES 1,2,3,** and **4** are designed with this in mind. You may choose to have the tables, which serve as the game boards, be consumable—meaning students can write on them. In this case, students mark the numbers using colored pencils or markers instead of counters.

Quiet Dice
Rolling dice can create lots of noise. To lessen the noise, consider using foam dice or padding students' workspaces with foam or fabric placemats.

TIME SAVER
Managing the Materials
For ease in managing the distribution of materials, place the required four dice (two labeled 0–5 and two labeled 5–10) and fifty counters (twenty-five of each color) in quart-size baggies (one baggie for each pair of students playing the game).

Overview
In this game, an addition table becomes the game board, encouraging students to practice their basic facts and work with addends up to 10. The game helps students increase their familiarity with reading an addition table, connect to previous conceptual understanding of addition, and improve their automaticity with facts. Students play in pairs, the winner being the first person to complete a continuous path (horizontally or vertically) across the table. As a variation, directions and the game board for *Multiplication Table Trail* are also provided.

Materials
- Addition Table 0–5 or 0–10 (REPRODUCIBLES 1 and 2) or Multiplication Table 1–6 or 0–10 (REPRODUCIBLES 3 and 4), 1 per pair of students

- counters, 50 per pair of students (25 of each color)

- dice (2 labeled *0–5*, 2 labeled *5–10*), 4 per pair of students

- *Addition Table Trail* or *Multiplication Table Trail* Game Directions (REPRODUCIBLES G-2A and G-2B), 1 per pair of students

Related Games
Game 3: Addition Tic-Tac-Toe

Game 9: Cross Out Singles

 See the Connections to the Common Core State Standards for Mathematics, page xv.

Adapted from *Real Math* by Peter Hilton, Joseph Rubinstein, Joan Moss, and Pede Bereiter (SRA/McGraw-Hill, 2007).

Key Questions

- Tell me about the game board. When playing, what did you notice about how the board is organized?

- What decisions did you have to make while playing this game?

- How did you determine where to place your counter?

Teaching Directions

Part I: The Connection

Relate the game to students' ongoing work.

Addition Table Trail assists students with the memorization of basic addition facts and builds their fluency and automaticity. Before playing the game, students need to be familiar with their basic facts and have some experience with using a completed addition table. Connect the game to students' previous work in mathematics around combining numbers. Review key vocabulary: *horizontal* and *vertical*.

Part II: The Teaching

Introduce and model the game to students.

1. Tell students they will be playing the game *Addition Table Trail* with a partner. To model the game, give each pair of students one Addition Table 0–10 (REPRODUCIBLE 2) and twenty-five game counters of the same color (note that pairs just need twenty-five counters at this point; later in the lesson each student will each get twenty-five, for a total of fifty per pair).

2. Explain the object of the game to students. Share, "The object of the game is to be the first to complete a continuous trail across the table." Show students what qualifies as a continuous path across the addition table. To do this, post an addition table where everyone can see it. Using a highlighter or bright

TEACHING TIP
Pairing Students
Prior to the game, determine how to pair students. One important factor is a student's current fluidity with addition facts. If pairing students with like abilities, consider having manipulatives available for pairs of students who may need them. If pairing students with differing abilities, think about how to make the game accessible yet challenging for both students. One idea is to have students who are just emerging in their facts use an abbreviated addition table to focus on facts one through five. For those who need more challenge, consider using an abbreviated version of a multiplication table with facts one through six (two regular 1–6 dice are used for this version). There could be three versions of the game by differentiating the content: addition facts one through five, addition facts zero through ten, and multiplication facts zero through five.

TECHNOLOGY TIP
The Addition Table for Modeling
You will need an enlarged addition table for modeling the game. Consider enlarging **REPRODUCIBLE 2** on a photocopier. Alternatively, interactive whiteboards often have addition tables in their tool kits. A documentation camera also works well for displaying the addition table and demonstrating the game.

Figure 2.1 Example of an addition table with a continuous trail horizontally, left to right.

Figure 2.2 An example of an addition table showing the two choices a player needs to make in covering the sum for the addends 2 + 8, 8 + 2.

Figure 2.3 An example of an addition table in which the player is moving vertically, from top to bottom.

marker (so students can easily see what is happening), draw an example of a continuous path. The path needs to connect two sides of the table, either vertically (the top and bottom sides of the table) or horizontally (the left and right sides of the table). While drawing, be sure to point out that the path can go up, down, forward, backward, or diagonally, as long as the squares are touching each other (see Figure 2.1).

3. Tell students the game is played with four dice, two with faces labeled *0–5* and two with faces labeled *5–10*. When it is your turn, select two of the four dice to roll. You may choose any combination of dice to roll: both *0–5*, both *5–10*, or one of each.

4. Roll the two dice you have selected. Explain that the numbers rolled are *addends*. If you roll a 2 and an 8, place a game counter where 2 + 8 intersect (or 8 + 2) on the table (the number 10) (see Figure 2.2).

5. Check for understanding by rolling two dice and having pairs of students point to the corresponding sums on their tables. Unless you roll doubles, students should be pointing to two squares on the addition table. Repeat this a number of times while circulating the classroom, checking in with pairs of students.

6. After you have determined that all students understand the numbers rolled are addends and how to locate the sums on the addition table, begin a game.

Part III: Active Engagement

Engage students to ensure they understand how to play the game.

7. Remind students, "For learning the game you will be playing *with* your partner, not against him or her. For this round, you and your partner need to decide if you are going to move from the top of the chart to the bottom (vertically—see Figure 2.3) or from left to right

(horizontally—see Figure 2.1) to make the continuous trail across the table." The paths may still connect diagonally.

8. Select and roll two dice, or ask a pair of students to each roll one. Announce to the class the numbers rolled. Write the addends where everyone can see them. For example, if you rolled a 3 and a 5, write *3 + 5* and *5 + 3*.

9. Instruct students to place a game counter on the corresponding sum on their addition table. In the previous example, the counter would go on either square numbered *8*, where 3 and 5 (or 5 and 3) intersect (see Figure 2.4).

10. Continue facilitating by taking the dice to different pairs of students around the classroom. Ask them to select two dice, roll them, and announce the addends. Each time, record the addends where all students in the classroom can clearly see them.

11. After several rounds, your recording of addends may look like this:

$$3 + 5 \ , \ 5 + 3$$
$$2 + 4 \ , \ 4 + 2$$
$$2 + 8 \ , \ 8 + 2$$

Try a few more so students get the idea of each roll of the dice leading to two sums (unless doubles are rolled) on the addition table. Emphasize that students should only cover one square (sum) each turn. Soon a path will begin to emerge and strategies will come into play.

12. Circulate, asking pairs of students to point out the continuous trail they are creating across the addition table. Use this time to clarify understanding of continuous trails. When a pair of students has made a trail across the addition table, enough practice has likely happened and understanding of the "how" to play is solid.

TEACHING TIP
Emphasize Collaboration
For Part III, "Active Engagement," students should test the game out in teams of two *with* their partner, not playing against him or her. The goal is for students to work together in understanding *how* to play the game and the math that is involved. When students have the opportunity to play the game independently (Part IV), they then can play each other.

+	0	1	2	3	4	5	6	7	8	9	10
0	0	1	2	3	4	5	6	7	8	9	10
1	1	2	3	4	5	6	7	8	9	10	11
2	2	3	4	5	6	7	8	9	10	11	12
3	3	4	5	6	7	8	9	10	11	12	13
4	4	5	6	7	8	9	10	11	12	13	14
5	5	6	7	8	9	10	11	12	13	14	15
6	6	7	8	9	10	11	12	13	14	15	16
7	7	8	9	10	11	12	13	14	15	16	17
8	8	9	10	11	12	13	14	15	16	17	18
9	9	10	11	12	13	14	15	16	17	18	19
10	10	11	12	13	14	15	16	17	18	19	20

Figure 2.4 An example of an addition table showing the two choices a player needs to make when covering the sum for the addends 3 + 5, 5 + 3.

TEACHING TIP
Recording the Addends
Record the addends where all students can see them, typically on the board. This is especially helpful to the visual learners in the classroom. Recording also provides an opportunity to highlight the commutative property of addition, which states that the order of two or more addends does not matter; the sum remains the same.

TEACHING TIP
The Importance of Practice
Some students will want to offer their reasoning as to why they choose to cover one sum over the other. Resist discussing strategy, skill, and luck at this time. Wait until all students have had many days of practice with the game before engaging in this conversation.

+	0	1	2	3	4	5	6	7	8	9	10
0	0	1	2	3	4	5	6	7	8	9	10
1	1	2	3	4	5	6	7	8	9	10	11
2	2	3	4	5	6	7	8	9	10	11	12
3	3	4	5	6	7	8	9	10	11	12	13
4	4	5	6	7	8	9	10	11	12	13	14
5	5	6	7	8	9	10	11	12	13	14	15
6	6	7	8	9	10	11	12	13	14	15	16
7	7	8	9	10	11	12	13	14	15	16	17
8	8	9	10	11	12	13	14	15	16	17	18
9	9	10	11	12	13	14	15	16	17	18	19
10	10	11	12	13	14	15	16	17	18	19	20

Figure 2.5 One player uses one color of counters to build his path vertically; the other player uses another color of counters to build her path horizontally. In this example, the player moving vertically won because he was the first to complete a continuous path.

Part IV: The Link
Students play the game independently.

13. Set up students for independent practice with the game. At this point, each pair of students has approximately twenty-five same-color game counters and a completed addition table. Now give each pair another twenty-five game counters of a different color (each pair should now have fifty counters, twenty-five of each color) and four dice (two labeled *0–5* and two labeled *5–10*). Explain that they will be given the opportunity to play the game on their own.

14. Tell students they will continue playing in pairs; however, this time they will play each other (versus as a team). One player will move up and down the board in a horizontal fashion and the other player will move across the board in a vertical fashion (refer back to Figures 2.1 and 2.3). Both partners' paths will likely have zigzags in them as discussed. Make sure each player uses a different color counter so their paths can be clearly distinguished from each other (see Figure 2.5). The first player to make a continuous trail to the opposite side of the addition table is the winner.

15. Distribute the directions (REPRODUCIBLE G-2A) to students as needed; give them time to play at least three to four rounds over the next few class periods.

MATH WORKSHOP AND SUMMARIZING THE EXPERIENCE

Teach this game at the beginning of the week to the whole class, then make it an integral part of your math workshop (for more on math workshops, see Chapter 5 in *From Reading to Math* by Maggie Siena). Build in time to observe students playing the game. Note their individual skill level and the strategies being utilized; come together later in the week to discuss both strategy and how the game aided in automaticity and fact facility. Refer to your notes during the discussion. Ask questions such as:

- How did the game become easier for you as you played more rounds?

- What made the game challenging?

- How might the game be more challenging?

- What properties of mathematics were you practicing as you rolled the dice and created equations from the numbers?

ASSESSMENTS

Using Language Frames

Addition Table Trail does not produce a product, so you will want to tell students how you will be assessing their learning. One suggestion is to provide students with language frames. Tell students you will be listening to them speak and use their mathematics vocabulary. Language frames for this game might be:

_____ is the sum of _____ + _____.

When you combine _____ and _____, you get a total of _____.

_____ and _____ are the addends, so _____ is the sum.

How Do You Feel About Your Basic Facts?

After students have played *Addition Table Trail* for a week or two, ask students how they are feeling about their basic facts. Do they feel more confident knowing the facts and knowing them quickly? Have students respond orally or in a math journal.

DIFFERENTIATING YOUR INSTRUCTION

Addition Table 0–5

Modify the addition table for younger or struggling students so that they are only practicing facts zero through five. **REPRODUCIBLE 1** has been provided for this purpose. Only two dice (labeled 0–5) are needed. Encourage students to use their unused counters as manipulatives for facts with which they are struggling. For example, if a student rolls a 2 and a 4, she can group her unused counters accordingly (see Figure 2.6).

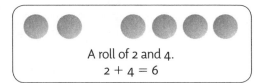

A roll of 2 and 4.
$2 + 4 = 6$

Figure 2.6 Encourage struggling students to use their unused counters to support their understanding of basic facts.

Multiplication Table Trail

As a variation for higher grades, directions and reproducibles for playing *Multiplication Table Trail* are included (**GAME DIRECTIONS G2-B** and **REPRODUCIBLES 3** and **4**).

Addition Tic-Tac-Toe

Recommended Grades 1–3
Time Instruction: 45–60 minutes
Independent Play: 20–30 minutes

TIME SAVER
Managing the Materials
For ease in managing the distribution of materials, place the required twenty-four tiles (twelve of each color) in quart-size sandwich bags (one bag for each pair of students playing the game). Clip the two paper clips to each *Addition Tic-Tac-Toe* Game Board. Note that larger paper clips stay put and get lost less frequently.

TEACHING TIP
Consumable *Addition Tic-Tac-Toe* Game Boards
To ensure that game boards can be used repeatedly, laminate them. Alternatively, distribute consumable game boards—copies on which students can write. In this case, instead of using color tiles to cover the boards, students color the spaces with markers or crayons as they play the game. This gives students the opportunity to save their work for later reflection (see "Math Workshop and Summarizing the Experience" at the end of this lesson).

See the Connections to the Common Core State Standards for Mathematics, page xv.

Overview
Addition Tic-Tac-Toe is a two-player game that provides practice in combining two addends up to the sum of twenty-five. Students need to be familiar with how basic tic-tac-toe or Bingo-type games are played. The winner is the player who places four counters in a row, column, or diagonal.

Materials
- paper clips, 2 per pair of students
- tiles, 24 per pair of students (12 of each color)
- *Addition Tic-Tac-Toe* Game Board, Completed (REPRODUCIBLE 5), 1 per pair of students
- *Addition Tic-Tac-Toe* Game Directions (REPRODUCIBLE G-3), 1 per pair of students

Related Games
Game 7: Close to 100 (the variation Close to 20)
Game 13: Fifteen-Number Cross-Out

Key Questions
- Tell me one of your strategies in playing *Addition Tic-Tac-Toe*.
- If you are the first player to go in this game, what addends do you place the clips on and why?
- Which is more important in playing *Addition Tic-Tac-Toe*: playing to win, playing to block, or both? Explain.

Adapted from *Teaching Arithmetic: Lessons for Addition and Subtraction, Grades 2–3* by Bonnie Tank and Lynne Zolli (Math Solutions, 2001).

Teaching Directions

Part I: The Connection

Relate the game to students' ongoing work.

Addition Tic-Tac-Toe gives students practice in combining numbers with sums to twenty-six. Connect the game to activities or worksheets students have done that involve combining two addends. Also, familiarize students with the classic game of tic-tac-toe. Ask, "Who has played tic-tac-toe before?" Find out what students know about playing the game. Point out that the game involves two concurrent modes of thinking: playing to win and playing to block one's opponent from winning. Review key vocabulary: *horizontal*, *vertical*, and *diagonal*.

Part II: The Teaching

Introduce and model the game to students.

1. Tell students they will be playing the game *Addition Tic-Tac-Toe* with a partner. First introduce the game board (REPRODUCIBLE 5).

2. Refer back to the discussion students had about the classic game of tic-tac-toe. Ask students, "What are the similarities and differences you see between the game board you use for tic-tac-toe and the game board we are using for *Addition Tic-Tac-Toe*?" Examples of student responses:

   - The *Addition Tic-Tac-Toe* Game Board is larger—it has five rows and five columns (the classic game has only three rows and three columns).

   - The spaces on the *Addition Tic-Tac-Toe* Game Board have numbers in them (the classic game's spaces are blank; in this game, the numbers are considered sums).

   - There are numbers at the bottom of the *Addition Tic-Tac-Toe* Game Board (these numbers are addends; players select addends that correspond to the sums).

 TEACHING TIP
Displaying the Game Board
There are several ways to display the *Addition Tic-Tac-Toe* Game Board when introducing it. Consider placing the game board on a document camera or an overhead projector. Alternatively, copy the game board and simply have students gather around you in concentric circles (an option that works well is to have one circle of students seated and one standing).

TEACHING TIP
Using Paper Clips to Mark Addends
Students may think that because they are using paper clips, they need to fasten (clip) the paper clips to the bottom of their game board. It is helpful to clip the paper clips onto their corresponding game board when storing the game materials; if the paper clips are already attached to the board, students can then slide the clips back and forth across the addends they select. However, if the clips are not attached, clipping paper clips to the game board can distract from the game and is not necessary; in this case, students can simply place the paper clips on top of the number (addend).

The advantage of using paper clips is students can cover a number without hiding it from view. They will also not get confused with the counters (color tiles) being used. An alternative to paper clips is sticky notes. Students can move the sticky note without damaging the game board, and the adhesive on the note should last many rounds of play.

3. Explain to students that instead of marking the spaces on the game board with Xs and Os (like the classic game of tic-tac-toe), they will use color tiles.

4. Refer students to the list of numbers at the bottom of the *Addition Tic-Tac-Toe* Game Board. Emphasize that these are the addends. Each player selects two addends and marks the sum on the game board using a color tile. The goal is to connect five sums in a row (horizontally), column (vertically), or corner-to-corner (diagonally).

5. Ask, "How can we keep track of the addends we choose to combine?" Explain to students that they can use paper clips to mark the addends. Place two paper clips on two addends on the board to demonstrate. Then, take a color tile and place it on the corresponding sum of the two addends on the board.

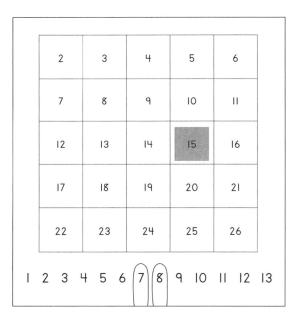

Figure 3.1 An example of a game board in play; the player has selected addends 7 and 8 and marked the sum, 15, with a color tile.

6. Now demonstrate a round of playing the game. Designate yourself as Player 1 and the students as Player 2. Start by placing the two paper clips on two of the addends at the bottom of the game board. Cover the sum with a color tile (see Figure 3.1 on the previous page).

7. Next, ask a student to move just *one* of the paper clips to a different addend and cover the corresponding sum with a color tile.

8. Continue playing until a player connects five spaces, either in a row, column, or diagonal. In the event that neither player has connected five spaces and there are no more sums to be covered, declare the game a tie.

9. When students are ready to play in pairs, move on to the "Part III: Active Engagement" part of the lesson. If students would benefit from playing another round collectively, play again as an entire class.

Part III: Active Engagement

Engage students to ensure they understand how to play the game.

10. Send students off in pairs to play the game of *Addition Tic-Tac-Toe*. Give each pair of students an *Addition Tic-Tac-Toe* Game Board (REPRODUCIBLE 5), two paper clips, and twenty-four color tiles, twelve in each color.

11. Circulate, observing students play and asking questions to check their understanding. Questions include:

- Help me understand why you made that move.
- What will your next move be?
- What sum are you hoping to cover next?

Part IV: The Link

Students play the game independently.

12. Set up students for independent practice of the game. Make sure each pair has the appropriate

TEACHING TIP
The Same Addends
Point out that sometimes the two paper clips can be placed on the same addend. For example, both paper clips have to be on number 13 to get the sum of 26 on the game board (adding 13 and 13 is the only way to arrive at 26).

DIFFERENTIATING YOUR INSTRUCTION
If some students are not yet ready to play this game in pairs, team up two pairs to create a group of four to play.

TEACHING TIP
The Importance of Asking Questions
Asking key questions assists you in understanding how or if students are developing strategies. When you ask key questions, students get to hear other students' thinking and further develop their own understanding of the content.

DIFFERENTIATING YOUR INSTRUCTION

There are several ways to modify the game according to the levels and needs of your students.

Change the Operation

Change the instructions so that students have the option of either adding or subtracting the two numbers they select. Students continue to mark the appropriate sum on their game boards.

Make Your Own Game Board

Have students create their own game boards, randomly filling in the spaces with the numbers 2–26. **REPRODUCIBLE 6** (a blank *Addition Tic-Tac-Toe* Game Board) has been provided for this purpose. As the teacher, you can also use the blank game board to create additional boards at varying levels.

Omit the Addends

Offer a completed game board without the addends listed at the bottom. Students have to determine the necessary addends before playing.

materials. Explain that they will be given the opportunity to play the game on their own.

13. Distribute the directions (**REPRODUCIBLE G-3**) to students as needed; give them time to play at least three to four rounds over the next few class periods.

MATH WORKSHOP AND SUMMARIZING THE EXPERIENCE

Teach this game at the beginning of the week to the whole class, then make it an integral part of your math workshop (for more on math workshops, see Chapter 5 in *From Reading to Math* by Maggie Siena). Build in time to observe students playing the game. Note their individual skill level and the strategies being used. Come together later in the week as a class to discuss students' learning; refer to your notes during the discussion. Ask students to share some of their strategies and explore them with their peers.

ASSESSMENTS

What Are Three Facts That You Found Challenging?

Have students share which facts they found challenging. Post these on a chart. Then, invite students who consider themselves an expert on a particular fact to place their initials next to that fact. Have these students share their thinking or a strategy that helped them feel like an expert. An example dialogue might be:

Student: [Places her initials by 6 + 9.]
I think of this problem as five plus ten instead of six plus nine.

Teacher: Why did you think of it that way?

Student: [Takes fifteen tiles and divides them into a group of six and a group of nine.] If you take one from the six group and move it to the nine group [moving the tile] you have a group of five and a group of ten. Five and ten are much easier to add than six plus nine. Nines are a ten minus one, so it works.

Teacher: Thank you for sharing your thinking with us.

Writing Prompt

If students have used consumable game boards, ask them to respond to the writing prompt, "Identify one move you made in this round of play that you think was a wise move. Explain why." Have each student share his or her response with another classmate or post the responses where everyone can read them.

Anything but Ten!

Overview

In *Anything but Ten!*, the hundreds chart becomes the game board. The object of the game is to be the first player to make it to one hundred *without* rolling combinations of ten (as the game name declares, *Anything but Ten!*). Students depend upon and strengthen their mental math skills while developing automaticity in basic addition facts 0–6. Probability is also explored.

Materials

- Hundreds Chart (REPRODUCIBLE A), 1 per pair of students
- dice (1 labeled *0–5*, 1 labeled *5–10*), 2 per pair of students
- counters (each a different color), 2 per pair of students
- *Anything but Ten!* Game Directions (REPRODUCIBLE G-4), 1 per pair of students

Related Games

Game 1: A "Mazing" 100

Game 5: Build Ten

Game 32: Tens Go Fish

Key Question

- What combinations of ten are possible with two dice—one with faces labeled *0–5* and another with faces labeled *5–10*?

- What is the largest sum you could have in *Anything but Ten*? What is the smallest sum you could have in this game?

Recommended Grades K–2

Time Instruction: 45–60 minutes
Independent Play: 15–20 minutes

 TEACHING TIPS
Don't Have Dice?
If you do not have dice labeled *0–5* and *5–10*, consider these options:

- Convert wooden cubes to dice. Place small, round, numbered stickers on each face of wooden cubes.

- Use Numeral Cards instead of dice. Photocopy a set labeled *0–5* on one color of paper and a set labeled *5–10* on another (see **REPRODUCIBLE B, NUMERAL CARDS 0–10**). Instead of dice, players draw one card of each color during their turn.

Quiet Dice
Rolling dice can create lots of noise. To lessen the noise, use foam dice or pad students' workspaces with foam or fabric placemats.

Transparent Counters
When deciding what to use for counters, opt for pieces that are transparent. In this way, the number is still visible on the chart when a counter is placed on it. This is especially helpful for students who struggle with number patterns.

 See the Connections to the Common Core State Standards for Mathematics, page xv.

TEACHING TIP
Pairing Students
When pairing students for this game, consider placing students of similar abilities together to ensure both students are engaged in the mathematics. One student, for example, wouldn't be making all the decisions for the game because of her strength in number sense and computation, while the other becomes a bystander. However, after students have had experience in playing the game numerous times on numerous occasions, partnering them with someone who has *different* thinking provides students with an opportunity to grow in their mathematical understandings.

TEACHING TIP
Recording Combinations of Ten
When soliciting combinations of ten, students will likely not suggest the combinations in a specific order; however, try to record the combinations in an organized way to help students see the pattern of the addends.

Teaching Directions
Part I: The Connection
Relate the game to students' ongoing work.

To connect to students' prior learning, remind them of the importance of ten in the numbering system. Have them review counting to ten, counting by tens, and combinations of ten.

Part II: The Teaching
Introduce and model the game to students.

1. Tell students they will be playing the game *Anything but Ten!* with a partner. Have students sit with their partner, either at their desks or on the floor in a class circle.

2. First, ask students to suggest all the combinations of ten. Record the combinations where everyone can see them. Your recording should look similar to this:

Combinations of 10

5 + 5

4 + 6   6 + 4

3 + 7   7 + 3

2 + 8   8 + 2

1 + 9   9 + 1

0 + 10   10 + 0

3. Next, explain to students that they will be rolling two dice. If they roll a combination of ten, they will have to start over. Point out that the dice are not ordinary dice.

4. Distribute one of each type of die to each pair of students. Let students inspect the dice. Ask, "What do you notice about these dice? What is different about them?"

5. After students have discovered that one die is labeled with numerals *0–5* and the other *5–10*, have them practice rolling both dice. Tell students to stop rolling when they roll a

combination of ten. Give both partners the opportunity to roll until they roll a combination of ten.

6. Have students set the dice in front of them so the materials are no longer in their hands. Ask, "Who got a combination of ten on their first roll?" Give students an opportunity to share how many rolls it took. Emphasize that at some point, each of them rolled a combination of ten.

7. Now show students the Hundreds Chart (REPRODUCIBLE A). Explain that this will be their game board. They will begin at zero, the space just before the chart begins. Demonstrate this by placing two counters (each a different color) on a class hundreds chart, just before zero.

8. Explain that each player gets a turn to roll both dice and combine the numbers. If the number is *not* a combination of ten, the player moves that many spaces. If the number rolled *is* a combination of ten, the player must remain at or go back to zero.

9. If the player rolls a number that is not a combination of ten, the player has the choice to end his or her move or roll again. Players can continue to choose to roll and move their counter, keeping in mind that if their roll is a combination of ten, they will have to start over.

10. The winner is the first player to reach 100 or beyond on the game board (hundreds chart).

11. Model a round of play for everyone. Think out loud as you roll, sharing your thought process about whether to roll again or end your turn. For example, you might say, "Hmmm.... How many combinations of ten are possible with the dice? I know there are eleven ways to make ten but there are fewer ways to make ten with the dice. I've rolled ___ times. Hmmm.... I should roll again or perhaps I'll play it safe."

TECHNOLOGY TIP
The Hundreds Chart
An interactive whiteboard can be used to display the hundreds chart; this chart is available in the tool kit of most interactive whiteboards. Usually, there are two hundreds charts available—one is interactive and one is not. Either will serve as a useful tool for introducing this game. Alternatively, place a copy of the hundreds chart under a document camera.

TEACHING TIP
Logic Versus Luck
It might be jarring at first for students to realize that even if they roll a combination of ten on their first roll (and were not taking a risk but rather taking their turn), they still must remain on or go back to zero—it's all part of playing the game!

TEACHING TIP
Thinking Out Loud
Thinking out loud is helpful when modeling for students how to play a game. Tell students you are going to think aloud. They do not need to answer, but rather watch you think—just like they watch a cartoon or movie and think!

DIFFERENTIATING YOUR INSTRUCTION

If some students are not yet ready to play this game in pairs, team up two pairs to create a group of four to play.

Part III: Active Engagement

Engage students to ensure they understand how to play the game.

12. Let students know that now it is their turn to play the game. You will be there to answer any questions and clear up any confusion they may have. Make sure each pair of students has a game board (REPRODUCIBLE A), dice, and two counters (each a different color).

13. Circulate, observing students play. After a student rolls the dice, observe how he or she moves along the game board. Ask yourself questions like the following:

    - Does the student jump ahead?

    - Does the student count on, square by square?

    - Is the student accurate?

    - Are the errors being made computational or are they made while moving spaces?

    Each of these observations helps you determine who you might want to pull into a smaller guided instruction group and/or any intervention or modified instruction that may be needed.

Part IV: The Link

Students play the game independently.

14. Set up students for independent practice of the game. Make sure each pair has the appropriate materials. Explain that they will be given the opportunity to play the game on their own.

15. Distribute the directions (REPRODUCIBLE G-4) to students as needed; give them time to play at least three to four rounds over the next few class periods.

MATH WORKSHOP AND SUMMARIZING THE EXPERIENCE

Teach this game at the beginning of the week to the whole class, then make it an integral part of your math workshop (for more on math workshops, see Chapter 5 in *From Reading to Math* by Maggie Siena). Build in time to observe students playing the game. Note their individual skill level and the strategies being utilized. Come together as a class later in the week to discuss students' learning; refer to your notes during the discussion. Begin with, "Share what you learned while playing the game *Anything but Ten!*" Then, revisit the eleven ways to make ten and discuss how many of those combinations were available in this game.

DIFFERENTIATING YOUR INSTRUCTION

To change the game and further challenge students, have them add three addends instead of two. In this case, use three dice labeled *1–6*.

ASSESSMENT
Practicing Basic Facts

Consider using *Anything but Ten!* as one of the many ways for students to practice their basic facts. After administering a preassessment of students' automaticity of basic addition facts, introduce the game and have students play it for several weeks, then administer the test again. Determine whether the game assisted with both accuracy and speed on basic addition facts and if other interventions need to be offered.

Build Ten

Recommended Grades K–2
Time Instruction: 45–60 minutes
    Independent Play: 15–20 minutes

TIME SAVER
Managing the Materials
For ease in managing the distribution of materials, place the required die, two base ten rods, and twenty base ten cubes in quart-size sandwich bags (one bag for each pair of students playing the game).

TEACHING TIP
Quiet Dice
Rolling dice can create lots of noise. To lessen the noise, use foam dice or pad students' workspaces with foam or fabric placemats.

See the Connections to the Common Core State Standards for Mathematics, page xv.

Overview

In this game, students practice counting up to ten. Each player begins with a base ten rod. Player 1 rolls a die and places the corresponding number of ones cubes against his or her base ten rod. Player 2 does a similar move; players alternate turns until both have reached ten. *Build Ten* naturally lends itself to classroom discussions: Which combinations of numbers equal exactly ten? Which go over?

Materials

- die (labeled *1–6*), 1 per pair of students
- base ten rods, 2 per pair of students
- base ten cubes, 20 per pair of students
- *Build Ten* Game Directions (REPRODUCIBLE G-5), 1 per pair of students

Related Games

Game 4: Anything but Ten!

Game 32: Tens Go Fish

Key Questions

- How many more do you need to make ten?
- What number are you hoping to roll next? Why?

Teaching Directions

Part I: The Connection

Relate the game to students' ongoing work.

This game is ideal for students whose facility with ten is tentative. It is also a fantastic way to introduce students to base ten manipulatives if they are unfamiliar with them.

Part II: The Teaching

Introduce and model the game to students.

1. Tell students they will be playing the game *Build Ten* with a partner. Decide how you will model the game (see the corresponding Technology Tip for options).

2. Show students the tens rod. Hold up an actual rod (even if you are using an interactive whiteboard) so students can make the connection between the manipulative and what is being presented on the whiteboard.

3. Ask students, "What do you know about the tens rod?" Possible responses include:

   - "That it means ten."

   - "It takes ten of those small cubes to make that stick of ten."

4. Next show students the ones cube. Ask students, "What do you know about the ones cube?" Possible responses include:

   - "It is smaller than the ten."

   - "The ones cube means just one."

   - "I know if you line up ten ones cubes it will look like a tens rod except apart."

5. Explain the directions to students. Each player will take turns rolling the die and placing the corresponding number of ones cubes against his or her base ten rod. The first person to build ten is the winner.

6. Model a round. Roll the die and collect the corresponding number of ones cubes. Carefully

TECHNOLOGY TIP
Using an Interactive Whiteboard
To model this game, you may either gather students around a table and use the base ten rods or alternatively use an interactive whiteboard. For the latter, select base ten blocks and dice from the tool kit. Create a page with a die, a tens rod, and a ones cube. Clone the ones cube until you have enough cubes to model the game.

place the ones cubes next to each other, against the tens rod, so that all the manipulatives are touching. This will help students see how many more ones cubes they need to get to ten (see Figure 5.1).

Figure 5.1 An example of how the manipulatives look if the number 3 is rolled.

7. Ask students, "How many more ones cubes are needed to reach ten?"

8. Roll again. If you roll a 4, add four more ones cubes (see Figure 5.2).

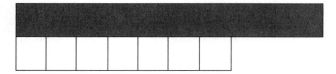

Figure 5.2 An example of how the manipulatives look after the numbers 3 and 4 were rolled.

9. Ask students, "How many more ones cubes are needed to reach ten?"

10. Discuss three plus four more is seven.

11. Using the example, on the next roll, a three is needed to make ten. For this game, an exact roll is not necessary, so if a 3, 4, 5 or 6 are rolled the player would add three and "build a ten." If a one or 2 are rolled, the game continues.

Part III: Active Engagement

Engage students to ensure they understand how to play the game.

12. Let students know that now it is their turn to play the game. You will be there to answer any questions and clear up any confusion they may have. Pair up students. Give each pair a die, two tens rods, and twenty ones cubes.

13. Remind students to take turns as they play. Players should have their tens rod in the workspace in front of them.

14. Circulate as students play. Encourage them to count, compute, and converse. Ask key questions such as:

    - "How many more until ten?"

    - "What was the sum of the first roll and the second roll?"

    - "I noticed you have [number of cubes], what numbers did you roll to get to _____?"

Part IV: The Link

Students play the game independently.

15. Set up students for independent practice of the game. Make sure each pair has the appropriate materials. Explain that they will be given the opportunity to play the game on their own.

16. Distribute the directions (REPRODUCIBLE G-5) to students as needed; give them time to play at least three to four rounds over the next few class periods.

TEACHING TIP
The Importance of Asking Questions
Asking key questions assists you in understanding how or if students are developing strategies. As students answer key questions, students get to hear other students' thinking and further develop their own understanding of the content.

DIFFERENTIATING YOUR INSTRUCTION
Reverse Build Ten
For more challenge and practice, have students play *Reverse Build Ten*. In this version, students play from ten to zero, practicing subtraction and counting back. Players begin with a tens rod and all ten of the ones cubes set out against it (see Figure 5.3). As players roll the die, they take away the corresponding number of ones cubes. The first player to reach zero wins the game. Have students journal about which version of the game they enjoyed more and why.

Figure 5.3 In *Reverse Build Ten*, players start with all ten ones cubes lined up against their tens rod.

MATH WORKSHOP AND SUMMARIZING THE EXPERIENCE
Teach this game at the beginning of the week to the whole class, then make it an integral part of your math workshop (for more on math workshops, see Chapter 5 in *From Reading to Math* by Maggie Siena). After students have played *Build Ten* several times, ask them to make a record of the games. This could be a class collection of equations that make ten and equations that are greater than ten. Students record the equations on poster-size pieces of paper titled, "Exactly Ten" and "Greater Than Ten." Display the two posters where everyone can see them. Alternatively, each student could make his or her own list of equations.

Circles and Stars

Recommended Grades 2–3

Time Instruction: 45–60 minutes
Independent Play: 20–30 minutes

TEACHING TIP
Quiet Dice
Rolling dice can create lots of noise. To lessen the noise, use foam dice or pad students' workspaces with foam or fabric placemats.

See the Connections to the Common Core State Standards for Mathematics, page xv.

Overview

This classic game helps students link their additive thinking to multiplicative thinking. It provides an introduction to the concept of multiplication by using what is familiar to students: repeated addition. A player rolls a die and draws the corresponding number of circles. The player then rolls the die a second time and draws the corresponding number of stars in each circle. The player records the two number sentences (addition and multiplication) that the model represents.

Materials

- die (labeled *1–6*), 1 per pair of students
- 12-by-18-inch sheet of white paper, 1 per pair of students
- pencil, 1 per pair of students
- *Circles and Stars* Game Directions (REPRODUCIBLE G-6), 1 per pair of students

Related Games

Game 18: Leftovers with 15

Key Questions

- Describe your mathematical illustration.
- How many groups do you have? How many are in each group?
- How will you record your work as an addition sentence?
- How will you record your work as a multiplication sentence?

Adapted from *About Teaching Mathematics, Third Edition: A K–8 Resource* by Marilyn Burns (Math Solutions, 2007).

Teaching Directions

Part I: The Connection

Relate the game to students' ongoing work.

Connect the lesson to previous content by telling students that today you will be showing them how multiplication is repeated addition. It is important that students hear you say, "*Circles and Stars* is a game linking additive thinking to multiplicative thinking. You will see how repeated addition is related to multiplication."

Part II: The Teaching

Introduce and model the game to students.

1. Tell students they will be playing the game *Circles and Stars* with a partner. Decide how you will model the game (see the corresponding Technology Tip for options).

2. Begin by asking a student to roll the die and report the number. If using an interactive whiteboard, students will be able to see, and reporting aloud will not be necessary.

3. Draw the corresponding number of circles where everyone can see them. Make each circle large enough to hold up to six stars. Point out the size to students. Say, "Notice the size I am drawing my circles; when you play the game you will need to make your circles about the size of a quarter."

4. Ask another student to roll the die and report the number to the class.

5. Draw the corresponding number of stars in each of the circles. If a 4 is rolled on the first roll and a 3 is rolled on the second roll, your drawing would look similar to this:

6. Next, link additive thinking to multiplicative thinking. Write an addition sentence and a

TECHNOLOGY TIP
Using an Interactive Whiteboard
To use an interactive whiteboard to model this game, create a page with one interactive dice and a star (cloned so that you have enough stars to model the game) or use the star stamp. If you don't have an interactive whiteboard, use an oversize die and record your work on the board or a piece of chart paper. Use this option to keep the work from getting erased for a while (in this way, students have an example of the game to refer back to as needed).

TEACHING TIP
When the First Roll Is One

If the first roll is one and hence one circle is drawn, students are often confused about what to write for the corresponding addition sentence. Show an example if one has not come up already. For example:

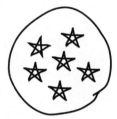

$6 + 0 = 6$

I group of 6

$1 \times 6 = 6$

TEACHING TIP
Why Use Both Sides of One Piece of Paper Instead of Two Pieces?

When students use the same piece of paper for their work, there is an increased chance that they will have conversations about the mathematics. At the same time, the teacher can examine each student's individual work to see who understands and the types of errors being made.

multiplication sentence for your drawing. Explain what you are doing. For the example in Step 5, say, "Three plus three plus three plus three equals twelve. This is the addition sentence for my drawing. Four groups of three is the multiplication sentence. Four times I wrote three stars."

$$3 + 3 + 3 + 3 = 12$$
$$4 \text{ groups of } 3$$
$$4 \times 3 = 12$$

7. Play another round, this time emphasizing the procedures of the game. Say, for example, "The first roll tells me how many circles to draw. The second roll tells me how many stars to draw. Last, I record the addition sentence and the multiplication sentence that describe my drawing."

8. When you feel like students have an understanding of how to play the game, pair them with a partner. Have them practice a few rounds (rolling the die, drawing corresponding circles and stars, and writing the addition and multiplication sentences).

9. Now give each pair a 12-by-18–inch piece of white paper and a pencil. Together with students, fold the paper so that it has eight sections. If this is problematic, prefold the paper for some or all students.

10. Explain that each student will use only one side of the paper. Have students choose their side and write *Circles and Stars* and their name in the top left-hand box.

Circles and Stars Blake			

Part III: Active Engagement

Engage students to ensure they understand how to play the game.

11. Let students know that it is now their turn to play the game. You will be there to answer any questions and clear up any confusion they may have. Pair up students.

12. Each student will play seven rounds of *Circles and Stars*. First, however, ask students to play one round of *Circles and Stars* with a partner, then check in with you or another adult in the room before moving on to the other six rounds.

13. Monitor students' understanding of the game procedures and the mathematics involved. Ask key questions including:

    - What does the first roll of the die tell you to do?

    - What does the second roll of the die determine?

    - Tell me about your work.

    - How is multiplication like addition?

    - How are you computing? (Show me how you are computing.)

Part IV: The Link

Students play the game independently.

14. Set up students for independent practice of the game. Distribute the game directions (REPRO-DUCIBLE G-6) to students as needed.

15. After each student has completed seven rounds of *Circles and Stars,* ask all students to turn in their work for review. Each pair of students should hand in one 12-by-18–inch piece of paper with seven rounds of *Circles and Stars* each, for a total of fourteen rounds.

TEACHING TIP

Understanding Student Thinking

Students have many different ways at arriving at their answers in this game. For example, consider the illustration shown. One student may say she counted from one to ten, touching each star as she counted. Another student may explain that he counted on from five, "Five, six, seven, eight, nine, ten." A third student may state, "Five plus five is ten." Yet another may conclude, "Two groups of five equals ten." In addition to understanding students' content knowledge, noting how students are thinking will help inform you of who might need to be further guided in smaller groups.

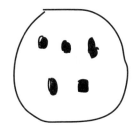

$$5 + 5 = 10$$
2 groups of 5
$$2 \times 5 = 10$$

DIFFERENTIATING YOUR INSTRUCTION

Developing students might record only the addition sentence independently. If this is the case, use each student's work to teach the connection to multiplication. On the other hand, for students who need more of a challenge, consider doing one of the following.

Record Three Sentences

Have students record *three* sentences—an addition sentence, multiplication, and division.

$$3 + 3 + 3 + 3 = 12$$

$$4 \times 3 = 12$$

$$12 \div 4 = 3$$

Total the Stars

Ask students to determine the total number of stars each person drew. The winner is the person with the most stars (the highest sum or product).

By How Much?

To increase the challenge, have students determine who had the higher number and *by how much* by recording a subtraction equation using the sum or product of each. For example:

Player 1: $4 \times 6 = 24$

Player 2: $5 \times 3 = 15$

Both players would record: $24 - 15 = 9$

Use a Different Die

To practice different facts, alter the die used (use two die labeled 4–9, for example).

MATH WORKSHOP AND SUMMARIZING THE EXPERIENCE

Teach this game at the beginning of the week to the whole class, then make it an integral part of your math workshop (for more on math workshops, see Chapter 5 in *From Reading to Math* by Maggie Siena). Later in the week, after students have played the game independently several times, present a chart titled "Circles and Stars" with the numbers 1–36 written on it. Have students place a tally mark next to the product of each round of their *Circles and Stars*. Model how to tally only the products and sums once per round. If students are unfamiliar with how to bundle tally marks, teach or remind them to bundle them in groups of five. This is always done best through demonstration.

    Discuss why some numbers have no tally mark. Numbers that cannot possibly have a tally are: 7, 11, 13, 14, 17, 19, 21, 22, 23, 26, 27, 28, 39, 31, 32, 33, 34, and 35, because the dice only contain numbers 1–6.

    Discuss why some numbers have fewer tally marks and other numbers have many. Some numbers have only two ways to make sums and products. An example is the number 10 (2 × 5 and 5 × 2). Other numbers have more ways to make sums and products, such as the number 12 (2 × 6, 6 × 2 and 3 × 4, 4 × 3).

Circles and Stars			
1	||	19	
2	||(	20	|||/
3	||	21	
4	﹢﹢﹢|	22	
5	|	23	
6	﹢﹢﹢ ||(/	24	|(|
7		25	|
8	|(	26	
9	﹢﹢﹢	27	
10	|(	28	
11		29	
12	﹢﹢﹢ (||	30	|||
13		31	
14		32	
15	|/|	33	
16	|	34	
17		35	
18	|||(	36	||

This *Circle and Stars* chart shows tally marks next to the products and sums students had in their rounds.

Close to 100
Variations: Close to 0, 20, and 1,000

Recommended Grades 1–5

Time Instruction: 60 minutes
Independent Play: 20–30 minutes

TEACHING TIPS

Enlarged Numeral Cards

A set of enlarged numeral cards is recommended to model this game. Use a photocopier to enlarge the cards provided in **REPRODUCIBLE B,** or alternatively use ten sheets of white copy paper or construction paper and write one of the 0–9 numerals on each (use a thick black marker so the numbers can be easily seen).

A Deck of Cards

For the purpose of this game, a deck of cards is four of each number. If using a deck of playing cards, the 0 will not be available. Aces represent the value of 1. Consider preparing decks of playing cards ahead of time, removing all the tens and face cards. The two jokers may remain as wild cards (meaning they can be any digit 0–9). Alternatively, show students how to sort the 10s and face cards out of their decks and then replace them when finished.

Coding Cards

Whether using numeral cards or a deck of playing cards, code each set to keep it complete. Do this by placing a small symbol in the corner of each set's card; use a different symbol for each set so that, if sets become mixed up, you can sort them more easily.

 See the Connections to the Common Core State Standards for Mathematics, page xv.

Overview

This card game and its variations focus on the base ten numbering system. For *Close to 100,* each player draws six cards and places the cards face up. Players then use the cards to construct two double-digit numbers that, when added, have a sum as close to one hundred as possible. Students record the corresponding equations on their recording sheets. The score of the round is determined by how far the sum is away from one hundred. After five rounds, the scores are totaled. The game fuses skill, strategy, and a bit of luck in supporting students' practice of place value, computation, and estimation. It's ideal for helping students build facility in number sense.

Materials

- enlarged Numeral Cards 0–9 (REPRODUCIBLE B), 1 set

- Numeral Cards 0–9 (REPRODUCIBLE B) plus four blank cards with *Wild Card* written on each, 1 deck per pair of students

  or

- playing cards (10s and face cards removed; Aces remain to represent a value of 1; Jokers may remain as wild cards), 1 deck per pair of students

- *Close to 100* Recording Sheet (REPRODUCIBLE 9), 1 per pair of students

- pencil, 1 per pair of students

- *Close to 100* Game Directions (REPRODUCIBLE G-7C), 1 per pair of students

Adapted from *Investigations in Number, Data and Space* by Susan Jo Russel, Andee Rubin and Cornelia Tierney (Dale Seymour Publications, 1998).

Related Games

See the variations included with this game.

Key Questions

To ask students:

- Tell me something you look for when you try to get close to one hundred.

- What numeral cards do you look for when playing this game?

- Explain how you are adding the two-digit numbers.

- How are you determining your score?

To ask yourself as teacher:

- Do students have a strategy or do they rely on guess and check?

- Do students consider the sum of the ones and the sum of the tens digit?

- Are students able to compute mentally with ease?

Teaching Directions

Part I: The Connection

Relate the game to students' ongoing work.

Connect the game of *Close to 100* to students' previous work with the hundreds chart and adding double-digit numbers.

Part II: The Teaching

Introduce and model the game to students.

1. Tell students they will be playing the game *Close to 100* individually, in pairs, or in threes. Explain that the goal of the game is to create two double-digit numbers that, when added, come as close to a sum of one hundred as possible.

2. Select six students to come to the front of the classroom. Hand each of them one

enlarged numeral card. Suggested numbers to start with are:

2　5　1　7　6　4

A CHILD'S MIND
Half of 100

Frequently, students first break one hundred in half and begin with a number close to half of one hundred. For example, a student may suggest the digits 5 and 1 make 51 and 4 and 6 make 46. In this case, students with the numeral cards 5, 1, 4, and 6 step forward and arrange themselves into the double-digit numbers: 51 + 46. Record the equation where everyone can see it: *51 + 46 = 97*.

TEACHING TIP
Exactly 100

It is likely students will initially come up with options that are close to one hundred even though the digit cards available, when combined, may total exactly one hundred. Accept all answers when introducing the game (this leads to more math practice in scoring of the game). Simultaneously, resist the temptation to teach strategies when playing this game. Rather, give students the opportunity to explore and discover their own strategies as they play. These strategies can then be shared and discussed during the summarizing part of the lesson.

3. Ask students to think about the numeral cards they see and suggest double-digit number combinations that come as close to a sum of one hundred as possible. When a suggestion is made, have the students holding the corresponding cards step forward and stand in order so that everyone else can see the double-digit numbers and the equation. Record the equations where everyone can see them. Students should compute the sum mentally.

4. Encourage students to get closer to one hundred. In the Half of 100 example, ask, "Is there a way we can use fifty as our first double-digit number and get even closer to the sum of one hundred?" Hopefully, students will see that replacing the 6 with a 7 will get them even closer to one hundred. Without erasing any previous suggestions, record the revised equation where everyone can see it:

$$51 + 47 = 98$$

The student with the 6 card then steps back and is replaced by the student holding the 7 card.

5. Eventually, the following four equations, which have the sum of exactly one hundred, should be suggested:

$$26 + 74 = 100$$
$$24 + 76 = 100$$
$$76 + 24 = 100$$
$$74 + 26 = 100$$

6. After several equations have been suggested and recorded, have the six students holding the oversize numeral cards return the cards and go back to their seats. Tell students that

they will now learn how to keep score during the game.

7. Create a column with the heading *Score* next to the recorded equations:

SCORE

51 + 46 = 97

51 + 47 = 98

26 + 74 = 100

24 + 76 = 100

76 + 24 = 100

74 + 26 = 100

8. Start with the equations with a sum of one hundred. Explain to students the score for these is zero because the sum is exactly one hundred. Record *0* in the score column next to each 100 sum. Emphasize that, in this game, the winner is the player with the lowest score.

9. In the first equation on the example list, the sum is 97. Tell students, "To determine the score, we need to find out how far away ninety-seven is from one hundred. We could do this by counting up or counting on from ninety-seven, or by subtracting and counting back from one hundred." When students offer the correct answer of 3, write this in the Score column next to the corresponding sum. Continue doing this until there is a score next to every equation. The example list will look like this:

SCORE

51 + 46 = 97   3

51 + 47 = 98   2

26 + 74 = 100   0

24 + 76 = 100   0

76 + 24 = 100   0

74 + 26 = 100   0

10. Now select one of the equations with a sum of one hundred. Label it *Round 1* and erase all the others. You will use the means of presentation to demonstrate how to total scores after the completion of three rounds.

ROUND 1	SCORE
26 + 74 = 100	0

11. Ask for another group of six volunteers to come to the front of the classroom. Select six numeral cards using the following criteria:

    a. Two of the six cards should be ones that were *not* used to total exactly one hundred in the previous round of play; in our example, we already used the 5 and the 1.

    b. Include 0 as one of the new numeral cards (this will set the stage for a discussion about using zero as a placeholder; note that if you're using a deck of playing cards you will not have a 0).

    c. For the remaining three cards, choose entirely new numbers.

12. Give each volunteer one of the six numeral cards. Discuss the use of the 0 card.

13. Once again, ask students to suggest double-digit number combinations that come as close to a sum of one hundred as possible. When a suggestion is made, have the students holding the corresponding cards step forward and stand in order so that students can see the two-digit numbers and the equation. Record the equations where everyone can see them.

14. Figure out the scores per Steps 8 and 9. Choose one of the equations and erase the others. Label it *Round 2.* Use this means of presentation to demonstrate how to total scores after the completion of three rounds.

15. Thank the volunteers and collect the enlarged numeral cards.

TEACHING TIP
Using Zero
Typically, we don't write the number 7 as 07. For this reason, in this game, a 0 may only be placed in the ones place but not the tens. For example, 70 would be allowed but not 07.

Part III: Active Engagement

Engage students to ensure they understand how to play the game.

16. Now give students an opportunity to explore the game in pairs. Select a new set of six enlarged numeral cards. Place the cards where everyone can see them clearly.

17. Invite students to talk with a partner. Which combinations of numerals would they pick to make two double-digit numbers that, when combined, would get them as close as possible to one hundred? Allow time for students to listen and learn. They should be given ample opportunity to explore the number combinations and computation involved.

18. Select a pair of students to share an equation aloud. Record it where everyone can see it. Label it *Round 3*. Remember to resist the temptation to discuss strategies; this can happen during the summarizing part of the lesson.

19. Three rounds are typically adequate for students to grasp how to play the game. After you have three equations listed and labeled by round (1, 2, and 3) where everyone can see them, take the opportunity to teach the final step of the game: adding the scores for a total. Tell students that when it's their turn to play the game, they will actually play five rounds and figure out the total score based on those five rounds. The player with the lowest total score is the winner.

Part IV: The Link

Students play the game independently.

20. Set up students for independent practice with the game. Each pair of students should be dealt six cards and given one *Close to 100* Recording Sheet (REPRODUCIBLE 9). Also distribute the game directions (REPRODUCIBLE G-7C) as needed.

TEACHING TIP
Pairing Students
After students have played the game several times and strategies have begun to emerge, you can be more purposeful when partnering students. Consider pairing students who use different strategies. For example, students who are using a strategy of halving (trying to make two numbers close to fifty so that when they're added, they are close to one hundred) might benefit from being partnered with students who look for the tens to total ninety and the ones to total ten. Likewise, students still clinging to random guess and check may benefit from working with a partner who uses the strategy of halving.

TEACHING TIP
The Importance of Practice
Refrain from discussing skill or strategies during the active engagement part of the lesson. The purpose is to give students as much practice as possible first; they will then have the opportunity to come back later and discuss their experiences (see "Math Workshop and Summarizing the Experience").

TEACHING TIP
Jokers as Wild Cards
After students understand the game and begin to play it independently, use the Jokers as wild cards—meaning, students can assign any number 0–9 to the Joker when it is drawn. If you're using numeral cards, include four blank cards with *Wild Card* written on each.

21. Give students time to play at least five rounds. When observing and talking with students as they play, ask key questions, such as:

- Tell me something you look for when you try to get close to one hundred.

- What numeral cards do you look for when playing this game?

- Explain how you are adding the double-digit numbers.

- How are you determining your score?

TEACHING TIP
The Importance of Asking Questions

Asking key questions assists you in understanding how or if students are developing strategies. As students answer key questions, students get to hear other students' thinking and further develop their own understanding of the content.

DIFFERENTIATING YOUR INSTRUCTION

There are several ways to modify the game according to the levels and needs of your students.

Score Variations

Introduce scoring variations. Have students record their score as less than or more than 100 using plus and minus signs. For example, if the sum of a round is 95, the player's score would be −5 because the sum is five less than 100. If the sum of the round is 103, the player's score would be +3. This scoring version offers more strategy and less luck to win the game.

Close to 0

Have students play *Close to 0*. A *Close to 0* Recording Sheets **(REPRODUCIBLE 7)** and *Close to 0* Game Directions **(REPRODUCIBLE G-7A)** have been provided for this version. *Close to 0* is played similar to *Close to 100*; however students practice subtraction. After drawing eight cards, students try to make two, three-digit numbers that, when subtracted, are close to 0.

Close to 1

Offer *Close to 1* for students who are working with decimals. The only difference with this version is now 0 may be used to hold the place of the tenths but not the hundredths. You may use the *Close to 0* Recording Sheets **(REPRODUCIBLE 7)** for this version.

Close to 20

Simplify the game and call it *Close to 20*. In this version, students draw four cards and select three to add. The objective is to have the three numbers be equal or close to 20. A *Close to 20* Recording Sheets **(REPRODUCIBLE 8)** and *Close to 20* Game Directions **(REPRODUCIBLE G-7B)** have been provided for this version. This version of the game is most applicable to younger students (grades 1–2); make counters accessible for students who may need a more tangible representation when combining numbers. Cubes or small discs work well.

Close to 1,000

Challenge students to play with three-digit addends in the variation *Close to 1,000*. For this version, students draw eight cards and use six of them in creating two triple-digit numbers to add, aiming for a sum of close to 1,000. A *Close to 1,000* Recording Sheets **(REPRODUCIBLE 10)** and *Close to 1,000* Game Directions **(REPRODUCIBLE G-7D)** have been provided for this version.

MATH WORKSHOP AND SUMMARIZING THE EXPERIENCE

Teach this game at the beginning of the week to the whole class, then make it an integral part of your math workshop (for more on math workshops, see Chapter 5 in *From Reading to Math* by Maggie Siena). Build in time to observe students playing the game. Note their individual skill level and the strategies being used. Come together as a class later in the week to discuss both strategy and how the game aided in automaticity and fact facility. Refer to your notes during the discussion. Begin a collection of equations that total exactly 100.

ASSESSMENTS

Writing Prompt

Have students pick what they feel is their best round in a game of *Close to 100*. Do they think skill or luck played a part in this being the best round? Ask them to write their thoughts in their journals.

Joe's Game

Distribute copies of the *Close to 100* Assessment: Joe's Game **(REPRODUCIBLE 11)**. Use this assessment to examine student thinking and determine students' facility with one hundred. The assessment can also guide you in selecting students who may benefit from small-group instruction. Students who are using underdeveloped strategies (more random approaches to reaching one hundred) might benefit from a lesson using a hundreds chart (a hundreds chart is available as **REPRODUCIBLE A** in this resource). Students who use a more sophisticated strategy, such as looking for the ones to make a ten and the tens to make ninety, could join a small group in which some of the game variations are taught and played (see "Differentiating Your Instruction" on the previous page).

Compare (Shake and Spill)

Recommended Grades K–1

Time   Instruction: 45–60 minutes
Independent Play: 20–30 minutes

Overview

Students who are learning to count and compare will benefit greatly from this game. Students, in pairs, take turns shaking and spilling a select group of two-color counters. Each time, students record whether there are more red counters, more yellow, or the same amount. The game can serve as a springboard for supporting students in writing number sentences to represent the data symbolically.

Materials

- two-color counters, 10 per student
- pencil, 1 per pair of students
- *Compare (Shake and Spill)* Chart (REPRODUCIBLE 12), enlarged for class use
- *Compare (Shake and Spill)* Chart (REPRODUCIBLE 12), 1 per pair of students
- *Compare (Shake and Spill)* Game Directions (REPRODUCIBLE G-8), 1 per student

Related Game

Game 21: More!

Key Questions

- What are you noticing about the combinations of ten?
- Would you classify the addends as odd or even?
- What do you notice about the sum of two odd numbers and two even numbers?

TEACHING TIP
Two-Color Counters
Two-color counters are counters that have a different color on each side. Typically, one side is red and the other is yellow.

CCSS → See the Connections to the Common Core State Standards for Mathematics, page xv.

Adapted from *About Teaching Mathematics, Third Edition: A K–8 Resource* by Marilyn Burns (Math Solutions, 2007).

Teaching Directions
Part I: The Connection

Relate the game to students' ongoing work.

Review the concept of comparison with students. To do so, preselect a few students who are wearing black sneakers and blue sneakers. Then, ask students to look around the classroom and make note of the color of their classmates' shoes. Invite the preselected group of students to the front of the classroom. Ask the students to note the color of each student's shoes. Ask questions such as:

- How many are wearing black sneakers?

- How many are wearing blue sneakers?

- Let's compare; how many more students are wearing _____ than _____?

Part II: The Teaching

Introduce and model the game to students.

1. Gather students on the floor in front of a board or easel. Explain to them that they will be playing the game *Compare* in pairs. During this game, they will be using and counting two-color counters.

2. Present the *Compare (Shake and Spill)* Chart (REPRODUCIBLE 12), large enough for everyone to see. A piece of lined chart paper works well and takes little preparation.

MORE RED	SAME	MORE YELLOW

3. Show students a two-color counter. If they have never used the manipulative before, give

TEACHING TIP
Arranging Students
For the modeling part of this game, having students sit in a circle or on the perimeter of a rectangular space (rug) works best. This gives room in the middle for students to see the counters as they are being spilled and tallied.

TECHNOLOGY TIP
Using an Interactive Whiteboard

For the purpose of modeling the game, instead of two-color counters, you can use an interactive whiteboard. In the whiteboard's tools, you'll find two-color counters that can flip and land randomly when tapped. An interactive coin could be substituted as well.

TEACHING TIP
Shake and Spill

It is important to take time to demonstrate how to shake and spill counters properly to prevent students from throwing and scattering them in the process. Consider giving each student a paper plate or placemat to use as a target—when they spill their counters, all the counters should land on the plate or placemat.

TEACHING TIP
Bundling Tally Marks

When there are five tally marks in one column of the chart, teach students how to bundle the marks. To do so, place the fifth mark diagonally across the other four marks to create a "bundle" of five marks.

one to each student and provide about thirty seconds for them to play with it.

4. Select a volunteer to come to the middle of the group. Tell the student to cup his hands. Place six counters in the student's hands; have the rest of the class count the counters aloud, "One, two, three, four, five, six," as you place them.

5. Point out to students that carefully cupped hands allow them to shake the counters without spilling any. Demonstrate this, shaking your cupped hands in front of your body with small up and down arm movements.

6. Give students the opportunity to practice shaking their hands. Have them pretend that they have six counters in their hands and shake; the volunteer with actual counters does the same.

7. Tell students to shake their cupped hands for about three seconds, then spill. To spill the counters, students should gently uncup their hands onto the work surface. Have the volunteer demonstrate, spilling his counters on the rug.

8. When the volunteer spills his counters, make sure students do not attempt to touch them. Instead, task students with observing the counters. Ask, "Are there more red, more yellow, or is it the same amount of both red and yellow?" Place a tally mark on the chart indicating the results.

9. Repeat Steps 7 and 8 multiple times until one column on the chart has five tallies. Each time, select another volunteer to demonstrate shaking and spilling. Make sure all students have the opportunity to see the counters spill out and to help report the results.

Part III: Active Engagement

Engage students to ensure they understand how to play the game.

10. Now give students the opportunity to explore the game in pairs. Give each pair of students six counters, a copy of the *Compare (Shake and Spill)* Chart (REPRODUCIBLE 12), and a pencil.

11. Instruct students to take turns shaking and spilling the counters. Say, "One person will shake and spill. Both will agree on the results. The other person will place the tally on the chart. Alternate turns."

12. Give students time to practice playing the game. Walk around the classroom while students are actively engaged. Make note of their conversations and thinking. After students have had a reasonable amount of time playing the game, bring them back together as a class.

Part IV: The Link

Students play the game independently.

13. Set up students for independent practice with the game. Each pair of students should be given ten counters, a pencil, and a copy of the *Compare (Shake and Spill)* Chart (REPRODUCIBLE 12).

14. Explain that, this time when students play the game, they should first decide how many counters they want to shake and spill. They have the option of using six, seven, eight, nine, or ten counters.

15. Observe and talk with students as they play. When playing with ten counters, ask key questions to help students recognize that two odd numbers make an even and two even numbers make an even. Your questions might be:

    - What are you noticing about the combinations of ten?

    - Would you classify the addends as odd or even?

TEACHING TIP
Emphasize Collaboration
Explain to students that they will be playing in teams of two with their partner, not against him or her. The goal is for students to work together to understand how to play the game and the math involved.

TEACHING TIP
The Importance of Giving Students Roles
When practicing the game in pairs, one student should shake and spill the counters while the other records the results. Dividing the tasks ensures that each student has an active role. Students should alternate roles with each turn.

TEACHING TIP
Pairing Students
For this game, pair students with someone of like ability. Pairing students with similar mathematical skills may allow for more differentiation options and will afford optimum access to the mathematics involved in playing the game.

TEACHING TIP
Posting a Class Chart
Having students transfer their work to a class chart aids in accountability and provides a collection of data. If some students didn't have an opportunity to finish a round or were unable to investigate all four numbers (6, 7, 8, 9 and 10) they can still see the data and participate in the closure/reflective process of *Compare*.

- What do you notice about the sum of two odd numbers and two even numbers?

16. Students should play twenty rounds with each group of counters before selecting a new number of counters to shake.

17. Post a class chart (an enlarged version of REPRODUCIBLE 12) to which students can transfer their work.

MATH WORKSHOP AND SUMMARIZING THE EXPERIENCE

Teach this game at the beginning of the week to the whole class, then make it an integral part of your math workshop (for more on math workshops, see Chapter 5 in *From Reading to Math* by Maggie Siena). Build in time to observe students playing the game. Note their individual skill level and the strategies being used. Come together later in the week and hold a discussion about the mathematics involved in the game. Refer to your notes during the discussion. Ask students to notice which numbers never come up with both colors the same. This leads to the concepts of doubles and odd and even numbers.

Refer to the class chart and identify all the possible color combinations for each column. Record corresponding number sentences (see Figure 8.1). If using two-color counters with red on one side and yellow on the other, Figure 8.1 shows the seven different combinations.

MORE RED	SAME	MORE YELLOW
＋＋＋ ＼＼＼＼	＼／＼	＋＋＋ ＼＼＼
6 red + 0 yellow		2 red + 4 yellow
5 red + 1 yellow	3 red + 3 yellow	1 red + 5 yellow
4 red + 2 yellow		0 red + 6 yellow

Figure 8.1. An example of a class chart in summarizing the experience for a game of *Compare (Shake and Spill)* using six counters. The tally marks indicate that twenty shake-and-spills were done.

Cross Out Singles

Overview

During this game, students practice addition while using logical reasoning coupled with probability. To begin, one player rolls a die. All players write the number rolled in a square of their choice on their game board. Another player rolls the die and, again, all players record the number in a square of their choice on their game board. Players take turns rolling the die until all nine squares have been filled in. Players then find the sums of the number strings (the numbers in the rows, columns, and diagonal on their game board). They record the sums in the circles on the game board. Finally, players examine their sums, crossing out any sums that only appear once (hence the game's name, *Cross Out Singles*). Players add up the sums in the remaining circles. The total is each player's score for the round. The winner is the player with the highest score for all three rounds. The game includes two versions for the game board to allow for differentiated instruction.

Materials

- die (labeled *1–6*), 1 per pair of students
- *Cross Out Singles* Game Boards (REPRODUCIBLE 13), 1 array enlarged for class use
- *Cross Out Singles* Game Boards (REPRODUCIBLE 13), 1 per pair of students
- pencil, 1 per student
- *Cross Out Singles* Game Directions (REPRODUCIBLE G-9), 1 per pair of students

Recommended Grades 2–4
Time Instruction: 30–45 minutes
Independent Play: 20–30 minutes

 TEACHING TIP
Quiet Dice
Rolling dice can create lots of noise. To lessen the noise, use foam dice or pad students' workspaces with foam or fabric placemats.

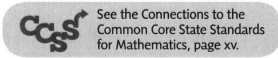 See the Connections to the Common Core State Standards for Mathematics, page xv.

Related Games

Game 10: Cross Out Sums

Game 13: Fifteen-Number Cross-Out

Key Questions

- Tell me about your strategy.

- What would be the ideal number to roll first? Why? Where would you place it?

- What is the largest/smallest sum you can achieve in this game using a 1–6 die? Explain.

Teaching Directions

Part I: The Connection

Relate the game to students' ongoing work.

Build background for the introduction to the concept of singles by asking students, "Have you ever heard a commercial about a fast-food restaurant having a single-, double-, or even triple-patty hamburger? What does it mean to have a single-patty burger compared with a double or triple?" Another connection might be, "Let's think about the game of baseball or kickball. Many of you play kickball at recess or have participated in, attended, or watched a game of baseball. What does it mean when players are up at bat and they hit a single?"

Part II: The Teaching

Introduce and model the game to students.

1. Explain to students that they will be learning the game *Cross Out Singles*. Ask students to help define what the word *singles* means. Help them understand that, in this game, they must cross out sums that only appear on their recording sheets once; these are considered the single sums.

A CHILD'S MIND
Defining *Single*

When discussing the meaning of the word *single*, the definitions children volunteer will vary depending on their age and experiences. They might suggest *one* like a "single slice of pizza." A child might describe how a line of students moves through the hallway or the cafeteria—in a "single file" line. Students may say *single* refers to a digit 0–9—a "single digit." Still others may say a single is "one song" released by an artist or that the word means "alone" as in living by yourself. Accept all of the ideas that are a definition of *single*. Explain that a mathematician's definition of the word *single* means one.

2. Next, place an enlargement of one of the game boards (REPRODUCIBLE 13) where everyone can see it. Tell students this will be their game board. The objective will be to record addends in the squares, add the number strings (both as rows, columns, and diagonal), and record the sums in the circles.

3. Model how the recording is done. First have a student roll a die. Have another student or group of students decide which square on the array should be used to record the number on the die. Record the number in the selected square.

4. Repeat Step 3 eight more times. Involve various students in the rolling of the die and the placement of the number. Emphasize that once a number is recorded on the array, it may not be moved to another square.

5. After all nine squares are filled, ask students to find the sums of the number strings: the numbers in the rows, columns, and diagonal. Work together to record the sums in the corresponding circles.

6. Now ask students to look at the array and identify any sums that are not repeated in the circles. Sums listed only once (the number appears in only one circle) are considered "singles." Cross out these sums.

TECHNOLOGY TIP
Using an Interactive Whiteboard
You can also use an interactive whiteboard to display the game board. To do so, create a table of three squares by three squares; the squares need to be large enough to be viewed easily by students. Draw or use the circle tool to add the seven circles to the game board. Also, enable the interactive die (when tapped, it will generate a number).

TEACHING TIP
Using the Die for Modeling Purposes
For modeling purposes, use a demonstration-size die or use the die on an interactive whiteboard. This ensures that every student can see the number rolled.

TEACHING TIP
Encouraging Talk
When finding sums of the number strings (the rows, columns, and diagonal), encourage students to talk about their computation. It is important for students to be able to articulate how they combine the numbers (adding left to right, doubling, combining ones, combining tens, and so forth). It is equally valuable for other students to see and hear how a classmate is computing. As students explain their thinking, record each student's thinking by writing the number string and noting how they are combining the numbers. For example, in the number string $3 + 5 + 3 = 11$, a student might explain her addition processes as, "I know my doubles and three plus three is six. Five and six is eleven." You would then record:

$$3 + 5 + 3 = 11$$
$$6$$
$$5 + 6 = 11$$

7. Ask students, "How many circles are left?" Have students total the sums in the circles that remain. This total is their score. For example:

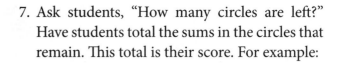

$$11 + 11 + 10 + 11 + 10 = 53$$

The player's score for this round is 53.

8. Point out that, in this game, the player with the highest score after three rounds is the winner.

9. Play another round of the game as a whole class (repeat Steps 2–8). This time, you might find that students consider more carefully the squares in which they record the numbers rolled. Refrain from discussing student strategies until the summarizing part of this lesson.

Part III: Active Engagement

Engage students to ensure they understand how to play the game.

10. Now give students an opportunity to explore the game in pairs. Distribute one copy of the *Cross Out Singles* Game Boards (REPRODUCIBLE 13) to each pair of students. Remind students that this is their game board.

11. Roll the die. Give pairs of students time to record the number rolled in one of the squares on their *Cross Out Singles* Game Board.

12. Repeat Step 11 eight more times. Remind students that once a number is recorded in a square, it may not be erased or moved to another square.

A CHILD'S MIND
Placing the Number

As students become more familiar with the game, do not be surprised if some students have strategies and opinions about "good" placement and "poor" placement of numbers on the array. Refrain from discussing strategies during this part of teaching the lesson. Tell students they will have an opportunity to share their strategies and thinking later in the week, giving everyone ample time to play the game and develop their own ideas.

TEACHING TIP
Pairing Students

Pairing students with someone of like ability or similar strategies may help level the playing field in this game. Ultimately, this game involves skill, strategy, and luck; overdesigning your pairings of students will not influence the success or failure of students playing the game. If you find that students are reluctant to explore this game in pairs, you might need to model another round (repeat Steps 2–8).

13. After all nine squares are filled, ask students to work in pairs to find the sums of the number strings (the rows, columns, and diagonal). Make sure they record the sums in the corresponding circles on their game boards.

14. Ask students to cross out any sums that appear only once in the circles (the "singles").

15. Have students work in pairs to total the sums in the circles remaining.

16. Now give students time to compare their game boards. Ideas for comparing include:

    - Pairs find another pair of students who share the same grand total. Compare game boards; are the nine numbers placed in the same squares? How are the game boards similar or different?

    - Pairs trade game boards with another pair of students. They check the mathematics and then compare their rounds.

Part IV: The Link

Students play the game independently.

17. Set up students for independent practice with the game. Each student should be given one copy of the *Cross Out Singles* Game Boards (REPRODUCIBLE 13). Each pair or group of students should also have one die. Distribute the game directions (REPRODUCIBLE G-9).

18. Determine how many rounds students should complete. The game boards are set up for three consecutive rounds. However, if time is limited, this could be modified. When observing and talking with students as they play, ask key questions such as:

    - Tell me about your strategy.

    - What would be the ideal number to roll first? Why? Where would you place it?

    - What is the largest/smallest sum you can achieve in this game using a 1–6 die? Explain.

TEACHING TIP
Common Strategies
That Students Use

One common strategy students often use is to place the first number, no matter what it is, in the middle of their game board and the next number in one of the corners. While interviewing students, I have learned they are using logical reasoning. They recognize that those same numbers are likely to be rolled again in the next six rolls. After the middle addend has been determined, placing the same numerals in the corners will result in the same sum. This is an example of the commutative property. This might lead to a lesson on this mathematical law, which states that the order of the digits doesn't affect the sum. This strategy and others will assist students in moving forward in their thinking and/or will serve as a revisit of content and concepts learned.

DIFFERENTIATING YOUR INSTRUCTION

Cross Out Singles: 4-by-4 Array

To provide more challenge, instead of using a three-by-three array, use a four-by-four array. **REPRODUCIBLE 14** is provided for this purpose. If using this game board, students need to add four addends and record sums in nine circles.

MATH WORKSHOP AND SUMMARIZING THE EXPERIENCE

Teach this game at the beginning of the week to the whole class, then make it an integral part of your math workshop (for more on math workshops, see Chapter 5 in *From Reading to Math* by Maggie Siena). Build in time to observe students playing the game. Note their individual skill level and the strategies being utilized. Have students cut out and post their best round on a classroom chart. Give students time to think about the chart. Which round is the winning round? Continue with a friendly discussion about the highest score.

ASSESSMENT

Writing Prompt

Have students pick what they feel is their best round in a game of *Cross Out Singles*. Do they think skill or luck played a part in this being the best round? Ask them to write about their strategies in their journals.

Cross Out Sums

Overview

This game gives students practice at basic addition facts as well as reinforces the commutative property of addition. Students draw three cards and arrange two of the numbers to build equations. They then cross off the corresponding sums on the game board. Play continues as long as there is at least one of the sums to cross off on the game board. The game ends in two ways: (1) when all the sums are crossed off or (2) when the numbers do not result in any of the remaining sums on the board. The game includes two versions of the game board to allow for differentiated instruction.

Materials

- enlarged Numeral Cards 1–10 (REPRODUCIBLE B), 1 set

- Numeral Cards 1–10 (REPRODUCIBLE B), 1 deck per pair of students

  or

- playing cards (face cards and Jokers removed; Aces remain to represent the value of 1), 1 deck per pair of students

- *Cross Out Sums* Game Board, Version 1 (REPRODUCIBLE 15), enlarged for demonstration purposes

- *Cross Out Sums* Game Board, Version 1 (REPRODUCIBLE 15), 1 per pair of students

- *Cross Out Sums* Game Directions (REPRODUCIBLE G-10), 1 per pair of students

Recommended Grades 1–2

Time Instruction: 45–60 minutes
Independent Play: 20–30 minutes

TEACHING TIPS
Enlarged Numeral Cards
A set of enlarged numeral cards is recommended to model this game. Use a photocopier to enlarge the cards provided in **REPRODUCIBLE B,** or alternatively use ten sheets of white copy paper or construction paper and write one of the 1–10 numerals on each (use a thick black marker so the numbers can easily be seen).

A Deck of Cards
For the purpose of this game, a deck of cards is four of each number 1–10. If using a deck of playing cards, the Ace represents the value of 1. Consider preparing decks of playing cards ahead of time, removing the face cards and Jokers.

Reusable Game Boards
Instead of making consumable copies of the *Cross Out Sums* Game Board, consider laminating a set or placing copies in plastic sleeves and providing dry erase pens.

 See the Connections to the Common Core State Standards for Mathematics, page xv.

Related Games

Game 3: Addition Tic-Tac-Toe

Game 13: Fifteen-Number Cross-Out

Game 23: Oh No! 20!

Key Questions

- What sums are coming up often? Why do you think that is happening?

- Why do you think some numbers occur only once on the board, whereas others occur many times?

Teaching Directions

Part I: The Connection

Relate the game to students' ongoing work.

Connect the game of *Cross Out Sums* to addition practice. Tell students that the game they will be playing will help them practice basic facts.

Part II: The Teaching

Introduce and model the game to students.

1. Explain to students that they will be learning the game *Cross Out Sums*. To play the game, they will use a deck of numeral cards. Mix up a set of enlarged numeral cards and stack them.

2. Draw three cards from the top of the stack. Flip over all three cards and place them where students can see them clearly. For example, you might draw and display the following cards:

| 7 | 6 | 2 |

3. Explain to students they need to create three equations, each equation using two of the numbers. Each equation should also have a different sum. Move the cards around to form the various equations. For the three cards drawn in the example, the equations might be:

$$7 + 6 = 13 \qquad 6 + 2 = 8 \qquad 2 + 7 = 9$$

4. Now show students an enlarged version of the *Cross Out Sums* Game Board, Version 1 (REPRODUCIBLE 15). Ask students, "What do you notice about this game board?" Make sure students note that some numbers occur more than once.

5. Bring students' attention back to the equations they formed with the three numeral cards. Explain that they now need to cross out the sums on the game board. In the example, students would cross out numbers 13, 8, and 9.

6. Place the three cards used in a discard pile. Draw three new cards from the top. Flip over all three cards and place them where students can see them clearly.

7. Work together as a class to move the three cards around to form three equations.

8. On the game board, cross out the sums of the three equations.

9. Repeat Steps 6–8 until there is no sum to cross out. When you reach an example of a sum that has already been crossed off, explain to students that they should not stop; as long as one of the three sums is still not crossed out, the game continues. The game ends when either (1) all sums are crossed out on the game board or (2) none of the cards drawn equal any of the remaining sums on the game board.

 DIFFERENTIATING YOUR INSTRUCTION

Two versions of the *Cross Out Sums* Game Board are provided. To introduce the game, use Version 1. This helps eliminate some of the complexity of the game and allows students to focus more on the computation and less on their strategy of crossing numbers off the game board.

TEACHING TIP
If a Number Appears More Than Once
Some numbers occur more than once on the game board. Students must only cross out one appearance of the number, even if it appears multiple times on their game board.

2	3	4	5	6
7	~~8~~	~~8~~	9	10
10	10	11	11	11
12	12	~~13~~	14	15
16	17	18	19	20

Part III: Active Engagement

Engage students to ensure they understand how to play the game.

10. Now give students an opportunity to explore the game in pairs. Distribute a deck of numeral cards and one copy of the *Cross Out Sums* Game Board (Version 1) to each pair of students.

11. As students play, circulate around the room, making sure students' computations are accurate. Observe if students are understanding and following the procedures of the game.

Part IV: The Link

Students play the game independently.

12. Set up students for independent practice with the game. Explain there are three ways to play the game: individually, in collaborative pairs, or in competitive pairs. Consider giving students the choice of which way to play the game. Students should be given one copy of the *Cross Out Sums* Game Board (**REPRODUCIBLE 15**). Each pair or group of students should also have one deck of numeral cards. Also, distribute the game directions (**REPRODUCIBLE G-10**) as needed.

13. When observing and talking with students as they play, ask key questions such as:

    • What sums are coming up often? Why do you think that is happening?

    • Why do you think some numbers occur only once on the board whereas others occur many times?

TEACHING TIP
Competitive Play

To play the game in competing pairs, the pair who ends the game first is the winner. To end the game, either the last remaining sum is crossed out or all three sums on a single turn have been crossed off previously.

DIFFERENTIATING YOUR INSTRUCTION

Cross Out Sums Game Board, Version 2 (Tic-Tac-Toe)

A second game board, *Cross Out Sums* (Version 2) (**REPRODUCIBLE 16**) is also provided. A bit more complex, this game board can be used to play *Cross Out Sums* similar to the way one plays the classic game tic-tac-toe. The objective is to be the first to cross off sums in a five-in-a-row fashion (horizontal, vertical, or diagonal).

MATH WORKSHOP AND
SUMMARIZING THE EXPERIENCE

Teach this game at the beginning of the week to the whole class, then make it an integral part of your math workshop (for more on math workshops, see Chapter 5 in *From Reading to Math* by Maggie Siena). Build in time to observe students playing the game. After students, have had many opportunities to play either version of the game, bring them together for a class discussion. Ask students, as you did when you circulated, "Why do you think the game board has some numbers listed more than once?" Guide students in discussing combinations and breaking apart numbers. Consider creating a chart for students to record the equations they formed during the game. You might do this for each number or numbers you want to investigate further. For example, a chart for the number 10 might look like this:

$$\underline{\text{Ways to Make } 10}$$

$0 + 10$	$10 + 0$
$1 + 9$	$9 + 1$
$2 + 8$	$8 + 2$
$3 + 7$	$7 + 3$
$4 + 6$	$6 + 4$
$5 + 5$	

Digit Place
(A Secret Number Quest)

Recommended Grades 3–5

Time Instruction: 30–45 minutes
Independent Play: 20–30 minutes

TIME SAVER
Reusable Recording Sheets
Instead of making consumable copies of the *Digit Place* Recording Sheet, laminate a set or place copies in plastic sleeves and provide dry erase pens. Alternatively, use whiteboards or pencil and paper to create the recording sheet. Some options (that is, paper and pencil) are better than others in terms of keeping a record of students' work.

See the Connections to the Common Core State Standards for Mathematics, page xv.

Overview

This game develops students' number sense and encourages practice in place value and deductive reasoning. To start, one player selects a secret number. The other player or players try to figure out the number through a series of guesses. After each guess, the player with the secret number reveals whether the number guessed shares a digit with the secret number. If it does, the player also reveals whether the place value is correct. Play continues until the number is guessed correctly. Needing only pencil, paper, and a partner, this game is a great one to play at home as well!

Materials

- *Digit Place (A Secret Number Quest)* Recording Sheet (REPRODUCIBLE 17), 1 per group of students

- *Digit Place (A Secret Number Quest)* Game Directions (REPRODUCIBLE G-11), 1 per group of students

- pencil, 1 per group of students

Related Game

Game 7: Close to 100

Key Questions

- After this round, what do you know for sure?

- Are there any digits that might be eliminated?

- Are there digits we should keep the same but change the place? Why? How do you know?

Teaching Directions

Part I: The Connection

Relate the game to students' ongoing work.

Connect the math to previously taught concepts of place value and digits. Emphasize the use of logic skills.

Review the meaning of the words *place value* and *digits*. Write the digits 0–9 where everyone can see them. Ask students to name two-digit numbers that can be created from the ten digits.

Explain the meaning of a palindrome (that is, 11, 22, or 33). Tell students that palindromes are not allowed in the *Digit Place* game even though they are two-digit numbers. In *Digit Place,* you must choose numbers that have two different digits.

Part II: The Teaching

Introduce and model the game to students.

1. Tell students they will be playing the game *Digit Place* in pairs or in small groups. During the game, one player chooses a two-digit number (the digits must be different numbers!) and keeps it a secret. The other players work together to make guesses and figure out the number. Display an enlarged version of the *Digit Place* Recording Sheet (REPRODUCIBLE 17) for everyone to see.

2. Explain that for the purpose of learning the game, you will start by sharing the secret number with everyone. Choose the number 42.

3. Next, show students how you record a guess. Say, "Let's pretend my partner guessed fourteen. I record the number fourteen in the Guess column." Write *14* in the Guess column of the enlarged recording sheet (REPRODUCIBLE 17).

4. Now add information about how many digits and places are correct based on the number 14 guess. Say, "I now write a one in the Digit

column because one of the digits, the four, is correct. I write a zero in the Place column because the four in fourteen is not in the correct place. The four is in the ones place, not the tens place." Your chart will look like this:

Guess	Digit	Place
14	1	0

5. Continue demonstrating making guesses and writing corresponding information on the chart until the secret number is figured out. Make many different guesses and carefully narrate your reasoning as you record. After seven guesses, your chart might look something like this:

Guess	Digit	Place
14	1	0
80	0	0
67	0	0
20	1	0
45	1	1
40	1	1
42	2	2

6. Choose another secret number and play another round with the class, this time not revealing your number ahead of time. As students guess numbers, record each number and the digits and places.

7. Each time a guess and new information are shared, ask students, "What do you know for sure?" This encourages them to reflect on the information in the chart and use it to guide their next guess.

TEACHING TIP

Remembering the Secret Number

In some cases a student might forget the secret number he chose, or students might feel the secret number has been changed partway through the game; to ensure that neither transpires, have players write the secret number on a sticky note and place it on the back of the recording sheet. When the secret number is guessed, it can be revealed easily.

8. Encourage students to share their thinking out loud when they guess a number. Ask key questions such as:

- After your last guess, what do you know for sure?

- What digits might be eliminated?

- What digits need to be repeated in the next guess but in a different place?

9. After students determine the secret number, play one more round (round three) as a class.

Part III: Active Engagement

Engage students to ensure they understand how to play the game.

10. Now give students an opportunity to explore the game in small groups of four (two pairs).

11. Explain to students that one pair will decide on a secret number. The other pair will make guesses and discuss after each guess "what they know for sure." Working together helps students avoid errors in conveying information about digit and place.

12. Give each group a copy of the *Digit Place* Recording Sheet (REPRODUCIBLE 17). As students play, circulate, observing and assisting as needed. Provide enough time for each pair of students to have a turn at being the secret number selector and the guesser.

13. At this time, it is not necessary to discuss skill or strategies in playing the game. Students should have more independent practice first.

Part IV: The Link

Students play the game independently.

14. Set up students for independent practice with the game. Decide if students will work in groups of twos or fours. Distribute one copy of the *Digit Place* Recording Sheet (REPRODUCIBLE 17) per group. Also, distribute the *Digit Place* Game Directions (REPRODUCIBLE G-11) as needed.

TEACHING TIPS

The Importance of Practice

Refrain from discussing skill or strategies during the "active engagement" part of the lesson. The purpose is to give students as much practice as possible first; they will have the opportunity to come back later and discuss their experiences (see the "Math Workshop and Summarizing the Experience" part of the lesson).

Encouraging "Stop and Think"

It is important, in this part of the lesson, to encourage students to stop and think. This is true of both pairs of students. The students who possess the secret number need to stop and think before responding to the other pair's guesses: What digit is correct? Is it in the correct place? The pair who is making guesses needs to stop and think, "What do I know for sure?" before making another guess.

How Many Players?

During this game, students can play in pairs or small groups of four (two pairs). Consider having students first work in small groups; after students are familiar with the game and have developed a greater understanding of the concept of digit and place, have them play with a partner.

Grouping Students for Play

Once students understand the procedural side of the game, consider grouping them in like ability groups. This will afford the opportunity to differentiate for students who need a challenge while giving the remaining students an opportunity to move through the game at a rate that supports the development of their understanding of place value and logic.

DIFFERENTIATING YOUR INSTRUCTION

There are several ways to modify the game according to the levels and needs of your students.

Three-Digit Place

To increase the challenge, students can play *Digit Place* with a three-digit number. This requires more sophistication in both strategy and skill. Remind students that the digits must all be different; numbers (palindromes) such as 333, 383, 388, and 883 are not allowed even though they are three-digit numbers.

Collective Competition

Introduce students to the idea of a "Class Records Chart." Use the chart to record collective and/or individual records throughout the year. Post a *Digit Place* chart and the fewest rounds until guessed. Students can then add and update the chart as records are broken. Using sticky notes to post the records works well because they can be removed and replaced with the new record.

Scoring Attempts

Introduce scoring to the game. Players get 1 point for each attempt made. After a complete round, players tally the number of attempts. The player and/or team with the lowest number of points is the winner.

TEACHING TIP
Play It at Home!

The game *Digit Place* can be played at home easily because the materials are so accessible. For home use, *Digit Place* needs only a pencil, paper, and partner. Send home copies of the game directions **(REPRODUCIBLE G-11)** as necessary.

MATH WORKSHOP AND SUMMARIZING THE EXPERIENCE

Teach this game at the beginning of the week to the whole class, then make it an integral part of your math workshop (for more on math workshops, see Chapter 5 in *From Reading to Math* by Maggie Siena). Build in time to observe students playing the game. Note their individual skill level. Come together as a class later in the week and play another collective game (just as you did in the model lesson). This time, record the digits 0–9 above the chart. After each guess, ask students, "What do you know for sure?" If the number 0 is in the digit column, the students can determine that neither digit is in the number. When his happens, cross off the digits in the listing above the chart. This reflective and organizational approach will further help some students move forward in their playing of the game. The example round from the model lesson would look like this:

~~0~~ 1 2 3 4 5 ~~6~~ ~~7~~ ~~8~~ 9

Guess	Digit	Place
14	1	0
80	0	0
67	0	0
20	1	0
45	1	1
40	1	1
42	2	2

Equation Building

Overview

This game promotes practice with how all four operations work. Students need to be familiar with the four operations (addition, subtraction, multiplication, and division) to play. To start, each player lines up either twenty red playing cards or twenty black playing cards. Player 1 rolls the dice and creates equations from the numbers rolled. Player 1 then turns those cards face down that share the same answer or answers as his equations. Player 2 takes her turn. The first player to turn all twenty cards of his or her color face down is the winner. Students will soon discover that not all the answers to the equations will result in turning a card face down; answers with decimals or numbers larger than ten will not have a matching face card.

Materials

- dice (1 labeled *0–5*, 1 labeled *5–10*), 1 of each per pair of students

- deck of playing cards (face cards and Jokers removed; Aces remain to represent the value of 1), 1 per pair of students

- paper and pencil

Related Games

Game 29: Take Five, Make Ten!

Game 30: Target 300 (A Multiplication Game)

 See the Connections to the Common Core State Standards for Mathematics, page xv.

Recommended Grades 3–5

Time Instruction: 45–60 minutes
Independent Play: 20–30 minutes

 TEACHING TIPS

Preparing Cards

This game requires actual playing cards in order to have both red and black cards. Prepare decks of playing cards ahead of time, removing all the face cards and sorting them into a group of red cards and a group of black cards. For the purpose of this game, a complete deck of cards will have two of each card, 1 (Ace)–10.

Quiet Dice

Rolling dice can create lots of noise. To lessen the noise, use foam dice or pad students' workspaces with foam or fabric placemats.

Don't Have Dice?

If you do not have 0–5 and 5–10 dice, consider these options:

- Convert wooden cubes to dice. Place small, round, numbered stickers on each face of wooden cubes.

- Use numeral cards instead of dice. Photocopy a 0–5 set on one color of paper and a 5–10 set on another (see **REPRODUCIBLE B, NUMERAL CARDS 0–10**). Instead of dice, players draw one card of each color on their turn.

Key Questions

- What operations make numbers increase (grow)? Decrease?

- What operation may result in something other than a whole number? Why is that?

Teaching Directions

Part I: The Connection

Relate the game to students' ongoing work.

Remind students of the four operations—addition, subtraction, multiplication, and division. Emphasize that two of them are increasing operations (addition and multiplication) and two are decreasing operations (subtraction and division).

Part II: The Teaching

Introduce and model the game to students.

1. Tell students they will be playing the game *Equation Building* in pairs. Gather students around a table or floor space.

2. Ask for two volunteers, sitting opposite one another, to be Player 1 and Player 2. Present them with a deck of playing cards (all face cards—King, Queen, and so forth—should be removed from the deck beforehand; Aces remain to represent the value of 1).

3. Ask Player 1 to place all twenty red cards face up, in numerical order, in front of her. Ask Player 2 to place all twenty black cards face up, in numerical order, in front of him.

4. While Player 1 and Player 2 organize their cards, continue by telling students they will take turns rolling the dice. The two numbers that they roll will be used in building equations.

5. Ask Player 1 to roll the dice and create equations using the two numbers rolled. She may use any one of the four operations (addition, subtraction, multiplication, division) as long as the answer results in a whole number.

Encourage the rest of the class to help Player 1 as needed.

6. Ask Player 1 to say the equations out loud. For example, if a 3 and 6 are rolled, the possible equations would be:

$$3 + 6 = 9$$
$$3 \times 6 = 18$$
$$6 - 3 = 3$$
$$6 \div 3 = 2$$

7. For demonstration purposes, record the equations where all students can see them.

8. Ask Player 2, "Do you agree with Player One's equations and answers?" If not, have players and the class work together to come to an agreement.

9. Now ask Player 1 to go back to her line of red cards. She needs to turn over the numbers used in the *answers* of her equations. In the example, cards 2, 3, and 9 should be turned over (so they are now face down on the table).

10. Explain that the goal of the game is to be the first player to turn all twenty cards face down.

11. Play another round, this time asking Player 2 to roll the dice and build equations from the numbers rolled. Repeat Steps 5–9. As another example, let's say that a 2 and a 5 are rolled. Students help Player 2 create corresponding equations. Record the equations where everyone can see them. In this example, the four equations would be:

$$2 + 5 = 7$$
$$2 \times 5 = 10$$
$$5 - 2 = 3$$
$$5 \div 2 = 2.5$$

Player 2 then turns cards 3, 7, and 10 face down.

 TEACHING TIP
Answers Without Cards
For answers in which a card does not exist (such as 18), nothing needs to be done. In addition, as students play more rounds, some answers will no longer have corresponding cards (the cards will have already been turned face down). If this is the case, once again, nothing needs to be done in response to those answers.

TEACHING TIPS

Recording the Equations

Encourage students to record their equations. Make scratch paper or mini-whiteboards readily accessible for this. Recording helps students organize their thinking and supports those who gain from seeing the mathematics. Have students record a round of *Equation Building* to turn in for review.

Pairing Students

For this game, pair students with someone of like ability. Pairing students with similar mathematical skills may allow for more differentiation options and will afford optimum access to the mathematics involved in playing the game.

12. Continue playing, with players taking turns rolling the dice and creating the equations, until students have an understanding of the game. This usually doesn't take many rounds; typically, students start to skip recording the equations and just call out the sum, difference, product, and quotient.

Part III: Active Engagement

Engage students to ensure they understand how to play the game.

13. Now give students an opportunity to return to their own tables or desks and explore the game in pairs. As students play, circulate, noting their computational fluency with the operations (this information can be used later to differentiate your instruction).

Part IV: The Link

Students play the game independently.

14. Set up students for independent practice with the game. Give each pair of students two dice and a deck of playing cards prepared per game specifications. Also, distribute the directions (REPRODUCIBLE G-12) as needed.

MATH WORKSHOP AND SUMMARIZING THE EXPERIENCE

Teach this game at the beginning of the week to the whole class, then make it an integral part of your math workshop (for more on math workshops, see Chapter 5 in *From Reading to Math* by Maggie Siena). Build in time to observe students playing the game. Note their individual skill level; come together as a class later in the week and give students the opportunity to reflect on their experiences in playing the game. Ask key questions, including:

· *Which operation often ended up with a fractional answer? Why does this happen?* Generating and posting the equations with whole-number quotients and equations with fractional quotients or quotients with remainders will help move some students forward in thinking about dividing. Often, students will state that a number cannot be divided; however, what they really mean is it cannot be divided evenly or with a whole number as the quotient. A class recording chart can serve as a point of reference when revisiting concepts developed around factors, multiples, odd/even, and the identity law of division.

· *Which operation often ended up with a number greater than ten? Why does this happen?* Students will respond with addition or, most likely, multiplication. Connect additive thinking to multiplicative thinking by revisiting the idea that multiplication is repeated addition (for example, $3 + 3 + 3 + 3 = 3 \times 4$).

   When answering the second question, consider starting two lists; one titled "Equations That Work in Equation Building" (equations that have answers that allow players to turn over cards) and the other titled "Equations That Don't Work in Equation Building" (equations that have answers that are either too big or have decimals, and hence do not have a matching card to turn over).

DIFFERENTIATING YOUR INSTRUCTION

One way to modify the game according to the levels and needs of your students is as follows; this version introduces strategy and teamwork to the game.

Equation Building: A Strategic/Collective Approach

1. Player 1 rolls the dice and creates equations. Player 1 then turns just one of the cards that matches an answer face down.

2. Player 2 then turns one of her cards that matches an answer face down. Her card needs to be a different number (answer) than the card Player 1 turned face down. For example, if Player 1 flipped over the sum, Player 2 could not flip over the sum but could flip over the difference, product, or quotient.

3. Play alternates until no cards can be turned face down.

4. Repeat Steps 1 and 2, this time with Player 2 rolling the dice and being the first to turn a card face down.

Students will begin to think about which operations result in numbers that work for the game of *Equation Building*.

TEACHING TIP
The Importance of Asking Questions

Asking key questions assists you in understanding how or if students are developing strategies. Key questions also prompt students to hear each other's thinking and further develop their own understanding of the content.

Fifteen-Number Cross-Out

Recommended Grades 2–4

Time Instruction: 45–60 minutes
Independent Play: 20–30 minutes

Overview

This game helps students learn to decompose numbers into two or more parts as well as provides addition practice for sums up to 12. Students first create lists of numbers. They then take turns rolling the dice, adding the numbers rolled, and announcing the sum. Players are tasked with decomposing the sum and choosing either the sum or numbers from the decomposition to cross out on their lists. The winner is the first player to cross out all his or her numbers. If both players are unable to cross out numbers, the player with the fewest numbers left on his or her list is declared the winner. The game includes a *Twenty-Number Cross-Out* Recording Sheet (REPRODUCIBLE 19) to allow for differentiated instruction.

Materials

- dice (labeled *1–6*), 2 per pair of students
- *Fifteen-Number Cross-Out* Recording Sheet (REPRODUCIBLE 18), 1 per student
- *Fifteen-Number Cross-Out* Game Directions (REPRODUCIBLE G-13), 1 per pair of students

Related Games

Game 3: Addition Tic-Tac-Toe

Game 7: Close to 100

Game 10: Cross Out Sums

TEACHING TIPS
Quiet Dice
Rolling dice can create lots of noise. To lessen the noise, use foam dice or pad students' workspaces with foam or fabric placemats.

Don't Have Dice?
If you do not have dice labeled *1–6*, consider these options:

- Convert wooden cubes to dice. Place small, round, numbered stickers on each face of the wooden cubes.

- Use numeral cards instead of dice. Photocopy a *1–6* set on two different colors of paper (see **REPRODUCIBLE B, NUMERAL CARDS, 0–10**). Instead of dice, players draw one card of each color on their turn.

See the Connections to the Common Core State Standards for Mathematics, page xv.

Key Questions

- Explain your reasoning for crossing off addends or sums. Why did you choose those addends to cross off?

- Is there a strategy you use in this game? What is it?

Teaching Directions

Part I: The Connection

Relate the game to students' ongoing work.

Introduce or review the term *decompose.* The simplest way to introduce the term is to provide examples of decomposition. Write the number *15* where everyone in the class can see it. Ask students to break the number apart into smaller chunks, in as many ways as possible. Your recording might look like this:

Emphasize to students when they break numbers apart, we call it *decomposition.* Write the term where everyone can see it (alternatively, post it on a word wall or have students note it in their math journal).

Part II: The Teaching

Introduce and model the game to students.

1. After decomposition has been introduced or reviewed, tell students they will be playing the game *Fifteen-Number Cross-Out.*

2. Start by writing five 5s where everyone can see them:

   5   5   5   5   5

3. Now add ten more numbers to the list. Introduce the three rules for adding ten more numbers:

1. The ten additional numbers may consist of any number 1–9, including more 5s.

2. Numbers may be repeated.

3. Not every number has to be used.

Your list might now look like this:

5 5 5 5 5 1 2 3 4 5 6 7 8 9 1

4. Label your list *Player 1/Teacher.*

5. Make a new list of five 5s under the previous list. Now ask students to add ten more numbers to the list by calling them out. Once again, the numbers may consist of any number 1–9, including more 5s. Numbers may be repeated; not every number has to be used. The second list might now look like this:

5 5 5 5 5 1 1 2 2 3 3 4 6 7 8

6. Label the second list *Player 2/Students.* Everyone should now be looking at two labeled lists, for example:

Player 1/Teacher:

5 5 5 5 5 1 2 3 4 5 6 7 8 9 1

Player 2/Students:

5 5 5 5 5 1 1 2 2 3 3 4 6 7 8

7. Now roll the two dice. Add the rolled numbers together and say the sum out loud. For example, if a 3 and 4 are rolled, announce the sum "seven."

8. Next explain that both players need to decompose the sum. Solicit combinations from the class. For the "sum seven," students might suggest the following combinations:

3, 4

6, 1

5, 2

2, 2, 3

9. Explain to students that players then can choose either:

   a. the sum

   or

   b. one of the combinations from the decomposition

   and cross the chosen numbers off their lists. Emphasize that both players cross off numbers; only one combination or sum can be crossed off on each list. The example lists might look like the following (Player 1 chose to cross out the sum; Player 2 chose to cross out the combination 2, 2, 3).

Player 1/Teacher:

5 5 5 5 5 1 2 3 4 5 6 ✗ 8 9 1

Player 2/Students:

5 5 5 5 5 1 1 ✗ ✗ ✗ 3 4 6 7 8

10. Repeat Steps 7–9.

11. After numbers are crossed off for the second roll of dice, introduce how the game can be won. Explain to students that there are two ways to win:

    a. The first player to cross out all the numbers on his or her list is declared the winner.

    or

    b. Both players reach a point at which they can no longer cross out numbers; the winner is then the player with the fewest numbers remaining on his or her list.

    If, during any of the rolls, one player is unable to cross off the sum or a combination from the sum, that player must wait until the next roll to cross off numbers.

TEACHING TIP
Alternatives to REPRODUCIBLE 18

Students can also create their own recording sheets using a blank piece of paper. Ask students to write the words *Fifteen-Number Cross-Out* at the top of their papers (write the words on the board for students to copy). Next, have them write their name followed by five 5s on one of the first lines of their paper. Then, students write their lists of ten numbers. Circulate to make sure students are setting up the game correctly.

TEACHING TIP
Recording Your Thinking

Encourage students to record their thinking; space has been provided for this after each list on **REPRODUCIBLE 18**. It is important for students to be able to articulate how they add and decompose the numbers. It is equally valuable for other students to see how their partners are computing.

TEACHING TIP
The Importance of Practice

After several rounds of play, students might also get a sense of how much of the game depends on luck, skill, or strategy. Refrain from discussing these topics during the active engagement part of the lesson. The purpose is to give students as much practice as possible first; they will then have the opportunity to come back later and discuss their experiences (see the "Math Workshop and Summarizing the Experience" part of the lesson).

Part III: Active Engagement

Engage students to ensure they understand how to play the game.

12. Now give students further opportunity to explore the game. This time, they will play individually against the teacher instead of collectively. Give each student a copy of the *Fifteen-Number Cross-Out* Recording Sheet (**REPRODUCIBLE 18**).

13. As Player 1, start your list where everyone can see it.

14. Invite students to add ten more numbers to their lists. Do the same with your list.

    Emphasize the three rules:

    1. The ten additional numbers may consist of any number 1–9, including more 5s.

    2. Numbers may be repeated.

    3. Not every number has to be used.

15. Circulate around the classroom, monitoring students' completion of the task and noting their understanding of how to set up the game. Clarify any confusion.

16. Roll the dice and announce the sum of the two numbers. Give students time to decompose the number and select whether they want to cross out the sum from their list or a combination of numbers. Do the same with your list.

17. Continue playing rounds of the game until students have a sound understanding of setting up the game, adding, decomposing numbers, and making decisions about what numbers to cross off their lists.

Part IV: The Link

Students play the game independently.

18. Set up students for independent practice with the game. Give each pair of students two dice and one copy of the recording sheet

(REPRODUCIBLE 18). Also, distribute the directions (REPRODUCIBLE G-13) as needed.

19. Give students time to play three games. When observing and talking with students as they play, ask key questions such as:

- Explain your reasoning for crossing off addends or sums. Why did you choose those addends to cross off?

- Is there a strategy you use in this game? What is it?

Make sure students are recording their thinking as much as possible.

MATH WORKSHOP AND SUMMARIZING THE EXPERIENCE

Teach this game at the beginning of the week to the whole class, then make it an integral part of your math workshop (for more on math workshops, see Chapter 5 in *From Reading to Math* by Maggie Siena). Come together as a class later in the week and give students the opportunity to reflect on their experiences when playing the game. Ask key questions such as, "Which numbers are best to place on your list? Why do you think so?"

TEACHING TIP
Pairing Students

For this game, pair students with someone of like ability. Pairing students with similar mathematical skills may allow for more differentiation options and will afford optimum access to the mathematics involved in playing the game.

DIFFERENTIATING YOUR INSTRUCTION

Two ways to modify the game according to the levels and needs of your students are as follows:

Twenty-Number Cross-Out

In this version of the game, students play with three 1–6 dice instead of two. Instead of adding ten numbers to their lists, they add fifteen. The same rules apply when selecting the numbers. **REPRODUCIBLE 19** is provided for use with this version of the game.

Cross-Out Limit

Place a constraint on the game that only two numbers may be crossed out at a time on each roll. This limit encourages students to think about how numbers can be decomposed into just two parts.

TEACHING TIP
The Importance of Asking Questions

Asking key questions assists you in understanding how or if students are developing strategies. Key questions also prompt students to hear each other's thinking and further develop their own understanding of the content.

Finding Factors

Recommended Grades 3–5

Time Instruction: 45–60 minutes
Independent Play: 20–30 minutes

Overview

This game reinforces students' learning of multiplication facts and their development of computational capacity. It should be played after students have developed a basic understanding of multiplication. To play the game, students take turns selecting numbers on the game board and identifying the number's factors. The first player selects and circles the number; the second player identifies and circles the number's factors. Students take turns until there are no longer any applicable numbers on the game board to circle. Students then tally their scores; a player's score is the total of all the numbers circled in his or her color. The player with the highest score is the winner. The game is played using a game board with numbers 1–30; a 1–50 game board is also included to allow for differentiated instruction.

Materials

- markers or crayons, 2 per pair of students (each a different color)

- *Finding Factors* Game Board, Version 1 (Numbers 1–30) (REPRODUCIBLE 20), enlarged for classroom use

- *Finding Factors* Game Board, Version 1 (Numbers 1–30) (REPRODUCIBLE 20), 1 per pair of students

- *Finding Factors* Game Directions (REPRODUCIBLE G-14), 1 per pair of students

TIME SAVER
Reusable Game Boards
Instead of making consumable copies of the *Finding Factors* Game Board, consider laminating a set or placing copies in plastic sleeves and providing dry erase pens.

See the Connections to the Common Core State Standards for Mathematics, page xv.

Adapted from *About Teaching Mathematics, Third Edition: A K–8 Resource* by Marilyn Burns (Math Solutions, 2007).

Related Games

Game 6: Circles and Stars

Game 18: Leftovers with 15

Game 26: Roll 6 for 100

Key Questions

- When it's your turn to select a number, what number do you look for and why?

- Are there any numbers on the game board you try to avoid? Why?

- Which numbers, 1–30, have many factors? Which numbers are prime or have only two factors, one and itself?

Teaching Directions

Part I: The Connection

Relate the game to students' ongoing work.

Students must have an understanding of multiplication to play this game. Review with them what the term *factor* means. Relate that *factor* has the word *fact* in it. Ask students to think about the multiplication facts. Write the number *12* where everyone can see it. Ask, "What are some facts you know that result in the product of twelve?" Record the facts as students offer them: *1 × 12, 2 × 6, 3 × 4.* Say, "These six numbers are factors of twelve." Write, *1, 12, 2, 6, 3, 4 are factors of 12,* so students can see the written word *factor.*

Part II: The Teaching

Introduce and model the game to students.

1. Tell students they will be playing the game *Finding Factors* in pairs. To begin, display an enlarged version of REPRODUCIBLE 20 (presented on the next page). Tell students that this will be their game board.

TECHNOLOGY TIP
Using an Interactive Whiteboard
An interactive whiteboard can be used to present the game board. To do so, prepare a table like the one in **REPRODUCIBLE 20**. After creating the table, lock it in place so it doesn't move around when students are interacting with it. Students will then be able to circle numbers on it.

FINDING FACTORS

1	2	3	4	5
6	7	8	9	10
11	12	13	14	15
16	17	18	19	20
21	22	23	24	25
26	27	28	29	30

Reproducible 20

TEACHING TIP
Thinking About Factors

To assist all students in thinking about the factors of 18 (1, 2, 3, 6, and 9), offer multiple ways to approach the task:

• Write equations with missing factors, for example:

$$18 \times \underline{\quad} = 18$$

$$2 \times \underline{\quad} = 18$$

$$\underline{\quad} \times 6 = 18$$

• Begin a conversation such as, "Eighteen is an even number. Tell me what you know about even numbers and factors."

• Record rectangular array models of the number like these:

$$(1 \times 18)$$

$$(2 \times 9)$$

X X X
X X X
X X X
X X X
X X X
X X X

$$(6 \times 3)$$

2. Explain that this is a two-player game. Each player needs a marker or a crayon of a different color. Player 1 selects a number and circles it with her marker. Player 2 then finds all the factors of that number, circling each factor with his marker. The game continues, players alternating until there are no factors left for the remaining numbers.

3. Next to your game board write, *Player 1: red. Player 2: blue.* Make sure you have a red and blue marker (if you use other colors, change the color you designate to each player).

4. Start by circling the number 18 with the red marker. Ask students, "What numbers are factors of eighteen?" Invite students to share their thinking with a partner, then hold a class discussion.

5. Return to the *Finding Factors* Game Board. Using the blue marker, circle the factors of 18 (1, 2, 3, 6, and 9). The game board will now have *18* circled in red and its factors circled in blue:

FINDING FACTORS

①	②	③	4	5
⑥	7	8	⑨	10
11	12	13	14	15
16	17	⑱	19	20
21	22	23	24	25
26	27	28	29	30

6. Play another round of the game, this time with the number 24. Circle 24 in blue (Player 2's color) on the game board.

7. Ask students, "What numbers are factors of twenty-four?" Invite students to share their thinking with a partner, then hold a class discussion.

8. Revisit the *Finding Factors* Game Board. This time, students will discover that some of the factors are already circled. Explain that, in this game, when a number is circled, it is "out of play" and cannot be circled again. Thus, for the number 24, the factors that can be circled are 4, 8, and 12. Circle them in red (Player 1's color).

FINDING FACTORS

①	②	③	④	5
⑥	7	⑧	⑨	10
11	⑫	13	14	15
16	17	⑱	19	20
21	22	23	㉔	25
26	27	28	29	30

9. Students may now be curious about the scoring or the goal of the game. Explain to them that the winner is the player with the highest score. Your score is the total of all the numbers circled in your color.

10. Invite students to compute the scores of the two players at this point in the game. Record the two number strings under the *Finding Factors* Game Board. For the numbers used in the examples here, the two number strings would be:

Player 1's Score: 4 + 8 + 12 + 18 = 42

Player 2's Score: 1 + 2 + 3 + 6 + 9 + 24 = 45

TEACHING TIP
Selecting Numbers with No Factors Left: An Illegal Move

As the game progresses, caution students about selecting a number with no factors left to circle in the *Finding Factors* Game Board. This may be a viable strategy; however, explain that, in this game, selecting a number with no remaining factors is an "illegal move." If an illegal move is made, the player loses his or her turn (meaning the other player goes twice in a row). However, the illegal number or move remains as part of the total.

TEACHING TIP
Pairing Students

For this game, pair students with someone of like ability. Pairing students with similar mathematical skills may allow for more differentiation options and will afford optimum access to the mathematics involved in playing the game.

Part III: Active Engagement

Engage students to ensure they understand how to play the game.

11. Increase students' opportunity to explore the game. Continue playing rounds, only this time, hand the markers to student volunteers. A student who volunteers to identify the next number is Player 1 and gets the red marker. Have another student volunteer (Player 2) circle the factors of the number using the blue marker.

12. Continue giving students an opportunity to play until there are no factors left for the remaining numbers, then ask students to determine who won. Remind students that they need to add all the numbers of the same color together to find their scores; the player with the highest score is the winner.

Part IV: The Link

Students play the game independently.

13. Set up students for independent practice with the game. Each pair of students should be given one copy of the *Finding Factors* Game Board (REPRODUCIBLE 20) and two markers or crayons, each a different color. Distribute the game directions (REPRODUCIBLE G-14) as needed.

14. Observe and talk with students as they play. Ask key questions such as:

    - When it is your turn to select the number, what do you look for?

    - Are there any numbers on the game board you try to avoid? Why?

15. Make sure students are showing their work when they compute their scores.

MATH WORKSHOP AND SUMMARIZING THE EXPERIENCE

Teach this game at the beginning of the week to the whole class, then make it an integral part of your math workshop (for more on math workshops, see Chapter 5 in *From Reading to Math* by Maggie Siena). Make it a requirement that students need to practice the game multiple times—both being Player 1, the first player to select a number, and being Player 2. It is important for students to have experience holding both positions to ensure a richer discussion later. Build in time to observe students playing the game. Note their individual skill level and the strategies being used. Come together as a class later in the week and hold a discussion about the mathematics involved in the game. Refer to your notes during the discussion. Ask the question, "Are there advantages to going first? If so, which number is the 'best' number to pick so that your opponent gets very few points?" Students will likely reply "Yes," and that number 29 is the best number to circle. The discussion should include concepts like *prime* and *composite*. By selecting the largest prime number on the game board, Player 1 accumulates 29 points, whereas Player 2 gets only 1 point. Player 1 has also made all the other prime numbers "illegal moves" and they are not desirable until later in the game.

ASSESSMENT
Writing Prompts
Have students write about their strategies in their journals. Provide writing prompts such as:

- If you have the first pick of a number in the *Finding Factors* game, what number would you circle and why?

- Is the number 25 a desirable number to choose? Why or why not?

DIFFERENTIATING YOUR INSTRUCTION
Figuring Out Scores
Tallying the players' scores is an opportunity for students to share their mental math. Some may need pencil and paper to compute. You may also decide that calculators should be made available for figuring out scores.

Version 2 (Numbers 1–50)
One way to modify the game according to the levels and needs of your students is to increase the range of numbers used in the game. **REPRODUCIBLE 21** offers a game board with numbers 1–50 for this purpose.

Greater Than, Less Than, Equal To

Recommended Grades K–4

Time Instruction: 45–60 minutes
Independent Play: 20–30 minutes

TEACHING TIPS

Manipulatives
For modeling this game, yellow wooden hexagons from pattern blocks sets work well. They are readily seen because of their size and have a weight that will be recognized and measured more easily using the scale. For playing the game, use small counters, interlocking cubes, or even pennies.

Enlarged Numeral Cards
A set of enlarged numeral cards is recommended to model this game. Use a photocopier to enlarge the cards provided in **REPRODUCIBLE B** or, alternatively, use ten sheets of white copy paper or construction paper and write one of the 0–10 numerals on each (use a thick black marker so the numbers can be seen easily).

A Deck of Cards
For the purposes of this game, a deck of cards is four of each number 0–10. If using a deck of playing cards, the 0 will not be available. Aces represent the value of 1. Consider preparing decks of playing cards ahead of time, removing all the face cards.

See the Connections to the Common Core State Standards for Mathematics, page xv.

Overview
Introduce this game after lessons on both basic addition and the concept development of equalities and inequalities. To play, pairs of students take turns drawing numeral cards and completing number sentences. Together, they determine which symbol (>, <, or =) goes with each sentence. The player with the greater sum keeps all four cards in that round. The player with the most cards at the end (ten rounds) is the winner. It's important to have balance scales accessible for supporting students' understanding of inequalities and equalities. Additional versions of recording sheets are also included to allow for differentiated instruction.

Materials
- balance scale, 1 per pair of students
- sticky notes labeled >, <, and =, 3 per pair of students
- manipulatives (see Teaching Tips)
- Numeral Cards 0–10 (REPRODUCIBLE B), 1 set enlarged for classroom use
- Numeral Cards 0–10 (REPRODUCIBLE B), 1 deck per pair of students
  or
- playing cards (face cards and Jokers removed; Aces remain to represent the value of 1), 1 deck per pair of students
- *Greater Than, Less Than, Equal To* Recording Sheet, Version 1 (Two Addends) (REPRODUCIBLE 22), 1 enlarged for class use

continued

- *Greater Than, Less Than, Equal To*
  Recording Sheet, Version 1 (Two Addends)
  (REPRODUCIBLE 22), 1 per pair of students

- *Greater Than, Less Than, Equal To* Game Directions (REPRODUCIBLE G-15), 1 per pair of students

Related Games

Game 8: Compare (Shake and Spill)

Game 21: More!

Key Questions

- Can you explain how _____ is greater than _____?

- How many more would you need for the two sums to be equal?

Teaching Directions

Part I: The Connection

Relate the game to students' ongoing work.

Equalities and Inequalities: Making Comparisons

1. Review the idea of equalities and inequalities through comparisons. To do so, use items in the classroom. For example, ask students to find one unsharpened and one sharpened pencil in their desk. Ask students to compare the two pencils. What do they notice? Students' observations might be the following:

   - "One is new and the other is used."

   - "One is longer and the other is shorter."

   - "One has a fresh eraser and the other eraser is worn."

2. Explain to students that during the game *Greater Than, Less Than, Equal To,* they will be comparing sums. Because sums have a numeric value, students will be able to tell which one is greater or less.

TEACHING TIPS

Arranging Students

For the demonstration area, have students make two concentric circles. In the first circle, students kneel or sit; in the second, students stand. This ensures that everyone can view the demonstration area.

A Balance Scale

Using a balance scale gives students a concrete visual for seeing the equalities and inequalities of the numbers being compared. If a balance scale is not available, create drawings on a board or space where all students can see them.

Using Manipulatives for Comparison

Using nonnumeric items for comparison, such as counters or interlocking cubes, may provide students more practice in counting the items when combining, whereas using pennies (which have a value of one) might allow them to rely more on their basic addition facts.

Equalities and Inequalities: Reviewing Concepts, Symbols, and Names

1. Review and introduce equalities and inequalities concepts, symbols, and names of signs. Do this through observation-style learning. Designate a table or desk as the demonstration area. Place a balance scale in the middle of the area.

2. Begin by showing students the balance scale. Point out that nothing, or zero, equals zero. Affix a sticky note with an equal sign to the middle of the scale so students can see the equality.

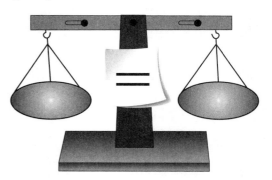

3. Next, place a counter on one side of the scale. Students should now see that one side of the scale has more than the other. Explain, "One side has more than the other. This is called an inequality."

4. Write the word *inequality* where all students can see it. Ask students to identify the root word. Most students will be able to see and hear the root word *equal* in inequality.

5. Discuss what inequality means. Record some of the students' words where everyone can see them. Typically, students will offer phrases and words such as the following:

    *   Not the same

    *   Not equal

    *   Unalike

6. Remove the sticky note with the equal symbol from the scale. Replace it with the sticky note showing the greater than (>) symbol.

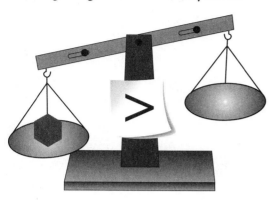

7. Ask students, "How can we get the scale back to a neutral or equal position?" Students will likely suggest removing the counter or adding a counter to the side with none.

8. Act on the suggestion of adding a counter. Place a counter on the side with nothing.

9. After the scale steadies, ask students, "What should the symbol in the middle read?" Replace the sticky note on the scale with a sticky note showing the equal symbol.

10. Now place a second counter on the same side of the scale. This action presents an opportunity to introduce the less than symbol. Remove the sticky note with the equal sign and place the sticky note with the less than symbol on the scale.

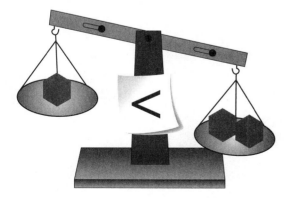

11. Continue the demonstration, having students help place counters on the scale, change the symbols, and read the symbols.

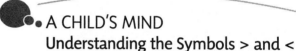

A CHILD'S MIND
Understanding the Symbols > and <
Precision of language when introducing the equality and inequality symbols is extremely important. Depending on the age and experiences of students, do not be surprised if they use words such as *alligator* or *arrow* to describe the symbols. Encourage students to use the correct names for the symbols.

Equalities and Inequalities: Recording Equations

1. The purpose of this part of the lesson is to take students from a more concrete model of equalities and inequalities (the balance scale) to an abstract representation (equations). Have students return to their seats and focus on the front of the classroom.

2. Recreate what you did previously with the balance scale, only this time, record the corresponding equations where everyone can see them, rather than using the sticky notes. Start by removing all counters from both sides of the balance scale and recording:

$$0 = 0$$

3. Then, place a single counter on one side of the scale, just as before. Tell students while writing, "When we add one counter, the mathematics that shows what we did is, zero plus one is greater than zero." Write:

$$0 + | > 0$$

4. Next, add one counter to balance out the scale. Tell students while writing, "Zero plus one is equivalent to zero plus one." Write:

$$0 + | = 0 + |$$

5. Last, add one more counter to one side of the scale. Tell students while writing, "Zero plus one is less than one plus one." Write:

$$0 + | < | + |$$

    Students should be able to see the scale's imbalance and, hopefully, link it to the equation that represents the inequality.

6. At this point in the lesson, your recording should look like this:

$$0 = 0$$
$$0 + | > 0$$
$$0 + | = 0 + |$$
$$0 + | < | + |$$

Ask students if they have questions and clarify any confusion.

Part II: The Teaching

Introduce and model the game to students.

1. Tell students they will be playing the game *Greater Than, Less Than, Equal To.* Place a set of enlarged numeral cards 0–10 near the scale and ask students to reassemble around the scale.

2. Display the first part of an enlarged version of the *Greater Than, Less Than, Equal To* Recording Sheet (REPRODUCIBLE 22) where everyone can see it.

Player 1 _____ + _____ ☐ Player 2 _____ + _____

3. Ask a student to draw two numeral cards from the stack of cards. Tell the student to turn over the cards, show them to everyone else, and read the numbers.

4. Record the numbers in the blanks under Player 1 on the recording sheet.

5. Ask another student to draw two more numeral cards from the deck. Tell the student to turn over the cards, show them to everyone else, and read the numbers.

6. Record the numbers in the blanks under Player 2 on the recording sheet.

7. Ask students, "Which symbol will make the number sentence true?" If your number sentence reads:

Player 1 __5__ + __2__ ☐ Player 2 __8__ + __1__

Students will likely know that seven (5 + 2) is less than nine (8 + 1). Place the less than symbol into the square on the recording sheet.

8. Repeat Steps 3–7 so students experience one more round with a different number sentence.

 TEACHING TIP
Arranging Students
For the demonstration area, have students make two concentric circles. In the first circle, students kneel or sit; in the second, students stand. This ensures that everyone can view the demonstration area.

 TEACHING TIP
Linking to the Concrete
When asking students to determine which symbol goes into the number sentence, it may be helpful to have student volunteers place counters on the balance scale. In the example provided, the inequality could be shown by placing five counters plus two more on one side of the scale, then eight counters plus one more on the other side.

Part III: Active Engagement

Engage students to ensure they understand how to play the game.

9. Now give students an opportunity to explore the game in pairs. Have students come up in pairs, draw numeral cards, and fill in the corresponding blanks on the recording sheet. Engage the rest of the class in determining whether the equation requires a greater than, less than, or equal to sign. Usually, five to six rounds of this is sufficient to ensure students have a sound understanding of the game.

10. Collect the number sentences that have been created. If they were written on the board, do not erase them because you will be using them in the link portion of the lesson.

Part IV: The Link

Students play the game independently.

11. Set students up for independent practice with the game. Each pair of students should be given a deck of numeral cards 0–10 and a copy of the recording sheet (REPRODUCIBLE 22). Also, distribute the game directions (REPRODUCIBLE G-15) as needed.

12. Before students start playing, draw their attention to the three sentences at the bottom of their recording sheets. Write the sentences where everyone can see them, next to the number sentences completed during the modeling of the lesson. Complete the sentences as a class, clarifying meaning if needed. Tell students that it is their responsibility to complete the sentences on their recording sheets after they've finished their game.

13. Explain that the player who has the greater sum gets to keep the cards for that round. Students play until their recording sheets are full (ten rounds).

TEACHING TIP
The Balance Scale

As students play the game independently, have one or two balance scales available for them to check their work. Be mindful that if students are not used to having this kind of learning tool available to them, they will likely need some time to experiment with it. You may want to introduce the balance scale to the class a few days before the lesson so that students can try it out prior to playing this game.

TEACHING TIP
Number Sentences on Recording Sheet

Draw students' attention to the three sentences at the bottom of their recording sheets. It is their responsibility to complete these sentences after they've finished the game.

Together we had: _____ equalities and

_____ inequalities.

_____ greater than (>).

_____ less than (<).

MATH WORKSHOP AND SUMMARIZING THE EXPERIENCE

Teach this game at the beginning of the week to the whole class, then make it an integral part of your math workshop (for more on math workshops, see Chapter 5 in *From Reading to Math* by Maggie Siena). Build in time to observe students playing the game. Note their individual skill level and use of the symbols; come together as a class later in the week and hold a discussion. Begin a class chart with two columns: Equalities and Inequalities. Have students record corresponding number sentences under each column, then select one of the equations in the Equalities column and ask key questions. For example, for the equation $3 + 5 = 4 + 4$ you could say, "Explain how this is true." A student might reply, "If you take one from the five and put it with the three, it's four plus four." Have the student use manipulatives to show her thinking visually.

Using an Interactive Whiteboard

If an interactive whiteboard is available, cloning pennies, circles, or squares assists in demonstrating how $3 + 5 = 4 + 4$. Students pull from the cloned virtual manipulatives and move the pieces accordingly.

DIFFERENTIATING YOUR INSTRUCTION

There are several ways to modify the game according to the levels and needs of your students.

Increase the Number of Addends

Have students play with three addends on each side of the equation. **REPRODUCIBLE 23** is provided for this purpose.

Change the Operation

Have students play the game with subtraction or multiplication instead of addition. The player with the larger difference or product takes all the cards for each round. Just as in the original version, the player with the most cards wins. **REPRODUCIBLE 24** and **REPRODUCIBLE 25** are provided for this purpose.

Hit the Target
(Mental Multiplication)

Recommended Grades 4–5

Time Instruction: 30–45 minutes
Independent Play: 20–30 minutes

Overview

This game uses students' estimating ability and their multiplication skills, providing practice with number sense and mental multiplication. Playing in pairs, students first choose a target range and multiplicand. They then pick multipliers that they think, when multiplied by the multiplicand, will get a product between the target range numbers. The objective of the game is to hit the target (get a product between the target range numbers). Needing only pencil, paper, and a partner, this game is a great one to play at home as well!

Materials

- paper and pencil, 1 per student
- *Hit the Target* Game Directions (REPRODUCIBLE G-16), 1 per pair of students

Related Games

Game 20: Missing Addend or Factor (Salute!)

Game 25: Pathways (and the variation, Times Ten)

Game 30: Target 300 (A Multiplication Game)

Key Questions

- How are you selecting your initial number—the multiplicand?
- After the multiplicand is determined, how do you choose a multiplier? What is your thinking as you choose a multiplier?
- What strategies are you using when you compute mentally?

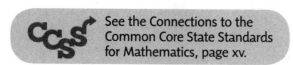

See the Connections to the Common Core State Standards for Mathematics, page xv.

Teaching Directions

Part I: The Connection

Relate the game to students' ongoing work.

This game uses students' estimating ability and their multiplication skills. Review or introduce terms like *multiplicand* and *multiplier* with students. Playing games that depend on mental math skills like *Missing Factor* (also known as *Salute!*), *Pathways,* or *Times Ten* will help students brush up on their skills.

Part II: The Teaching

Introduce and model the game to students.

1. Explain to students they will be playing the game *Hit the Target* in pairs. Tell them that the goal of the game is to get a number in the target range in as few tries as possible. For modeling purposes, start with the target range of 650–700. Post this where everyone can see it.

2. Ask two students to volunteer to be Player 1 and Player 2. Ask Player 1 to pick a number between three and twenty-nine. Explain that this will serve as the *multiplicand.* Write the number where everyone can see it. For example, the student might pick twelve as the multiplicand. Your recording should look like this:

   Target Range: 650–700

   Multiplicand: 12

3. Ask Player 2 to pick a number that he thinks, when multiplied by the first number, will get a product between the target range of 650–700. Explain that this number will be the *multiplier.*

4. Record the number sentence where everyone can see it. For example, if Player 2 picks the number 50, write:

   $12 \times 50 =$

TEACHING TIP
Powers of Ten
Remind students of the powers of ten to help them mentally compute with more confidence, speed, and accuracy. Because 12 x 5 is a basic fact, students can employ the powers of ten to 12 x 50, making it easier to calculate.

5. Invite the class to solve the number sentence. Students should compute mentally. After the students agree on the product, record the answer:

$$12 \times 50 = 600$$

6. Ask students, "Does the product hit the target? Why or why not?"

7. It is most likely students will not hit the target on the first try. If this is the case, ask Player 2 to select another number to serve as the multiplier. Remind students that the multiplicand stays the same; the multiplier changes. Play several rounds, regardless of whether students hit the target. Your recording might look like this:

Target Range: 650–700

Multiplicand: 12

$$12 \times 50 = 600$$

$$12 \times 60 = 720$$

$$12 \times 55 = 660$$

Part III: Active Engagement

Engage students to ensure they understand how to play the game.

8. Now give students the opportunity to explore the game in pairs. Help pairs in determining who will be Player 1 and Player 2. Have Player 1 get a pencil and Player 2 get scratch paper.

9. Announce a new target range and write it where everyone can see it. For example, you might choose the range 820–870. Write:

Target Range: 820–870

10. Ask students to write the target range at the top of their scratch paper.

11. Continue guiding students through the game. Instruct Player 1 in each pair to pick a multiplicand—a number between one and one hundred. Player 1 should write the multiplicand on the scratch paper.

12. Now instruct Player 2 in each pair to pick a multiplier—a number that she thinks, when multiplied by the first number, will get a product in the target range. Tell Player 2 to write the number sentence on the paper.

13. Have each pair work together to solve the number sentence. Encourage students to use both mental and paper-and-pencil mathematics as a way of showing their thinking at arriving at a product.

14. Have pairs discuss: Does the product hit the target? Why or why not? Proceed with one of the following, depending on the outcome:

    a. If the product does *not* hit the target, have pairs repeat Steps 12 and 13, with Player 2 picking another multiplier. Explain that play should continue until a product is reached that hits the target (lands within the range).

    b. If the product hits the target, have players switch roles; Player 2 now picks a multiplicand and Player 1 picks the multiplier.

15. Some pairs may hit the target with the first multiplier whereas others may go through several multipliers. A round is considered completed when both players have hit the target once. Then, a new target range can be determined and, again, players should each hit the target once. As students complete their rounds, ask a few pairs to share their number sentences by writing them where everyone can see them. This provides an opportunity for students to see an assortment of ways to hit the target.

Part IV: The Link

Students play the game independently.

16. Set up students for independent practice with the game. Each pair should have paper and pencil. Also, distribute the game directions (REPRODUCIBLE G-16) as needed.

TEACHING TIP
The Importance of Practice
Refrain from discussing skill or strategies during the active engagement part of the lesson. The purpose is to give students as much practice as possible first; they will then have the opportunity to come back later and discuss their experiences (see "Math Workshop and Summarizing the Experience").

TEACHING TIP
Pairing Students
For this game, pair students with someone of like ability. Pairing students with similar mathematical skills may allow for more differentiation options and will afford optimum access to the mathematics involved in playing the game.

TEACHING TIP
Emphasize Collaboration

Explain that students will be playing in teams of two with their partner, not against him or her. The goal is for students to work together to understand how to play the game and the math involved.

TEACHING TIP
Using Target Range Posters

If using the poster option for students to select target ranges, place some parameters on when students can post their work. If they post as they go, then a provision needs to be in place that, after a round of play is posted, the multiplier may *not* be selected again by any other pair of students in the classroom. Alternatively, have students work on a set of posted target ranges, but post their number sentences at a later-determined time. This ensures that all students get an opportunity to work with the target range before seeing their classmates' findings.

17. This time, pairs get to choose their target range (see the list of options for doing so).

> ### Options for Determining Your Target Range
>
> - *Make a class decision:* As a class, pick the target range or ranges.
>
> - *Roll a die:* Roll a 1–6 die three times. Combine the three numbers to form as large a three-digit number as possible. For example, if a 1, 5, and 2 are rolled, the largest number would be 521. Then, add fifty to the number to create the target range. In the example, the target range would be 521–571.
>
> - *Create target range posters:* Post various target ranges on poster paper (one target range per sheet) around the classroom. Have students pick a target range, play the game, then record their number sentences under the corresponding target range on the poster. This option gives students the opportunity to see how their peers are hitting the target.

18. Give students time to play at least three games with predetermined ranges. When observing and talking with students as they play, ask key questions such as:

- When a multiplicand is determined, how do you choose a multiplier?

- What is your thinking as you choose a multiplier?

- What strategies are you using when you compute mentally?

- Are there advantages to being Player 1 in this game? Player 2? Explain.

MATH WORKSHOP AND SUMMARIZING THE EXPERIENCE

Teach this game at the beginning of the week to the whole class, then make it an integral part of your math workshop (for more on math workshops, see Chapter 5 in *From Reading to Math* by Maggie Siena). Build in time to observe students playing the game. Note their individual skill level and the strategies being used, then come together as a class later in the week and hold a discussion about the mathematics involved in the game. Refer to your notes during the discussion. If posters have been used, ask students to select a poster to discuss. Ask key questions such as: "What strategies did you use when calculating mentally? Which initial numbers (multiplicands) are easy to work with? Why? What makes them easier?" Play another collective round of *Hit the Target* as done in "Active Engagement." Ask students to share their thinking not just about computation, but also about the strategies used in selecting the multiplicand and multipliers.

TEACHING TIP
Using Target Range Posters for Whole-Class Discussion

When student work is posted and referred to, students are more vested in the summarizing discussion that ensues. The posted work also helps you focus your discussion; choose one target range (poster) to discuss in depth. Discussions can lead to a number of concepts, such as revisiting the commutative property ($25 \times 26 = 650$ and $26 \times 25 = 650$) and moving on to the distributive property [$5 \times 130 = 650$ because 130 is five 26s or $5 \times (5 \times 26) = (5 \times 5) \times 26$]. Doubling and halving is another concept that likely will emerge ($26 \times 26 = 676$ and hits the target, so 13×52 might appear on the corresponding poster).

DIFFERENTIATING YOUR INSTRUCTION
Changing Target Ranges

To modify this game according to the levels and needs of your students, simply change target ranges. Consider using ranges that begin with an even hundred such as 200–250 or 300–350 for students who are struggling. Likewise, make the mental estimation in the game more challenging by narrowing the range from fifty to thirty (for example, 650–680) or selecting ranges that do not begin at a round hundred (for example, 735–785). This strategy helps make the mathematics both accessible yet challenging for all.

Using a Die to Determine the Target Range

If you choose to roll a die to determine the target range, consider using a die labeled 4–9 to increase the challenge. The rolls will result in larger numbers, further challenging students' mental computation skills as well as their estimating abilities.

TEACHING TIP
Play It at Home!

The game *Hit the Target* can be played easily at home because the materials are so accessible. For home use, *Hit the Target* needs only a pencil, paper, and partner. Send home copies of the *Hit the Target* Game Directions **(REPRODUCIBLE G-16)** as necessary.

How Close to 0?

Recommended Grades 2–4
Time Instruction: 45–60 minutes
Independent Play: 20–30 minutes

TEACHING TIP
Quiet Dice
Rolling dice can create lots of noise. To lessen the noise, use foam dice, or pad students' workspaces with foam or fabric placemats.

TIME SAVER
Reusable Game Boards
Instead of making consumable copies of the *How Close to 0?* Game Board, laminate a set or place copies in plastic sleeves and provide dry dry erase pens.

Overview

This game provides practice in subtraction as well as strategy and logical reasoning. Both players start with one hundred and try to get as close as possible to zero in seven rounds of the game. During Round 1, players take turns rolling a die, assigning the rolled number a ones or tens value, and subtracting the quantity from one hundred. During the six following rounds, players subtract the number from the previous difference. The player closest to zero by Round 7 is the winner; if a player reaches or goes below zero before Round 7, the other player wins. With slight modifications, this game can also be played with decimals.

Materials

- die (labeled 1–6), 1 per pair of students
- *How Close to 0?* Game Board (REPRODUCIBLE 26), 1 copy per pair of students
- *How Close to 0?* Game Directions (REPRODUCIBLE G-17), 1 per pair of students
- pencil, 1 per pair of students

Related Games

Game 18: Leftovers with 15
(the variation Leftovers with 100)
Game 27: Roll for $1.00
Game 30: Target 300 (A Multiplication Game)

Key Questions

- How do you decide whether to use a number as a ten or a one?
- How are you getting the difference?

Adapted from *Teaching Arithmetic: Lessons for Addition and Subtraction, Grades 2–3* by Bonnie Tank and Lynne Zolli (Math Solutions, 2001, 128).

Teaching Directions

Part I: The Connection

Relate the game to students' ongoing work.

During preparation for this game, review place value (tens and ones) and computation (subtraction). Then, show students a retail catalog or Web site that sells products that interest them (toys, video games, and so on). Invite students to pretend they have a hundred dollar bill. They need to use their hundred dollar bill to make seven separate purchases from the catalog or Web site. Emphasize that the goal is *not* to save any of the money, but rather to spend it all, getting as close to zero as possible with their seven purchases. Students' attempts at doing this will get them excited to play the game *How Close to 0?*

Part II: The Teaching

Introduce and model the game to students.

1. Explain to students that they will be playing the game *How Close to 0?* The goal of the game is to have a number as close to zero as possible after seven rounds. However, if they reach or go below zero *before* the seventh round, they lose!

2. Display a portion of the *How Close to 0?* Game Board (REPRODUCIBLE 26) where everyone can see it. Write the number *100* in the Player 1, Round 1 box. Connect this number to the one hundred dollars the students had to spend on seven purchases (see "The Connection" presented earlier).

3. Roll the die. Explain that each time the die is rolled, the player must assign a ones value or a tens value to the number. For example, if 3 is rolled, it could be used as a 30 or a 3.

4. Next, subtract the number from one hundred. The new number becomes the starting number for Round 2. The game board should

look like this if the number rolled is 3 and you assign the tens value to it:

	Player 1
Round 1	100 −30 ——— 70
Round 2	70
Round 3	

5. Play Round 2, rolling the die and once again pondering with students about which value to assign the number, ones or tens? Subtract the number from seventy and carry the new difference down for Round 3.

6. As the game develops, seize opportunities to discuss place value. During Round 4 of the sample game presented to the left, when a 6 is rolled, some of the students know the 6 has to be a 6 rather than a 60. Encourage those students to share their thinking.

7. After modeling seven rounds of the game with students, walk through the scoring. The player closer to zero after seven rounds is the winner. If a player reaches or goes below zero before the seventh round, the other player wins and the game is over.

Part III: Active Engagement

Engage students to ensure they understand how to play the game.

8. Now give students the opportunity to explore the game in pairs. Give each pair of students a *How Close to 0?* Game Board (REPRODUCIBLE 26).

9. Explain that you are going to play two rounds together with Player 1 as a class, this time showing all the possible ways to play. Make a chart like the following, where everyone can see it.

	Player 1
Round 1	100 −30 ——— 70
Round 2	70 −5 ——— 65
Round 3	65 −40 ——— 25
Round 4	25 −6 ——— 19
Round 5	19 −2 ——— 17
Round 6	17 −10 ——— 7
Round 7	7 −4 ——— 3

Sample game.

Round 1	100		100	
Round 2				

10. Roll a die. Have students assign a ones value or a tens value to the number rolled and record it on their game board in the Player 1, Round 1 box.

11. On the chart where everyone can see it, record both possibilities—the number with a ones value assigned to it and the number with a tens value assigned to it. For example, if a 5 is rolled, your chart should look like this:

Round 1	100 −5 — 95		100 −50 — 50	
Round 2				

12. Tell students they should have written one of the above as their Round 1. Quickly circulate the classroom to check for understanding.

13. Instruct students to bring down the difference of Round 1 to begin Round 2. Do the same on the class chart.

14. Roll the die again. This time have students assign a ones value or a tens value to the number rolled and record it on their game board in the Player 1, Round 2 box.

15. Record all the possibilities on your chart for Round 2. For example, if a 2 is rolled, your chart should now look like this:

Round 1	100 −5 — 95		100 −50 — 50	
Round 2	95 −2 — 93	95 −20 — 75	50 −2 — 48	50 −20 — 30

A CHILD'S MIND

Bringing Down the New Number

Most difficulties with the format of How Close to 0? begin when students forget to bring down the new number for the next round's starting number. A way to emphasize this is to highlight the step on the game board you've displayed. Emphasize that the difference in Round 1 becomes the starting number in Round 2, the difference in Round 2 becomes the starting number in Round 3, and so on.

TEACHING TIPS
Provide Hundreds Charts

For students who need support in this game, it may be tempting to provide calculators; instead of doing this, make sure hundreds charts are accessible. A hundreds chart (**REPRODUCIBLE A**) is included in this resource.

Recording Your Thinking

In this game, each player is accountable for the mathematics in one of the game board columns—both the computation and the writing representing the thinking. Emphasize that students should take turns recording their number sentences. One student should not be doing all the recording.

Pairing Students

When pairing students for this game, consider placing students of similar ability together. Like ability ensures mathematical engagement of both students. One student, for example, won't be making all the decisions for the game because of her strength in number sense and computation while the other becomes a bystander. However, after students have had experience in playing the game numerous times on several occasions, partnering them with someone who has *different* thinking provides students with an opportunity to grow in their mathematical understandings.

16. Point out to students that there can be four potential differences at this point of play: 93, 75, 48, or 30. At this point of instruction, students should be secure in how to play the game and are ready for independent practice.

Part IV: The Link

Students play the game independently.

17. Set up students for independent practice with the game. Each pair of students should have a *How Close to 0?* Game Board (**REPRODUCIBLE 26**), die, and pencil. Also, distribute the *How Close to 0?* Game Directions (**REPRODUCIBLE G-17**) as needed.

18. Provide students time to play two rounds and multiple games in the days that follow. When observing and talking with students as they play, elicit thinking around concepts of place value and subtraction by asking key questions such as:

- How does place value play a role in this game?

- When you are subtracting a multiple of ten from any number, what happens to the ones place? Why does it remain unchanged?

19. Take note of how students are subtracting. Are they counting backward or using a procedure such as regrouping? Are they subtracting correctly? What are some common errors?

MATH WORKSHOP AND SUMMARIZING THE EXPERIENCE

Teach this game at the beginning of the week to the whole class, then make it an integral part of your math workshop (for more on math workshops, see Chapter 5 in *From Reading to Math* by Maggie Siena). Build in time to observe students playing the game. Note their individual skill level and the strategies being used. Come together as a class later in the week and hold a discussion about the students' strategies. Ask, "Why did you decide to assign the ones value to a number? The tens value?" Their answers can lead to a discussion about probability and likeliness.

ASSESSMENT
Writing Prompts

After students have become familiar with the game, have them revisit or play a game of *How Close to 0?* Then, have them select one of the Rounds 1–7 and write about it. What value did they assign to the number rolled in this round? Why?

DIFFERENTIATING YOUR INSTRUCTION
Playing with Decimals

To make this game more challenging, practice with decimals. Change the beginning number from from one hundred to ten and play the game. This time players must assign a value of ones or *tenths* to the numbers rolled.

Leftovers with 15
Variation: Leftovers with 100

Recommended Grades 3–5
Time Instruction: 45–60 minutes
Independent Play: 20–30 minutes

TEACHING TIP
Quiet Dice
Rolling dice can create lots of noise. To lessen the noise, use foam dice, or pad students' workspaces with foam or fabric placemats.

TIME SAVER
Managing the Materials
For ease in managing the distribution of materials, place the fifteen color tiles, six paper plates, one cup, and one die in gallon-size plastic bags (one bag for each pair of students playing the game).

See the Connections to the Common Core State Standards for Mathematics, page xv.

Overview

This game supports students in developing the concept of division and remainders (leftovers). Students start by creating a division problem. One student rolls the die and distributes fifteen tiles equally among the corresponding number of plates. The student records the problem, keeps the tiles that are the remainder, and the next student starts off using *only* the tiles that are on the plates. Students take turns modeling and recording division problems. The game continues until no tiles are left to divide. At the end of each game, each student adds up the tiles held as remainders. The student with the highest sum is declared the winner. As part of summarizing the game, students record their relevant division problems on a classroom chart titled "Leftovers with a Remainder of 0."

Materials

- color tiles, 15 per pair of students
- small paper plates or round coffee filters, 6 per pair of students
- die (labeled *1–6*), 1 per pair of students
- cup, 1 per pair of students
- pencil and ruled paper
- *Leftovers with 15* Game Directions (REPRODUCIBLE G-18A), 1 per pair of students

Related Game

Game 12: Equation Building

Adapted from *Teaching Arithmetic: Lessons for Introducing Division, Grades 3–4* by Maryann Wickett, Susan Ohanian, and Marilyn Burns (Math Solutions, 2002, 48).

Key Questions

Procedural questions related to play:

- How many plates will you lay out?

- How many tiles are in each group?

- How many tiles are left over or remaining?

- How you will record this? Show me.

- How many tiles will you begin
  the next round with?

Mathematical concept questions:

- Which numbers result more
  easily in remainders?

- Are some numbers difficult to get
  a remainder for? Why is this?

Teaching Directions

Part I: The Connection

Relate the game to students' ongoing work.

Review the concept of division and remainders. Ask students to think about a time when they have had to share something. Discuss what they do when whatever they are sharing does not come out evenly. Students might suggest dividing or leaving out the remainder for fairness.

Part II: The Teaching

Introduce and model the game to students.

1. Explain to students that they will be playing the game *Leftovers with 15* in pairs. Ask students to gather around a demonstration area.

2. Roll a die. Explain that you will be making groups on paper plates. The number rolled determines how many plates or groups you will make. Place the corresponding number of paper plates out where all students can see them. For example, if a 4 is rolled, lay out four paper plates.

TEACHING TIP
Arranging Students
For the modeling part of this game, have students make two concentric circles. In the first circle, students kneel or sit; in the second, students stand. This ensures that everyone can view the demonstration area.

TEACHING TIP
The Word *Remainder*
If this is the first time students have been introduced to the word *remainder* and how to abbreviate it in a mathematical sentence, hold a conversation about leftovers being the tiles that remain or cannot be placed equally into a group.

TEACHING TIP
Returning Tiles to the Cup
Using the cup to hold the tiles that will be played in the next turn helps keep the game organized for students. Emphasize the importance of not skipping the step of transporting the tiles on the plates to the cup. This also ensures that the tiles on the plates don't get mixed up with the remainders (the leftovers), which students need to win!

3. Next, take a cup holding fifteen color tiles and distribute the tiles equally onto each plate (in the example using four plates, three tiles would be placed on each plate).

4. Keep the remaining tiles (in the example, there are three remaining tiles). Explain to students that the remainders—the leftovers—are no longer in play.

5. Now ask students, "How can we record a number sentence that describes what we just did?" Model the use of mathematical vocabulary. Based on the example, you would say, "Fifteen divided into four groups is three in each group, with a remainder of three." You would record:

$$15 \div 4 = 3 \text{ R } 3$$

6. Mark your turn by placing your initial or a T for teacher in front of your number sentence:

$$\text{T: } 15 \div 4 = 3 \text{ R } 3$$

Return *only* the tiles on the plates to the cup.

7. Now it is the students' turn. Play continues only with the tiles that were divided equally among the plates (the tiles that should now be in the cup). In the example, this means there are twelve tiles to work with. Ask one student to roll the die, another to lay out that many paper plates, and a third to divide the twelve tiles equally onto the plates. Record the sentence to explain what happened and mark it with a *C* for class. For example, if the number 6 is rolled, six paper plates would be placed on the table. The twelve tiles would then be divided equally, two on each plate. The recording would look like this:

$$\text{C: } 12 \div 6 = 2 \text{ R } 0$$

8. Demonstrate another round of play, once again using *only* the tiles that are on the plates (in this example, twelve). Emphasize the importance of keeping the reminders out of play and marking each turn with an initial.

9. Explain that the game continues until there are no more tiles to divide or the number rolled is larger than the remaining tiles. At the end of the game, players calculate their scores by counting the number of remainder tiles each player collected. The winner is the player with the most remainders (also referred to as *leftovers*).

Part III: Active Engagement

Engage students to ensure they understand how to play the game.

10. Now give students the opportunity to explore the game in pairs. Give each pair of students the appropriate materials.

11. Circulate, observing students. Watch how they manipulate the materials. Listen to how they talk about the mathematics. Look to see if they are recording a number sentence that reflects the round correctly.

12. Close this section of the lesson with presenting a chart titled "Equations with a Remainder of 0." Ask students to record collectively the equations they discovered that have no leftovers (a remainder of zero).

Part IV: The Link

Students play the game independently.

13. Set up students for independent practice with the game. Make sure each pair of students has the appropriate materials. Also, distribute the *Leftovers with 15* Game Directions (REPRODUCIBLE G-18A) as needed.

14. Give students time to play at least one game. When observing and talking with students as they play, ask key procedural questions about playing the game before moving to math content questions (see "Key Questions" listed at the beginning of this game).

TEACHING TIPS
Pairing Students
For the first round of playing this game, pair students who have different levels of understanding of the concept of division. This strategy helps students focus on the procedures for playing the game. After students have been introduced to the game and have an understanding of the procedural side of it, then pairings should reflect students with similar fact automaticity, which allows you to differentiate learning.

Developing Math Vocabulary
As you circulate, listen for and encourage the vocabulary you want students to be using. Post language objectives— words students should be using in their conversations. For this game, language objectives include *leftover*, *remainder*, and *difference*. When you hear students use the word *leftover*, take the opportunity to remind them that the word mathematicians use is *remainder*.

Managing the Materials
Because of the number of materials used in this game, consider ways for students to manage them best. Per the Time Saver tip presented earlier, sort materials beforehand in gallon-size plastic bags. Determine an area where each pair of students can go to find and return the materials.

A CHILD'S MIND
To Rush or Not?
Some students may rush through the game, skipping the use of plates and tiles to model the division. Remind these students of the importance of being methodical. Being systematic will lead to fewer errors and greater understanding when the numbers become more challenging.

DIFFERENTIATING YOUR INSTRUCTION

Consider the following two ways to increase the challenge of this game:

Leftovers with 20 or 25

Play this game exactly as instructed in *Leftovers with 15*, only use twenty or twenty-five tiles (you can set the number as you wish).

Leftovers with 100

This game ups the challenge but only requires a pencil and paper. Players start by selecting and dividing a number 1–20 into the starting number of one hundred. The remainder becomes the first player's score. The second player subtracts the remainder from the start number to determine the next "new" start number. The game continues until the start number is zero. Players then add up their remainders to determine the winner. Complete directions for this version of the game are in **REPRODUCIBLE G-18B**.

TEACHING TIP
Discussing the "Equations with a Remainder of 0" Chart

When reviewing the classroom chart, highlight the following problems:

$$12 \div 1 = 12$$
$$12 \div 2 = 6$$
$$12 \div 3 = 4$$
$$12 \div 4 = 3$$
$$12 \div 6 = 2$$

Note that twelve is a number students will get "stuck" on when they play the game, because only the number 5 will produce a remainder (when using a 1–6 die). Use this opportunity to introduce lessons around common multiples and composite numbers.

15. Collect students' papers. Beforehand, decide whether students should hand in one paper per pair or whether each student should record on his or her own sheet of paper.

MATH WORKSHOP AND SUMMARIZING THE EXPERIENCE

Teach this game at the beginning of the week to the whole class, then make it an integral part of your math workshop (for more on math workshops, see Chapter 5 in *From Reading to Math* by Maggie Siena). Build in time to observe students playing the game. Note their individual skill level. Come together as a class later in the week and hold a discussion about the mathematics involved in the game. Refer to your notes during the discussion. Ask students, "Where is the math in *Leftovers*?" Students may need help arriving at what mathematical concepts were needed, developed, and practiced, so be prepared to help build their vocabulary and guide their thinking. Concepts to address include one-to-one correspondence (counting), division or sharing, and the idea of a remainder and how to record a division problem with remainders.

Making Moves on the Hundreds Chart

Overview

During this game, the hundreds chart serves as the game board. Students roll a specially labeled die to determine the corresponding number of spaces to move on the chart. The starting place is in the margin to the left of the square marked one (where zero would be) and the objective is to be the first to land exactly on the square numbered ninety-nine. Students gain practice in addition and subtraction as well as develop a deeper understanding of the structure of a hundreds chart, leading to ease of computation. The chart provides a visual representation for students; it serves as both a record of the game moves and a symbolic representation of numbers.

Materials

- Hundreds Chart (REPRODUCIBLE A), 2 per pair of students

- game markers (counters or interlocking cubes of two different colors, for example), 2 per pair of students

- die (labeled *+10, +10, +10, −10, +1, −1*), 1 per pair of students

- *Making Moves on the Hundreds Chart* Game Directions (REPRODUCIBLE G-19), 1 per pair of students

- pencil and paper, 1 per pair of students

CCSS See the Connections to the Common Core State Standards for Mathematics, page xv.

Recommended Grades 1–2

Time Instruction: 45–60 minutes
Independent Play: 20–30 minutes

 TEACHING TIPS

Making the Special Die
There are several options for making the die required in this game:

- *Relabel existing dice:* Use small round stickers to relabel existing dice.

- *Write on wooden cubes:* Using a permanent marker, label each face of a wooden cube.

- *Use spinners:* As an alternative to dice, create spinners.

Reusable Game Boards
Instead of making consumable copies of the hundreds chart, laminate a set of charts or place copies in plastic sleeves. Have each student keep a nonconsumable hundreds chart in his or her folder or cubby (whichever classroom organization tool is being used).

Quiet Dice
Rolling dice can create lots of noise. To lessen the noise, use foam dice or pad students' workspaces with foam or fabric placemats.

Adapted from *Teaching Arithmetic: Lessons for Introducing Place Value, Grade 2* by Maryann Wickett and Marilyn Burns (Math Solutions, 2002, 104).

Related Games

Game 1: A "Mazing" 100

Game 2: Addition Table Trail

Game 27: Roll for $1.00

Key Questions

- How many more tens do you need to move your marker to reach ninety-nine?

- How many more ones do you need to reach a multiple of ten?

- What is the distance between the two players?

Teaching Directions

Part I: The Connection

Relate the game to students' ongoing work.

Introduce the hundreds chart to students if they have not yet used it. Distribute a chart (REPRODUC-IBLE A) to each pair of students. Ask students what they notice about how it is organized. If students are already familiar with the hundreds chart, re-mind them of work done around patterning. Have them take out their individual hundreds charts or display a classroom hundreds chart. Review the fact that the columns count by tens.

Part II: The Teaching

Introduce and model the game to students.

1. Tell students they will be playing the game *Making Moves on the Hundreds Chart* in pairs. Their game board will be the hundreds chart. The objective of the game is to be the first player to land exactly on the square numbered 99.

2. Gather students around a large table or floor space to model the game.

3. Have a student volunteer assist in the demon-stration of the game. Give the special die to the student. Ask her to inspect the die and re-port to the class what she sees. Have the class discuss how this die is different from others.

TECHNOLOGY TIP
Using an Interactive Whiteboard
Most interactive whiteboards have a hundreds chart as part of the tools; use this for the modeling part of the game. Use the highlighter tools as your game markers, tracing your moves as you go. Use the "fun" highlighting tools, such as the star or smiley face as a stamp, and have students touch each number square as they make their moves, marking their path. It's okay if the highlighting overlaps—in fact, it helps the visual learners see the moves.

TEACHING TIP
Arranging Students
For the modeling part of this game, have students make two concentric circles. In the first circle, students kneel or sit; in the second, students stand. This ensures that everyone can view the demonstration area.

4. Record the faces of the die where everyone can see them:

Faces of the die: +10, +10, +10, –10, +1, –1

5. Explain that students will take turns rolling the special die. They will move their game marker the corresponding number of squares on the hundreds chart.

6. Place two game markers in the margin next to the number 1 square on the hundreds chart. Have the student volunteer roll the die and move her game marker the corresponding number of squares.

7. Ask the class to describe the move using a number sentence. For example, if a +10 was rolled, the class would share, "Zero plus ten is ten."

8. Record the move where everyone can see it. Label the move *Player 1*. Emphasize that an important part of the game is recording your moves.

9. Now roll the die as Player 2 and move the corresponding number of squares. Record your move next to Player 1. For example, if you rolled a +1, the recording would now look like this:

Player 1   Player 2
0 + 10 = 10   0 + 1 = 1

10. Continue to model the game; after each player's turn, ask the class to describe the move using a number sentence, then record it.

11. After several rounds of play, your recording might look like this:

Player 1   Player 2
0 + 10 = 10   0 + 1 = 1
10 + 10 = 20   1 + 10 = 11
20 – 1 = 19   11 + 10 = 21
19 + 10 = 29   21 – 1 = 20

12. Play enough rounds for students to understand how to move on the hundreds chart

Start	1	2	3	4	5	6	7	8	9	10
	11	12	13	14	15	16	17	18	19	20
	21	22	23	24	25	26	27	28	29	30
	31	32	33	34	35	36	37	38	39	40
	41	42	43	44	45	46	47	48	49	50
	51	52	53	54	55	56	57	58	59	60
	61	62	63	64	65	66	67	68	69	70
	71	72	73	74	75	76	77	78	79	80
	81	82	83	84	85	86	87	88	89	90
	91	92	93	94	95	96	97	98	99	100

End

TEACHING TIP
Impossible Moves
Sometimes, a corresponding move on the hundreds chart will not be possible. For example, if a –1 is rolled as the first roll of the game, the player will not be able to move his game marker. Or, if the player is on square 98 and rolls a +10, the player will not be able to move his game marker. In the case of an impossible move, the player loses a turn.

TEACHING TIP
Rule Reminder
Remind students that they always start their move on the game board where they left off with their last move, meaning they always begin a new number sentence (equation) with the sum or difference of their previous move.

based on the roll of the die, as well as how to record the corresponding number sentences.

13. Close by reminding students of the game's objective: You want to be the first player to get to square 99 exactly.

Part III: Active Engagement

Engage students to ensure they understand how to play the game.

14. Now give students the opportunity to explore the game in pairs. Give each pair a hundreds chart and special die. Make sure students have pencil and paper as well; remind them of the importance of recording their moves. They should title their work, *Making Moves on the Hundreds Chart.*

15. Circulate as students engage in play. Ask them questions such as the following:

- Who is ahead and by how much?

- How many tens did you roll to get to that space?

- How many more tens do you need to roll to reach the row of nineties?

- How far away from the next ten are you?

- How many spaces separate you from your partner and how do you know? (This can be a more challenging question!)

Part IV: The Link

Students play the game independently.

16. Set up students for independent practice with the game. Each pair should have the necessary materials; this time, when students play together, each should use their own game board (hundreds chart). Also, distribute the game directions (REPRODUCIBLE G-19) as needed.

17. Students play the game until one player reaches 99 exactly.

TEACHING TIP
Pairing Students
For this game, partner students of varied abilities and facility with the hundreds chart. Because the game involves luck (as a result of rolling a die), students will not be at an advantage or disadvantage playing alongside a peer who has a different skill level for adding and subtracting.

TEACHING TIP
The Hundreds Chart
During the active engagement part of this lesson, students share a hundreds chart; however, when playing independently in pairs, have each student use his or her own hundreds chart. Using separate charts facilitates independent practice and flexibility among pairings of students; it may also simplify the management of materials.

MATH WORKSHOP AND SUMMARIZING THE EXPERIENCE

Teach this game at the beginning of the week to the whole class, then make it an integral part of your math workshop (for more on math workshops, see Chapter 5 in *From Reading to Math* by Maggie Siena). Build in time to observe students playing the game.

Come together as a class later in the week and hold a discussion about the mathematics involved in the game. Use the sample round from when you modeled the game or select a round produced by a pair of students. Ask students to separate the equations into like functions. For example, using the number sentences produced from modeling the game, group all the equations that have +10:

Player 1	Player 2
0 + 10 = 10	0 + 1 = 1
10 + 10 = 20	1 + 10 = 11
20 – 1 = 19	1 + 10 = 21
19 + 10 = 29	21 – 1 = 20

+10 Group

0 + 10 = 10

10 + 10 = 20

19 + 10 = 29

1 + 10 = 11

11 + 10 = 21

Look for patterns. Ask key questions such as the following:

- What happens to the tens digit when we add ten?

- What happens to the ones digit when we add ten?

- Is this always true? (Students can test their hypothesis on a larger number.)

TEACHING TIP
Recording Your Moves

Students typically record between twenty and thirty number sentences before reaching 99. Emphasize the importance of recording your moves as number sentences. These notations help students articulate their thinking and are equally valuable for other students to see how their partner is computing. Consider collecting students' work at the end of each game. The work can be used as a way to examine the combination of equations that add up to 99, or as proof of a record-holding game if you keep classroom records. Challenge students to have the fewest or the most moves to get to 99. Post the students' work; it can serve as the record to beat.

DIFFERENTIATING YOUR INSTRUCTION
Play Backward!

Using the hundreds chart, have students start on the square numbered 99 and play to 0. This strategy allows for more practice in subtraction—often a more challenging function for students to understand. For this alternate way of play, a change in the die faces is required: −10, −10, −10, +10, −1, +1.

Missing Addend or Factor (Salute!)

Recommended Grades 2–5

Time Instruction: 45 minutes
Independent Play: 20–30 minutes

Overview

Missing Addend or Factor is also known as *Salute!* In the *Missing Addend* version, two players start by each drawing a card. On the third player's command ("Salute!"), the two other players place the card on their forehead, with the number facing outward. The third player studies both cards and announces the sum of the two numbers. The other two players try to determine the card they are holding by knowing the sum and seeing the other addend. The first player to call out the number he is holding wins both cards. The game continues until all the cards have been used. The player with the most cards then plays the role of Player 3, the player who calls out the sums. This strategy gives the player who was slower in calling out the missing addends another chance to improve his or her automaticity against a new player.

This game is an exercise in basic facts and builds automaticity as students memorize fact families. As a variation, players can also play *Missing Factor*, this time announcing the product of the two numbers instead of the sum (multiplication instead of addition).

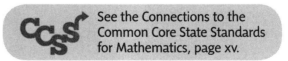

See the Connections to the Common Core State Standards for Mathematics, page xv.

Materials

- Numeral Cards 0–10 (REPRODUCIBLE B), 1 set enlarged for class use

- Numeral Cards 0–10 (REPRODUCIBLE B), 1 deck per group of three students

  or

- playing cards, 1 deck per group of three students (face cards and Jokers removed; Aces remain to represent the value of 1)

- *Missing Addend (Salute!)* Game Directions (REPRODUCIBLE G-20), 1 per group of three students

Related Games

Game 2: Addition Table Trail
(the variation Multiplication Table Trail)

Game 16: Hit the Target (Mental Multiplication)

Key Questions

- When you hear the sum announced, what do you do in your head to call out the missing addend?

- How did you get your answer so quickly?

- What did you have to know to "just know" the missing addend?

Teaching Directions

Part I: The Connection

Relate the game to students' ongoing work.

When students are not in the room, post basic addition equations where everyone can see them. Using sticky notes, cover up one of the addends in each equation. When students come into the room, ask them to think about the missing addends in each of the equations. Review each equation. As students offer the answer to each equation, ask how they knew what number was under the sticky note: "How did you determine the missing addend?"

TEACHING TIPS

Enlarged Numeral Cards

A set of enlarged numeral cards is recommended to model this game. Use a photocopier to enlarge the cards provided in **REPRODUCIBLE B** or use eleven sheets of white copy paper or construction paper and write one of the 0–10 numerals on each (use a thick black marker so the numbers can be seen easily).

A Deck of Cards

For the purpose of this game, a deck of cards is four of each number. If using a deck of playing cards, the Ace (1)–10 should be in play; if using the numeral cards, 0–10 will be available. Prepare decks of playing cards ahead of time, removing all the face cards. The two Jokers may remain as wild cards (meaning, they can be any digit 0–10). Alternatively, show students how to sort the face cards out of their deck and then replace them when finished.

Coding Cards

Whether using numeral cards or a deck of playing cards, code each set to keep it complete. Do this by placing a small symbol in the corner of each set's card; use a different symbol for each set so that, if sets become mixed up, you can sort them more easily.

TEACHING TIPS

Selecting Student Volunteers

Be deliberate about who you select as the student volunteers to demonstrate the game. Select students who are secure in their facts, because they will be put in a situation in which all of their peers are watching them.

Numbers to Start With

For the purpose of modeling the game, start with the numbers 3 and 7 because students likely are comfortable working with these combinations. Alternatively, select any two cards that you feel will reduce the risk of students not knowing the sum quickly and with ease. This strategy heightens the engagement of students.

Part II: The Teaching

Introduce and model the game to students.

1. Tell students they will be playing the game *Missing Addend* (also called *Salute!*) in groups of three. Explain that the goal of the game is to guess the missing addend; their clues are the known addend and a sum.

2. Select two students to come to the front of the classroom. Hand each of them one enlarged numeral card with the number side facing down. Emphasize that they are not to look at the number!

3. Explain to the students that when you say "Salute!" they should place their enlarged numeral card against their forehead with the number side facing outward (so the class can see the number, but the student holding the card cannot).

4. Say "Salute!" When the students have the cards to their forehead, explain to the rest of the students: "These two students do not know the numbers on their card. We must give them a clue. The clue is going to be the sum of the two numbers we see. What is the sum?"

5. Wait a few moments then ask the students to call out the sum in unison. If the cards are 3 and 7, the students would call out, "Ten!"

6. The two volunteers holding the cards now have two pieces of information: they know the sum and they know the addend (the card the other volunteer is holding). With this information, they can determine what number they are holding to their forehead. The first to call out the number he or she is holding (the missing addend) wins both cards.

7. Repeat Steps 2–6 for two more rounds or until you feel students have a firm grasp of the game procedures.

8. Now explain how the game is won. Explain to students, "After all the cards have been

used, the player with the *most* cards trades roles with the player calling out the sums. The player who had fewer cards remains in their role and has a new player to play against."

Part III: Active Engagement

Engage students to ensure they understand how to play the game.

9. Now give students the opportunity to explore the game in groups of three. Have each group determine who will play the role of calling out sums.

10. Instruct the players who are the sum callers (Player 3) to pick up a set of cards while the other two players choose a place in the room to play.

11. Now ask the sum callers (Player 3) to shuffle the cards and deal one to each player.

12. Give the command "Salute!" for play to begin.

13. Circulate, observing students as they play. Make certain that the groupings are allowing all students a level of success (all students have an opportunity to be both a player in the game and a sum caller). The game is designed so the student needing the most practice with recall of facts stays in a position to practice; however, it is also important those students have a chance to feel successful and practice calling the sums also.

Part IV: The Link

Students play the game independently.

14. Set up students for independent practice with the game. Each group should have the necessary cards. Also, distribute the game directions (REPRODUCIBLE G-20) as needed.

15. Have students play the game long enough to allow each student to be in both the role of sum caller and the role of addend guesser. Circulate and observe, making note of students' improvement in their automaticity. Make adjustments to the groups as necessary.

TEACHING TIPS

Determining Roles

There are several ways groups can determine their roles; one way is to have the student whose first name contains the most letters to be Player 3 (the player who calls out the sums).

Shuffling Cards

Younger students are typically not able to shuffle the cards. If this is the case, demonstrate how to mix the cards with your hands, being careful to keep all the cards facing the same direction (either face down or face up).

Managing Classroom Noise

Because this game has speed and efficiency woven into it, students tend to raise their voices to the point of shouting out the missing addend. Establish an acceptable volume level prior to play; remind students to use their "indoor" voices. Encourage the sum callers to *whisper* the sums.

DIFFERENTIATING YOUR INSTRUCTION

Missing Factor

As a variation, players can also play Missing Factor, this time stating the product of the two numbers instead of the sum (multiplication instead of addition).

MATH WORKSHOP AND SUMMARIZING THE EXPERIENCE

Teach this game at the beginning of the week to the whole class, then make it an integral part of your math workshop (for more on math workshops, see Chapter 5 in *From Reading to Math* by Maggie Siena). Build in time to observe students playing the game, noting student's individual skill level and competency in their basic facts. Gather new data to determine whether students have improved in their fact efficiency and accuracy. Come together as a class later in the week and conduct a lesson around fact families. Begin by asking students, "What are some of the fact families for the sum of ten?" As students offer ideas, record the ideas where everyone can see them.

Fact Families of Ten:

1, 9, 10

2, 8, 10

3, 7, 10

4, 6, 10

5, 5, 10

Students then might work in pairs to record the fact families for other sums 2–20.

More!

Overview

During this game, students play in pairs to build and compare visual representations of numbers. Players are dealt equally all the cards from a deck of playing cards. They each draw one card from their pile and compare the face value of the cards. The player with the greater value determines the difference between the two values and connects the corresponding number of interlocking cubes. As play continues, players continue to connect cubes; each player will have a stick of cubes when all cards have been played. Students then compare the lengths, count their stick of cubes, and record the amount.

Materials

- playing cards (Jokers removed; Aces optional and represent the value of 1), 1 deck per pair of students
- interlocking cubes, approximately 150 for each pair of students
- *More!* Recording Sheet (REPRODUCIBLE 27), 1 per pair of students
- pencil, 1 per pair of students
- *More!* Game Directions (REPRODUCIBLE G-21), 1 per pair of students

Related Games

Game 8: Compare (Shake and Spill)

Game 32: Tens Go Fish

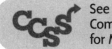 See the Connections to the Common Core State Standards for Mathematics, page xv.

Recommended Grades K–1

Time Instruction: 45–60 minutes
Independent Play: 20–30 minutes

 TEACHING TIP
A Deck of Cards
For the purpose of this game, a deck of cards is four of each number. When using a deck of playing cards, the zero will not be available. It is optional to include the Aces (representing a value of 1). The two Jokers may remain as wild cards (meaning, they can be any digit 1–13, with the Jack, Queen, and King representing the values 11, 12, and 13, respectively).

 TIME SAVERS
Coding Cards
Code each set of playing cards to keep them complete. Do this by placing a small symbol in the corner of each set's card; use a different symbol for each set so that, if sets become mixed up, you can sort them more easily.

Organizing Interlocking Cubes
For the purpose of this game, organize the sets of 150 cubes in tubs or containers that students can reach into easily with their hands. Have two pairs of students share a tub of interlocking cubes (so each tub contains approximately 300 cubes). Have students place the tub in the middle of a table so both players can access the cubes easily.

Key Questions

- How are you finding the difference?
- If you draw a ten, what card do you hope that your opponent draws? Why?
- When you compare numbers, what do you do?
- Do you prefer to count up or count back? Why?

Teaching Directions

Part I: The Connection

Relate the game to students' ongoing work.

Students' Familiarity with Playing Cards

It is important, before playing this game, to know how familiar students are with decks of playing cards. Ask students, "How many of you have played with playing cards?" Show students what you mean by playing cards. Hold up a number of different cards, including face cards. Inquire if students play cards at home. Depending on their age, some students may have many experiences with decks of playing cards; others will have limited experiences. If students seem inexperienced in playing with cards, explicit instruction is needed on how to shuffle, deal, and discard the cards before introducing the game.

Stories of Comparing

Ask students to think about a time when they were playing with a friend and they compared how many of something they had. Tell a story about your childhood memories of comparing. For example, "When I was seven, I would play with dolls with my friend, Michelle. We would count and compare how many dolls we had before putting them together to play. Now that I'm a grownup and have my own seven-year-old, he likes to compare his football and baseball card collections with his buddies. What do you like to compare?"

Have students turn to their partner and share their stories about collecting and comparing.

Part II: The Teaching

Introduce and model the game to students.

1. Gather students around a table or demonstration area of your classroom. Tell students they will be playing the game *More!* in pairs. Explain that the goal of the game is to build and compare visual representations of numbers.

2. Explain to students that during this game they'll be using a deck of playing cards. Every card in the deck has a value. Talk about the value of the face cards. For this game, the Jack is the number 11, the Queen is the number 12, and the King has the value of 13 (see the Teaching Tip for using the Ace). Write these values where everyone can see them and reference them when playing the game independently.

Value of Face Cards

J = 11

Q = 12

K = 13

3. Select two student volunteers, Player 1 and Player 2, to help with demonstrating how to play the game. Model how to shuffle and deal the playing cards. During an actual game, players will deal the entire deck of cards (fifty-two cards; meaning, each player will have twenty-six cards). For the purpose of modeling, limit the number of cards to twelve (so each player has six cards and six rounds are played).

4. Have the two players stack their cards in a neat pile, face down, in front of them.

5. Instruct each player to take the top card from their pile and turn it over.

6. Ask the students, "What number does each player have? Which player has more?" For example, if Player 1 turns over an 8 and Player 2 turns over a Jack, the response might be, "Player one has eight because the card shows

TEACHING TIPS

Arranging Students
For the modeling part of this game, have students make two concentric circles. In the first circle, students kneel or sit; in the second, students stand. This ensures that everyone can view the demonstration area.

Emphasize Card Value
When supporting students in understanding the value of each playing card, make the connection to collections of baseball cards. Each baseball card has a value and is worth something; in this game, each card has a number value and is worth that number.

Using the Ace Face Cards
It is optional to include the Ace face cards in this game. Depending on the experiences of your students, if you do include the Aces, assign these cards a value of one and add A = 1 to your list of face values.

Shuffling Cards
Younger students are typically not able to shuffle the cards. If this is the case, demonstrate how to mix the cards with your hands, being careful to keep all the cards facing the same direction (either face down or face up).

TEACHING TIP

If Cards Are the Same Value

If the cards drawn happen to be the same value, players put them aside, draw two new cards, and continue playing.

eight. Player two has eleven because a Jack has the value of eleven. Player two has more than Player one." Point to the list of card face values as necessary to remind students of the face card equivalents.

7. Now ask, "How many more?" In the previous example, Player 2 has three more than Player 1.

8. Explain that the player with the greater value now represents the difference in values using interlocking cubes. In the example, Player 2 then takes three interlocking cubes and snaps them together.

9. Repeat Steps 5–8, continuing to have players compare their cards and build the differences using interlocking cubes. Note that players should always add on to their existing train of interlocking cubes.

10. After all the cards have been played, each player will have a stick of cubes. Invite the players to compare their stick of cubes. Say, "For the scoring of the game of *More!*, you need to determine the difference in the length of the sticks of cubes." Elicit ideas about how to do this from students. Some of their thoughts might be to count each cube in each stick. Another might be to place the sticks side-by-side to see which one is longer or taller.

11. Check for understanding of the game procedures by prompting students with procedural questions such as: What do you do first? Then what? And last?

12. Play another round or game collectively if needed.

Part III: Active Engagement

Engage students to ensure they understand how to play the game.

13. Now give students an opportunity to return to their own tables or desks and explore the

game in pairs. First, have students organize themselves in their playing spaces. Cards should be shuffled, dealt, and stacked neatly in two piles (Player 1's cards and Player 2's cards). As students play, circulate, shifting your focus from the procedural side of the game to the mathematical processes (such as a student's computational fluency).

14. Have students play for a predetermined amount of time. Students will finish the game at varying times. When they do so, have them shuffle the cards and begin another game, even if they do not complete it. When time is up, students who are in the middle of a round can simply find the difference in their stick of cubes at that juncture in the game.

Part IV: The Link

Students play the game independently.

15. Now show students the *More!* Recording Sheet (REPRODUCIBLE 27). Explain that there are three important numbers to enter after each game:

    a. The total number of cubes in Player 1's stick of cubes.

    b. The total number of cubes in Player 2's stick of cubes.

    c. The difference between Player 1 and Player 2's totals.

16. Set up students for independent practice with the game. Make sure each pair of students has one deck of playing cards prepared per game specifications, access to interlocking cubes (see Teaching Tip included with materials list at beginning of this lesson), and one *More!* Recording Sheet (REPRODUC- IBLE 27). Also, distribute the game directions (REPRODUCIBLE G-21) as needed.

TEACHING TIP
Pairing Students
When pairing students for this game, place students of similar ability together. Although the game relies on luck of the cards, skill comes into play when students are determining the difference between the numbers. Pairing students of similar ability in number sense, patterning, and computation (addition/subtraction) increases mathematical engagement of all students while allowing them to move through the game at a rate that is comfortable and meaningful for them. Students who are more fluent in their basic facts will likely move at a faster rate, whereas those who are insecure in their facts will move more slowly and methodically.

DIFFERENTIATING YOUR INSTRUCTION

There are several ways to modify the game according to the levels and needs of your students.

Card Deck Variations

Decrease the number of cards in the decks. Students could play with half a deck, for example. This modification is especially helpful if you're limited by materials (especially interlocking cubes) and/or time.

Double More!

For students who need a computation challenge, introduce *Double More!* When playing this variation, each player turns over two cards at one time, finds the sum of the two cards, and then players find the difference between the two sums.

MATH WORKSHOP AND SUMMARIZING THE EXPERIENCE

Teach this game at the beginning of the week to the whole class, and then make it a fundamental part of your math workshop (for more on math workshops, see Chapter 5 in *From Reading to Math* by Maggie Siena). Throughout the week, ask questions such as "How many more?" "How many less?" and "What's the difference?" Throughout the year, connect to experiences with the game when making other comparison contexts, such as student height, temperature, or time.

Also, use the experience to revisit or launch data concepts such as range, median, and mode. Gather students together and ask them to record one of their totals from a game on a sticky note. Post the notes where everyone can see them. Organize the notes from smallest to largest value. Some numbers will have more than one note, so place them above each other like a line plot or bar graph:

Then, continue with revisiting or introducing data concepts of range, median, and mode. In the previous example, the range is forty-six because the difference between the smallest piece of data, 38, and the largest piece of data, 84, is forty-six. The median is fifty-seven because it is the middle number of the twenty-five pieces of data. Remember that if you have an even number of students participating, you may want to add a round. An even number of pieces of data can sometimes result in a number that is between two data points and likely a challenging concept for this age of students. The mode is sixty-two because it is the piece of data that occurs most often.

Odd or Even?

Overview

This game offers practice in addition as well as exploration of properties of odd and even numbers. Students work in pairs using a deck of playing cards. They start by taking the top two cards from the stack and placing the cards face side up, one overlapping the other. If the sum of the two cards is an even number, players "win" the cards and set them aside in their pile. Players then take two more cards from the deck. If the sum is odd, players take a third card from the deck and place it face up, once again overlapping it on the top card. Now if the top two cards are even, the players "win" these two cards and remove them from play. Play continues in this fashion, with players always looking at only the last two cards played. After all cards have been played, players count to see how many cards are in their pile versus the pile formed by the deck. The winner (the players or the deck) is the one with the most cards.

Materials

- playing cards, 1 deck per pair of students (face cards and Jokers removed; Aces remain to represent the value of 1)
  or
- Numeral Cards 1–10 (REPRODUCIBLE B)
- *Odd or Even?* Game Directions (REPRODUCIBLE G-22), 1 per pair of students

Related Games

Game 5: Build Ten

Game 7: Close to 100 (the variation Close to 20)

Game 8: Compare (Shake and Spill)

Adapted from *Second Grade Math: A Month-to-Month Guide* by Nancy Litton (Math Solutions, 2003, 206).

Recommended Grades K–2

Time Instruction: 45 minutes
Independent Play: 20–30 minutes

TEACHING TIP
A Deck of Cards
For the purpose of this game, a deck of cards is four of each number 1–10 (**REPRODUCIBLE B**). If using a deck of playing cards, remove the face cards and Jokers. Aces remain to represent the value of 1. Prepare decks prior to teaching the game or show students how to sort the face cards and Jokers out of their deck and then replace them when finished.

TIME SAVER
Coding Cards
Code each deck of playing cards to keep it complete. Do this by placing a small symbol in the corner of each set's card; use a different symbol for each set so that, if sets become mixed up, you can sort them more easily.

 See the Connections to the Common Core State Standards for Mathematics, page xv.

Key Questions

- What happens when you add two even numbers?

- What combinations must you add to get an even sum?

- What happens when you add one odd and one even number?

Teaching Directions

Part I: The Connection

Relate the game to students' ongoing work.

Math Books

Before launching this game, read a book or watch a video about odd and even numbers; suggestions include:

- *Even Steven and Odd Todd* by Kathryn Cristaldi

- There is a video titled *Odd Todd Even Steven* produced by the Waterford Institute (running time 1 min 30 seconds) and can be viewed at www.youtube.com/watch?v=fK6b9Zxte24

- *My Even Day* by Doris Fisher and Dani Sneed

- *One Odd Day* by Doris Fisher and Dani Sneed

One Odd Day is an especially nice fit for this lesson because the front cover features three overlapping cards. If using this resource, highlight this part of the cover and point out how the cards are overlapping. Determine the sum of the top two cards featured.

The Hundreds Chart

Revisit the hundreds chart (ideally, one is displayed in your classroom; see also REPRODUCIBLE A). Identify numbers that are even and odd. Consider having students do this on their own hundreds chart using two different colors of crayons and shading the odd and even numbers lightly. As a class, discuss the patterns that odd and even numbers make on the hundreds chart.

Part II: The Teaching

Introduce and model the game to students.

1. Gather students around a table or demonstration area of your classroom. Explain to students that they will be playing the game *Odd or Even?* in pairs. Note that the goal of the game is to improve one's understanding of even and odd numbers while simultaneously "sparring" with a deck of cards.

2. Model how to shuffle a deck of playing cards (remember that the face cards need to be removed prior to play) and place them neatly, face down, in a stack.

3. Take the top two cards from the deck and turn them over. Place them face side up, one just slightly overlapping the other.

4. Ask students to examine the two numbers on the cards. Is the sum of the two numbers odd or even?

   a. If the sum is an even number, remove both cards from play, placing them aside in a pile. Emphasize that these are the players' cards; they are playing against the deck and these cards are now theirs. Then, take two more cards from the deck and ask, "Is the sum of the two numbers odd or even?" Continue play accordingly.

The sum of these cards is the even number 8, so both would be removed from play.

   b. If the sum is an odd number, draw a third card from the deck and place it so that it overlaps the top card. If the two new top cards are even, again the players win those two cards and they get set aside in the player pile. Another card is drawn and

TEACHING TIPS

Arranging Students
For the modeling part of this game, have students make two concentric circles. In the first circle, students kneel or sit; in the second, students stand. This ensures that everyone can view the demonstration area.

Shuffling Cards
Younger students are typically not able to shuffle the cards. If this is the case, demonstrate how to mix the cards with your hands, being careful to keep all the cards facing the same direction (either face down or face up).

TEACHING TIP
Emphasizing Collaboration

Explain that students will be playing in teams of two *with* their partner, not against him or her. The goal is for students to play as a team against the deck, working together in understanding *how* to play the game and the math involved. It might be helpful to describe how such a partnership may look and sound.

TEACHING TIP
Using Manipulatives

Have manipulatives and other tools (cubes, counters, and hundreds charts) on hand to support students as needed in determining odd and even numbers. If students disagree regarding whether a sum is odd or even, have them use the manipulatives to explore the sum. For example, sort the corresponding number of counters into two equal groups. If there is one counter left over, the number is odd. Keep manipulatives on hand for when students play the game independently.

TEACHING TIP
Pairing Students

When pairing students for this game, place students of similar ability together. If students have similar abilities, the speed of the game will be more comfortable for both of them and will keep them both actively engaged.

placed so that it overlaps the remaining card. The remaining card becomes the beginning of "the deck's" cards.

The sum of the first two cards was an odd number 7, so a third card was drawn. The sum of the top two cards is now even (3 + 9 = 12), so these two cards are removed from play. The 4 card is placed in a separate deck.

5. Continue playing, repeating Step 4, until all the cards in the deck have been played.

6. To determine the winner, explain to students that they must count the number of cards they have in their pile, then they count the cards that are in the deck's pile. If there are more cards in their pile than in the deck's pile, they win!

Part III: Active Engagement

Engage students to ensure they understand how to play the game.

7. Now give students an opportunity to explore the game. Continue modeling the game; however, this time ask the students to participate as mathematicians. Note that it is their responsibility to compute the sum of the two cards and determine whether that sum is odd or even.

8. As students become more familiar with the game, give them an opportunity to guide the procedures of the game, having them point out the process and the rules as rounds are played.

Part IV: The Link

Students play the game independently.

9. Set up students for independent practice with the game. Each pair of students should have a deck of playing cards prepared to

game specifications. Also, distribute the game directions (REPRODUCIBLE G-22) as needed. Emphasize that students are working together in a partnership.

10. Give students time to play at least three games. When observing and talking with students as they play, ask key questions such as the following:

- When you get an even sum, what types of numbers are you adding?

- What types of number combinations result in odd sums?

MATH WORKSHOP AND SUMMARIZING THE EXPERIENCE

Teach this game at the beginning of the week to the whole class, then make it an integral part of your math workshop (for more on math workshops, see Chapter 5 in *From Reading to Math* by Maggie Siena). Build in time to observe students playing the game. Note their individual skill level and the strategies being used. Throughout the week, have students record their even and odd sums on a class chart, adding to the list as they play more rounds of the game. Come together as a class later in the week and hold a discussion about the mathematics involved in the game. Refer to the class chart. Discuss some of the properties of odd and even numbers. Ask key questions such as the following:

- What happens when you add two even numbers?

- What happens when you add two odd numbers?

- What happens when you add one of each (one odd and one even)?

Continue the discussion by posing questions about the probability of the game as well:

- Are you more likely to get even sums or odd sums in this game? Have students explain their thinking.

DIFFERENTIATING YOUR INSTRUCTION

There are several ways to modify the game according to the levels and needs of your students.

Remove High-Digit Cards

To make the game more simple, remove some of the high-digit cards like 7–10. During this version of the game, students practice facts with a sum of twelve or less.

Reverse Odd or Even

Switch it up and have players "win" the odd sums instead of the even ones. This can lead to a probability lesson: "What if the game rules were the opposite and you were collecting odd sums? Would it be harder to win, easier to win, or the same?"

Use Three Cards

To make the game more challenging, play with three addends instead of two. Play would follow the same procedures except players would begin with three cards.

Oh No! 20!

Recommended Grades 1–3
Time Instruction: 45–60 minutes
Independent Play: 20–30 minutes

TEACHING TIP
A Deck of Cards

For the purpose of this game, a deck of playing cards is four of each number 2–5 (cards 6–10 and Jokers removed) plus the face cards, assigned the following values:

Ace = 1

Jack = –5 (subtract 5)

Queen = 0

King: wild card (any number 1, 2, 3, 4, 5, –5, or 0)

Prepare decks of playing cards ahead of time, removing cards 6–10 and the Jokers. Alternatively, show students how to sort out cards 6–10 and the Jokers from their deck and then replace them when finished.

TIME SAVER
Coding Cards

Code each set of playing cards to keep it complete. Do this by placing a small symbol in the corner of each set's card; use a different symbol for each set so that, if sets become mixed up, you can sort them more easily.

Overview

This card game provides students practice in addition and subtraction, encouraging mental computation, number sense, and strategy. Pairs play a hand of four cards each, adding or subtracting card values strategically until one player's sum equals or exceeds twenty. The objective of the game is *not* to be the first player to get twenty or over. Careful modeling of the procedures of this game (which can be slightly tricky because face cards are assigned values beyond the norm) will help to ensure playing success—and get students hooked!

Materials

- playing cards (6, 7, 8, 9, 10, and Joker cards removed; face cards remain; Aces remain to represent the value of 1), 1 deck per pair of students

  or

- Numeral Cards 1–5 (REPRODUCIBLE B) plus four cards marked –5, four cards marked 0, and four wild cards, 1 deck per pair of students

- *Oh No! 20!* Game Directions (REPRODUCIBLE G-23), 1 per pair of students

Related Games

Game 7: Close to 100 (the variation Close to 20)

Game 10: Cross Out Sums

 See the Connections to the Common Core State Standards for Mathematics, page xv.

Key Questions

- How are you deciding on your next card to play?

- Which card do you like to keep in your hand just in case you might need it? Explain.

Teaching Directions

Part I: The Connection

Relate the game to students' ongoing work.

Students' Familiarity with Playing Cards

It's important, before playing this game, to know how familiar your students are with decks of playing cards. Ask them, "How many of you have played with playing cards?" Show students what you mean by playing cards; hold up a number of different cards, including face cards. Inquire if students play cards at home. Depending on their age, some students may have many experiences with decks of playing cards; others will have limited experiences. If students seem inexperienced in playing with cards, explicit instruction will be needed on how to shuffle, deal, and discard the cards before introducing the game. See how many students know the number value of an Ace (1). Show them a Jack, Queen, or King and ask them if they can see the face on the card. Point out that, "This is why we call these face cards."

Part II: The Teaching

Introduce and model the game to students.

1. Gather students around a table or demonstration area of your classroom. Tell students they will be playing the game *Oh No! 20!* in pairs. Explain that the objective of the game is to get your opponent to get to twenty or more before you do.

2. Explain to students that during this game they'll be using a deck of playing cards (or numeral cards, if you choose that option). Cards 6–10 and Jokers are removed; all other

TEACHING TIP
Arranging Students
For the modeling part of this game, have students make two concentric circles. In the first circle, students kneel or sit; in the second, students stand. This ensures that everyone can view the demonstration area.

TEACHING TIP
Emphasizing Card Value
When supporting students in understanding the value of each playing card, make the connection to collections of baseball cards. Each baseball card has a value and is worth something; in this game, each card has a number value and is worth that number.

TEACHING TIP
Shuffling Cards
Younger students are typically not able to shuffle the cards. If this is the case, demonstrate how to mix the cards with your hands, being careful to keep all the cards facing the same direction (either face down or face up).

cards have a value. From your set of playing cards, hold up a 5 card. Ask students, "What is the value of this card?" Continue with the 4, 3, 2, and Ace cards. By going in decreasing order, students are often able to deduce that the value of the Ace card is 1.

3. Talk about the value of the remaining face cards. Emphasize that these values are for the game of *Oh No! 20!* only. Write these values where everyone can see them and reference them when playing the game independently.

> Values of Face Cards
>
> Ace = 1
>
> Jack = -5 (subtract 5)
>
> Queen = 0
>
> King: wild card (any number 1, 2, 3, 4, 5, -5, or 0)

4. Review the values by holding up different cards and asking, "What is the value of this card for *Oh No! 20!?*"

5. Next, ask students to help in modeling the game. Ask a student sitting near you to partner with you as the Player 1 team. Ask two students seated across from you to partner as the Player 2 team.

6. Next, model how to shuffle and deal the deck of playing cards. Deal out four cards to each team. For the purpose of teaching the game, have teams turn their cards face up on the table. Tell students you want them to be able to see the cards while learning how to play the game.

7. Place the remaining cards stacked face down in the center of the demonstration area.

8. As Player 1 team, start by selecting a card from the four dealt and placing it in the middle of the demonstration area, face up. For example, one of your four cards might be a 3. Have Player 2 team do the same thing, selecting a

card from the four dealt to them and placing it face up next to the 3. Player 2 team might choose a 2 card. Player 2 team then needs to compute the two numbers, either adding or subtracting them. For example, 3 + 2 = 5. Both players then draw another card from the stack, so they always have four cards in their hand at the start of a next turn.

9. After this initial start of the game, return to the objective of the game. In the game of *Oh No! 20!,* you do not want to be the first player to get to or go over twenty, Which is why you might think or say, "Oh no! Twenty!" Rather, you want to get your opponent to get to or go over twenty.

10. Make sure students acknowledge and understand the basics of the objective, then proceed with playing the game. Here is an example of a portion of the game that might be played:

   a. Player 1 plays the 4 card by placing it in the middle of the playing area, then Player 1 replaces the 4 with a new card from the deck, which happens to be a Queen. Remind players they should always have four cards.

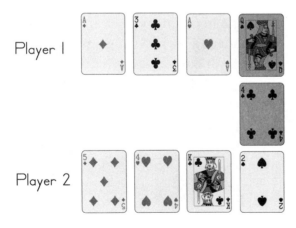

   b. Player 2 plays her 4 card. When Player 2 places the card in the middle of the table, ask all the students observing to add the 4s. Tell students, "Before the game continues, Player 2 must say the sum of the numbers."

c. After Player 2 and the other students confirm that the sum is eight, Player 2 then draws another card—a 2 card—from the stack (so that Player 2 continues to have four cards). The players' cards now look like this:

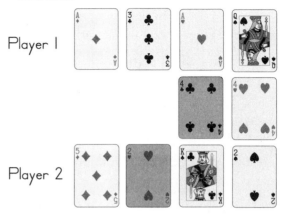

Values of Face Cards

For the purpose of this game, a deck of playing cards is four of each number 2–5 (cards 6–10 removed) plus the face cards, which are assigned the following values:

Ace = 1

Jack = –5 (subtract 5)

Queen = 0

King: wild card (any number 1, 2, 3, 4, 5, –5, or 0)

d. It is Player 1's turn again. Player 1 decides to play the 3 card and places it in the middle with the 4 and the 4. Player 1 must now compute the cards, adding the card played to the previous sum of eight. Player 1 announces the new sum, eleven, and draws another card (4) from the stack so that he continues to have four cards.

e. Player 2 decides to play the 5 card, adding it to the previous sum, eleven, and announcing the new sum, sixteen. Player 2 then draws another card (Ace) from the stack so that she continues to have four cards.

f. The players' cards now look like this:

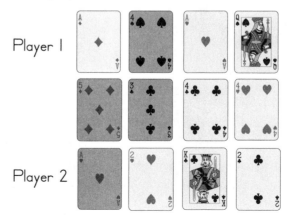

11. Now ask the class, "What card should Player 1 *not* play?" Hold a discussion about which card should not be played and why. Check to make sure students understand the objective of the game once again: if you are the first player to get twenty or more, you lose. In the previous illustration, the card not to play is the 4 card.

12. Continue play, which might unfold as follows:

    a. Realizing that the 4 card is *not* the card to play, Player 1 selects his Ace card to play and announces the new sum, seventeen. Player 1 draws another card, the Jack.

    b. Player 2 plays the 2 card and announces the sum, nineteen. (At this point the students observing will likely be catching on and getting excited that players are nearing twenty). Player 2 draws another card from the stack, this time a 3 card. The players' cards now look like this:

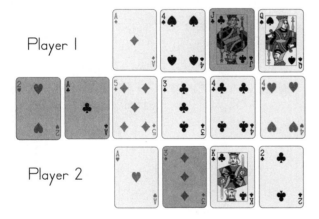

13. As players get close to twenty, take the opportunity to stop the game again and discuss what card to play next. In our example, Player 1 could play the Queen and stay at nineteen or his Jack and subtract five, taking the game back to fourteen. Decide as a class what Player 1 should do and continue play:

    a. Students like the idea of staying at nineteen, so Player 1 decides to play his Queen.

b. Player 2 can now only play one card to remain in the game. Ask students, "Which card can Player 2 now play to stay in the game?" Students have an opportunity to see how a wild card (King) is handled and how to assign its value. In this instance, the only possibility is to assign the King a negative five value, taking the game back to fourteen.

14. Continue play until a winner is announced. Encourage students to add their thoughts about the next plays. Note whether some students are beginning to use strategy and/or whether students are focused more on *not* getting twenty themselves, rather than trying to force their opponent to get to twenty or more.

Part III: Active Engagement

Engage students to ensure they understand how to play the game.

15. Now give students an opportunity to return to their own tables or desks and explore the game in two teams of two. First, have students organize themselves in their playing spaces. Cards should be shuffled, dealt, and neatly stacked.

16. This time, as students play, they should not play with their cards face up. Instead, each team should hold the cards so that only they can see them, not the opposing team. Not only will the game move quickly as a result, but this will encourage more strategic thinking about what cards to play next.

17. As students play, circulate, shifting your focus from the procedural side of the game to the mathematical processes (such as a student's computational fluency).

TEACHING TIPS
Pairing Students

When pairing teams of students for this game, place students of similar ability together. Although the game relies on the luck of the cards, skill and logical reasoning come into play when students are determining which cards to play. Pairing students of similar ability in logical reasoning and computation (addition/subtraction) will increase mathematical engagement of all students while allowing students to move through the game at a rate that is both comfortable and meaningful. Students who are more fluent in their basic facts will likely move at a faster rate whereas those who are insecure in their facts will move more slowly and methodically.

The Importance of Practice

Refrain from discussing skill or strategies during the active engagement part of the lesson. The purpose is to give students as much practice as possible first; they will then have the opportunity to come back later and discuss their experiences (see "Math Workshop and Summarizing the Experience").

Part IV: The Link

Students play the game independently.

18. Set up students for independent practice with the game, now playing individually in pairs. Make sure each pair of students has one deck of playing cards per the game specifications and the game directions (REPRODUCIBLE G-23), as needed.

19. After students have had opportunities to play multiple rounds, gather them together as a class once more. Explain that, as they are playing the game, they should think about the mathematics in the game of *Oh No! 20!*. Label the top of a piece of chart paper "Mathematics in the Game of *Oh No! 20!*," and use the chart when summarizing students' experiences with the game (see "Math Workshop and Summarizing the Experience" below).

MATH WORKSHOP AND SUMMARIZING THE EXPERIENCE

Teach this game at the beginning of the week to the whole class, and then make it a fundamental part of your math workshop (for more on math workshops, see Chapter 5 in *From Reading to Math* by Maggie Siena). Build in time to observe students playing the game, noting student's individual skill level and computational fluency. Come together as a class later in the week and hold a class discussion about students' experiences with the game. Add their thoughts to the chart, "Mathematics in the Game of *Oh No! 20!*" Encourage students to share strategies by asking them questions such as, "Do you save certain cards as you play the game? Jacks, Queens, Kings? If so, why?"

DIFFERENTIATING YOUR INSTRUCTION

There are several ways to modify the game according to the levels and needs of your students.

Record Your Equations
Add an additional step to the game in which students record the equations they form in each round.

Teams of Two
If some students are not yet ready to play this game in pairs, continue to team up two pairs to create a group of four to play.

Yes! 20!
Change the objective of the game so the first player to reach or have more than twenty is the winner.

Oh No! 99!
For this version, use all cards in the deck except Jokers. Assign the following values to the face cards:

Ace: +1 (add 1)

Jack: −10 (subtract 10)

Queen: +10 (add 10)

King: wild card (any number 2–10 or +1, +10, or −10)

Order Up 21!

Recommended Grade 5

Time Instruction: 45 minutes
Independent Play: 20–30 minutes

TEACHING TIPS
A Deck of Cards

For the purpose of this game, a deck of cards is four of each number Ace (1)–10. If using a deck of playing cards, the zero is not available. Prepare decks of playing cards ahead of time, removing all the face cards and Jokers. Alternatively, show students how to sort the face cards out of their deck and then replace them when finished.

Quiet Dice

Rolling dice can create lots of noise. To lessen the noise, use foam dice or pad students' workspaces with foam or fabric placemats.

TIME SAVER
Coding Cards

Whether using numeral cards or a deck of playing cards, code each set to keep it complete. Do this by placing a small symbol in the corner of each set's card; use a different symbol for each set so that, if sets become mixed up, you can sort them more easily.

See the Connections to the Common Core State Standards for Mathematics, page xv.

Overview

This game is ideal for students being introduced to the order of operations. It is flexible in both the number of players (one, two, three, or four) and the type of materials (a deck of playing cards, numeral cards 0–10, or four dice). After drawing four cards or rolling the four dice (two labeled *0–5* and two labeled *5–10*) students attempt to build an equation using all four numbers and applying the order of operations (parentheses, exponents, multiplication, division, addition, and subtraction). The objective is to build an equation that totals twenty-one. After each round, a player's score is determined by how far away their total is from twenty-one. After ten rounds, the player with the lowest score is declared the winner. This game requires mathematical stamina because students are constantly computing and toggling between functions!

Materials

- playing cards (face cards and Jokers removed; Aces remain to represent the value of 1), 1 deck per student, pair, or group of students

  or

- Numeral Cards 0–10 (REPRODUCIBLE B), 1 deck per student, pair, or group of students

  or

- dice (2 labeled *0–5*, 2 labeled *5–10*), 2 of each per student, pair, or group of students

- *Order Up 21!* Recording Sheet (REPRODUCIBLE 28), 1 per student or pair of students

continued

- *Order Up 21!* Game Directions (**REPRODUCIBLE G-24**), 1 per student, pair, or group of students

Related Games

Game 12: Equation Building

Game 26: Roll 6 for 100

Game 29: Take Five, Make Ten!

Key Questions

- What operations result in larger numbers?
- What operations result in smaller numbers?
- How do you build your equations?
- What do you look for first?

Teaching Directions

Part I: The Connection

Relate the game to students' ongoing work.

Before playing this game, review order of operations with your students. Do either one or both of the following practices.

Number Strings

After order of operations has been taught and practiced, write a number string where everyone can see it. Discuss what students know about working through the problem left to right. Place parentheses in the number string. Discuss how this affects the total.

For example, write:

$$1 + 2 \times 3 + 4$$

Next, introduce parentheses and continue to move them throughout the same equation:

$$(1 + 2) \times 3 + 4$$
$$1 + (2 \times 3) + 4$$
$$1 + 2 \times (3 + 4)$$

TEACHING TIP
Arranging Students
For the modeling part of this game, have students make two concentric circles. In the first circle, students kneel or sit; in the second, students stand. This ensures that everyone can view the demonstration area.

TECHNOLOGY TIP
Using an Interactive Whiteboard
If using an interactive whiteboard, use the cards that are available in the tools. Use cards 3, 4, 6, and 9 from the interactive tool kit. Move the cards into the order students suggest. Then record the equation, adding parentheses and functions to note students' thinking. The interactive dice could also be used. However, the dice in the whiteboard tool kit are standard 1–6 dice, so not all digits are available for demonstrating the game.

TEACHING TIP
Game Rules for Building Equations
- Players may use any combination of the four operations (addition, subtraction, multiplication, division).

- The numbers may be used in any order, but may be used only once. If a number is drawn/rolled twice, the number must be used twice in the equation.

- Parentheses may be used and numbers drawn/rolled may be used as exponents.

- Numbers may be used as fractions (see Differentiating Your Instruction at the end of this lesson).

- Equations must be accurate mathematically.

PEMDAS

Post the PEMDAS acronym in the classroom or refer to where it is posted. Review the order of operations: parentheses, exponents, multiplication, division, addition, subtraction. One way students might review this is by reciting the acronym and then stating all six words in order. Most classrooms have established catchy words or sayings to remember the order of operations. A common one is Please Excuse My Dear Aunt Sally.

Part II: The Teaching

Introduce and model the game to students.

1. Decide ahead of time whether students will be using numeral cards, playing cards, or dice to generate the four numbers in this game.

2. Gather students around a table or demonstration area of your classroom. Tell students they will be playing the game *Order Up 21!* either individually, in pairs, or in small groups.

3. Explain that the goal of the game is to build an equation that totals twenty-one using four numbers and applying the order of operations (parentheses, exponents, multiplication, division, addition, and subtraction).

4. With the materials you've decided to use (cards or dice), draw or roll four numbers. Post the numbers so all students can see them.

5. Review the rules for building an equation using the four numbers (see Teaching Tip).

6. Ask students to build equations using the four numbers. Encourage students to use parentheses in the equations to delineate order. Record the equations for everyone to see. If the four numbers posted are 3, 4, 6, and 9, the following equations may be suggested:

$$3 + 4 + 6 + 9 = 22$$

$$6 (9 \div 3) + 4 = 22$$

$$6 \times 3 + 9 - 4 = 23$$

$$6 (3 \times 4 - 9) = 18$$
$$6 + 3 (9 - 4) = 21$$
$$4 (6 - 3) + 9 = 21$$
$$9 (6 - 4) + 3 = 21$$

7. After you've solicited six to eight equations, take the opportunity to explain the scoring. Points are determined by how far away the total is from twenty-one. Scoring zero for the round means the player got exactly twenty-one. The goal is to have the lowest number of points after ten rounds. In our example, the first two equations have a score of 1 point because twenty-two is one more than twenty-one. If there was a total of twenty, the score would also be 1 point because twenty is one less than twenty-one.

Part III: Active Engagement

Engage students to ensure they understand how to play the game.

8. Now give students an opportunity to return to their own tables or desks and explore the game individually. The *Order Up 21!* Recording Sheets are not necessary yet; rather, students may use mini-whiteboards or a piece of scratch paper.

9. Roll the dice or draw cards and post the four numbers where everyone can see them. Ask students to build their equations individually. Remind students of the order of operations, PEMDAS.

10. After adequate time has passed and all students have recorded at least one equation, ask them to select one equation and place a star by it. Next, tell them to determine the score of that equation.

11. Have students play another round if necessary. If some students need additional support, consider having them work in pairs or small groups of four.

 TEACHING TIP
Scoring
Points are determined by how far away the total of the equation is from twenty-one. A score of 0 point means the player got exactly twenty-one. A score of 1 point means the player got either twenty or twenty-two. The goal is to have the lowest score.

 TEACHING TIPS
Exponents
Students will likely ask whether they may use a number as an exponent; they may.

Fractions
At this point, students are encouraged to create fractions that result in whole numbers, so a few improper fractions would work, such as $\frac{9}{3}, \frac{8}{4}, \frac{8}{2}$, and so forth. After more practice with the game, allow students to create fractions resulting in decimal answers. This strategy is a way to differentiate to provide challenge or more practice with decimals.

Students Who Finish First
As students work to build their equations, some students will get twenty-one sooner than others. Consider having those students continue their work. Challenge them to find additional equations that total twenty-one.

TEACHING TIP
Setting a Time Limit
Determine whether there will be a time limit for each round. When to abandon the numbers can be difficult for some students. However, teaching students to persevere and stick with solving for twenty-one can also prove challenging. Find a balance!

DIFFERENTIATING YOUR INSTRUCTION
There are several ways to modify the game according to the levels and needs of your students.

Order Up [Pick Your Number]!
Choose another number other than twenty-one for the total.

Build More Equations
Challenge students to build two equations totaling twenty-one or close to twenty-one for each set of four numbers.

Introduce Fractions
Allow numbers to be used as fractions that result in decimals.

Part IV: The Link
Students play the game independently.

12. Set up students for independent practice with the game. Decide whether students will play solo, in twos, threes, or fours. Make sure students have a deck of playing cards and the *Order Up 21!* Recording Sheet (REPRODUCIBLE 28). Also, distribute the game directions (REPRODUCIBLE G-24) as needed.

MATH WORKSHOP AND SUMMARIZING THE EXPERIENCE
Teach this game at the beginning of the week to the whole class, then make it a fundamental part of your math workshop (for more on math workshops, see Chapter 5 in *From Reading to Math* by Maggie Siena). Build in time to observe students playing the game. Note their individual skill level and how they are using the order of operations to their advantage. After students have had multiple experiences with the game, bring them together as a class to discuss their strategies. Ask them to explain how they build their equations and their thinking behind them.

ASSESSMENT
Blake and Jackson's Game
After students have played at least two complete games, give them an assessment (REPRODUCIBLE 29) to check their computational skills, logical reasoning, as well as correct use of the order of operations.

Pathways (Products Tic-Tac-Toe) Variation: Times Ten

Overview

During this two-player game, students get practice with some of the more challenging multiplication facts. Players select factors, multiply them, and cover the corresponding product on the game board. The objective of the game is to be the first player to complete a continuous pathway across the game board, from one side to the other. There are four different game boards from which to select based on the needs of your students. As a variation, *Times Ten* is offered. It, too, has four versions. It is played in the same manner as *Pathways,* but it incorporates multiplying by ten, thus providing practice with the powers-of-ten concept.

Materials

- *Pathways* Game Board (REPRODUCIBLES 30, 31, 32, or 33), 1 per pair of students

- paper clips, 2 per pair of students

- cubes, tiles, counters, or other game markers, 20 (2 sets of 10, each set a different color) per pair of students

- *Pathways* Game Directions (REPRODUCIBLE G-25A), 1 per pair of students

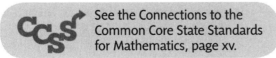 See the Connections to the Common Core State Standards for Mathematics, page xv.

Recommended Grades 4–5
Time Instruction: 45 minutes
Independent Play: 20–30 minutes

 TEACHING TIPS
Reusable Game Boards
Instead of making consumable copies of the game boards, laminate a set or place copies in plastic sleeves and provide dry erase pens to use during game play.

 TIME SAVER
Managing the Materials
For ease in managing the distribution of materials, place the two paper clips and the game markers in quart-size sandwich bags (one bag for each pair of students playing the game).

Adapted from *Teaching Arithmetic: Lessons for Extending Multiplication: Grades 4–5* by Maryann Wickett and Marilyn Burns (Math Solutions, 2001, 162).

TEACHING TIP
Arranging Students

For the modeling part of this game, have students make two concentric circles. In the first circle, students kneel or sit; in the second, students stand. This placement ensures that everyone can view the demonstration area.

TECHNOLOGY TIP
Enlarged Game Board

For modeling purposes, scan the game board and use your whiteboard tools ink layer so that you can interact with the board and use the markers to note your moves. Although not necessary, this tool helps everyone to see the demonstration more clearly.

Related Games

Game 2: Addition Table Trail (the variation Multiplication Table Trail)

Game 16: Hit the Target (Mental Multiplication)

Key Questions

- What space do you try to get first? Why?
- What factors will get you to that space?

Teaching Directions

Part I: The Connection

Relate the game to students' ongoing work.

This game is best played after the concept of multiplication has been solidified. Prior to playing this game, students should understand the relationship of addition and multiplication and know that multiplication is repeated addition. A game in the earlier grades that supports this concept development is *Circles and Stars* (Game 6).

Part II: The Teaching

Introduce and model the game to students.

1. Explain to students that they will be playing the game *Pathways* in pairs. The game will help them learn some of the more challenging multiplication facts as well as build automaticity. Emphasize that students will want to be quick and accurate with their basic facts.

2. Gather students around a table or demonstration area of your classroom. Show them the *Pathways* Game Board (REPRODUCIBLE 30, 31, 32, or 33). Explain that the numbers below the game board are the factors and the numbers on the grid are the products.

3. Take the two paper clips and place them on two factors (the numbers below the game board).

4. Multiply the numbers and cover the corresponding product on the game board with a game marker.

5. Next, move only one of the paper clips so that it covers a different factor. Multiply the two numbers and cover the corresponding product on the game board with a different color game marker.

6. Explain that play alternates between two players, with the goal being to create a pathway across the game board.

7. Show what qualifies as a pathway. Using the game markers, build examples of pathways across the game board. A pathway connects by sharing two sides or a corner of a square across the game board. Pathways need to move across the game board from left to right, not from top to bottom (although pathways will move up and down).

TEACHING TIP
The Same Factors
When modeling how to play this game, point out to students that placing the paper clips on the same factors is permitted, provided the corresponding product is still uncovered on the game board.

81	54	63	36	72
28	18	32	81	24
48	64	21	16	56
12	9	42	49	27

3   4   6   7   8   9

Part III: Active Engagement

Engage students to ensure they understand how to play the game.

8. Now give students an opportunity to explore the game. Have students remain in the arrangement around the demonstration area. This time, assign the seated students as Team 1 and the standing students as Team 2.

9. Ask students to think about how to make their moves purposeful to win the game.

10. Have a player from Team 1 position the two paper clips over two factors. The player's team then helps multiply the numbers and

DIFFERENTIATING YOUR INSTRUCTION

There are several ways to modify the game according to the levels and needs of your students.

Show Your Work

Encourage students to show you what they've learned. If using consumable game boards, have students record their moves with two different colors of crayons or markers, then have students explain their game with both equations and words.

Times Tables

Make completed times tables available for students who are struggling with some of their multiplication facts.

Times Ten

The game *Times Ten* is a variation of *Pathways* for students who need a challenge or for students who have mastered their basic facts and need practice with multiples of ten. **REPRODUCIBLES 34, 35, 36,** and **37,** and *Times Ten* Game Directions **(REPRODUCIBLE G-25B)** are provided for this purpose.

determine the product. The player covers the corresponding product on the game board.

11. A player from Team 2 now moves just one of the paper clips to cover a new factor. The player's team then helps determine the product and the player covers the corresponding product on the game board.

12. Play continues, with teams alternating turns, until a complete pathway has been built.

13. As students play, check for misunderstandings and moderate students so that all voices are heard and all students are engaged.

Part IV: The Link

Students play the game independently.

14. Set up students for independent practice with the game. Give each pair of students the necessary materials and a game board (REPRODUCIBLE 30, 31, 32, or 33). Also, distribute the game directions (REPRODUCIBLE G-25A), as needed.

MATH WORKSHOP AND SUMMARIZING THE EXPERIENCE

Teach this game at the beginning of the week to the whole class and then make it a fundamental part of your math workshop (for more on math workshops, see Chapter 5 in *From Reading to Math* by Maggie Siena). Build in time to observe students playing the game. Note their individual skill level and fluency with multiplication facts. After students have had several opportunities to play the game, group students to discuss the game. Group students according to the version of the game board with which they played (group sizes will vary). Ask groups to discuss their answers to the questions:

- Is there an advantage to going first? Explain.

- What number do you try to secure first? Why?

Then, have the class come back together as a whole and ask, "When do you play to win and when do you play to block?" Ask, "What other games involve both a 'play-to-win' and 'play-to-block' strategy?" Students will likely come up with the classic games Tic-Tac-Toe and Connect Four.

Roll 6 for 100

Overview

In this game, students build facility in mental math as well as make decisions along the way that rely on number sense. The goal of the game is to get one hundred or as close to it as possible (but not over!) through a combination of adding and multiplying the numbers rolled. The die may be rolled up to six times. After each roll, students record an addition equation/number string. At any time up to six rolls, a player can decide to end the round by using the roll as multiplication rather than addition. The other player may continue the round up to six rolls; the player closest to one hundred is the winner. An assessment is included with this game for those students who play it individually.

Materials

- die (labeled *1–6*), 1 per pair of students
- pencil and ruled paper
- *Roll 6 for 100* Recording Sheet (REPRODUCIBLE 38), 1 per student
- *Roll 6 for 100* Game Directions (REPRODUCIBLE G-26), 1 per pair of students

Related Games

Game 7: Close to 100

Game 9: Cross Out Singles

Game 16: Hit the Target (Mental Multiplication)

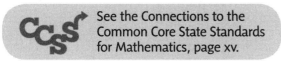

See the Connections to the Common Core State Standards for Mathematics, page xv.

Recommended Grades 3–5

Time Instruction: 30–45 minutes
Independent Play: 20–30 minutes

 TEACHING TIP
Quiet Dice
Rolling dice can create lots of noise. To lessen the noise, use foam dice or pad students' workspaces with foam or fabric placemats.

Key Questions

- How do you determine when to multiply and end your turn?

- If you have a sum of twenty, what number would you hope for on your next turn? Why?

Teaching Directions

Part I: The Connection

Relate the game to students' ongoing work.

Emphasize the importance of the number 100 in the number system. Ask students for real-life examples of number combinations that total one hundred. Ideas that may come up might be:

- ten dimes equal one hundred pennies or

- a football field has 100 yards and is divided into 1-yard increments.

Part II: The Teaching

Introduce and model the game to students.

1. Gather students around a table or demonstration area of your classroom. Explain to students they will be playing the game *Roll 6 for 100* in pairs. Note that the goal of the game is to get to one hundred or as close to it as possible (but not over!) through a combination of adding and multiplying the numbers rolled. You may roll the die up to six times.

2. Model how the game is played by first asking a student volunteer to roll the die and record the number where everyone can see it.

3. Invite another student to roll the die a second time. Have the student record this number next to the first number by forming and solving an addition equation. For example, if the first roll was a 4 and the second was a 3, the second student would write:

$$4 + 3 = 7$$

TEACHING TIP
Arranging Students
For the modeling part of this game, have students make two concentric circles. In the first circle, students kneel or sit; in the second, students stand. This placement ensures that everyone can view the demonstration area.

TECHNOLOGY TIP
Using an Interactive Whiteboard
When modeling this game, use the interactive die included with the whiteboard tool kit. Simply tap the die and record the number that comes up using the markers in the whiteboard tray.

4. Ask yet another student to roll the die a third time and create a new equation using the sum of the last. In the example, if the third student rolls a 6, her equation would be:

$$7 + 6 = 13$$

5. At this point, ask the class if they have another idea for how to represent the three rolls in an addition equation. Emphasize that the equation must only contain one equality symbol. Another way is to record each roll in a number string:

$$4 + 3 + 6 = 13$$

6. Now introduce the final rule of the game: at any time up to six rolls, a player may choose to multiply the previous sum by the rolled number instead of adding to it. When he does so, the player ends his round.

7. Remind students that the goal of the game is to reach the number 100 in six rolls or less. Emphasize that they cannot go over one hundred! Ask, "If the fourth roll turns out to be a six, would it make sense to multiply and have this be the final roll?" The consensus might be yes, but anything less than a 6 on the fourth roll would most likely be added to the number string.

8. Ask another student to roll the die a fourth time and record the equation/number string. Continuing with our example, if the fourth student rolls a 2, the recording reads:

$$4 + 3 = 7$$
$$7 + 6 = 13$$
$$13 + 2 = 15$$

or

$$4 + 3 + 6 + 2 = 15$$

9. Before the die is rolled a fifth time, emphasize that students need to think about the most logical move. If the fifth roll is a 1, it likely makes sense to add and hope that the sixth

TEACHING TIP
Using All Six Rolls?
Although six rolls is the maximum number of rolls allowed in each round, players do *not* have to use all six rolls of the die. However, they *do* have to multiply on their final roll.

roll is a bigger number to multiply and get closer to one hundred. On the other hand, if a 6 is rolled on the fifth turn, multiplying might make sense—fifteen multiplied by six is ninety. Again, let students decide collectively and do not interfere or coach too much at this juncture.

10. Ask a student to roll the die a fifth time. In our example, the fifth roll is a 3. Students decide to opt for a sixth roll. The recorded equations/number string thus far look like this:

$$4 + 3 = 7$$
$$7 + 6 = 13$$
$$13 + 2 = 15$$
$$15 + 3 = 18$$

or

$$4 + 3 + 6 + 2 + 3 = 18$$

11. In the sixth and final roll, a student rolls a 5. The only choice at this point (because six is the maximum number of rolls and the final roll must be multiplied) is to create a multiplication equation:

$$18 \times 5 = 90$$

12. Keep the equations for the first round of the game where everyone can see them.

Part III: Active Engagement

Engage students to ensure they understand how to play the game.

13. Now give students an opportunity to record their own equations/number string as you model a second round of the game. Make sure each student has pencil and paper. With each roll of the die, instruct students to record the number and compute. Model the recording for those students who may not have grasped how the recording should look and need to copy what you write.

TEACHING TIP
Modeling the Game
Because this is their first time ever playing the game, students will not yet be familiar with the pitfalls of the game; however, do not use this time to teach strategy. Rather, guide students to think about the computation intermingled with probability. Above all, refrain from too much guidance, no matter what students choose to do (add or multiply). Students will develop a sense of the game throughout the course of playing it often and frequently.

14. Initially, students' work should all look similar and result in the same sum. At some point, however, some students may decide to multiply the sum by the next number, therefore terminating their play in this round. Others may take all six rolls before multiplying.

- If the first four rolls are, 5, 2, 1, and 4, students' recording should be:

$$5 + 2 = 7$$
$$7 + 1 = 8$$
$$8 + 4 = 12$$

or

$$5 + 2 + 1 + 4 = 12$$

- If a 6 is rolled next, some students may elect to multiply and end the game with a total of seventy-two ($12 \times 6 = 72$). Others may choose to add and continue the game with a new sum of eighteen ($5 + 2 + 1 + 4 + 6 = 18$).

- Depending on your students, decide whether to post both ways on the board or let students continue independently in their recording and computing.

- One more roll is necessary for those students who wish to use all six rolls. On this roll, they must multiply.

15. Now have two student volunteers facilitate the modeling of the game procedures. Designate one student as Player 1 and the other as Player 2.

16. Player 1 starts first, rolling and recording until he has multiplied and hence completed his round. Then have Player 2 roll and record until she has completed her round. The rest of the class should stay engaged by checking the players' computation and comparing the ending totals. Who is the winner?

TEACHING TIP
The Importance of Practice
Refrain from discussing skill or strategies during the active engagement part of the lesson. The purpose is to give students as much practice as possible first; they will then have the opportunity to come back later and discuss their experiences (see the "Math Workshop and Summarizing the Experience" part of the lesson).

TEACHING TIPS
Providing Choice in Student Pairs

For this game, allow students to choose their partners or use a random strategy (such as pulling sticks with student names on them). Regardless of the pairings, students of varying abilities will be able to access the mathematics required to play the game because the game utilizes probability in the rolling of the dice as well as estimation and computation skills.

Recording Sheet

As an alternative to using the recording sheet (**REPRODUCIBLE 38**), have students create their own by folding a piece of paper in half lengthwise, forming two columns. Have the students label the first column *Player 1* and the second column *Player 2*. In addition to recording their equations, encourage students to write a statement about who wins each round and by how much.

DIFFERENTIATING YOUR INSTRUCTION

There are several ways to modify the game according to the levels and needs of your students:

Go Over One Hundred

Change the rules so that students are allowed to go over one hundred. This version alters the luck and strategy involved.

Individual Play

Students may play this game individually, competing against their last round in an effort to get closer and closer to one hundred.

Part IV: The Link

Students play the game independently.

17. Set up students for independent practice of the game. Make sure each pair of students has a die and one *Roll 6 for 100* Recording Sheet (**REPRODUCIBLE 38**). Also distribute the game directions (**REPRODUCIBLE G-26**) as needed. Emphasize that, after each round, students need to complete the scoring sentence frames on their recording sheet:

Scoring
_____ had _____. _____ had _____. _____ won because _____ is _____ closer to 100 than _____.

MATH WORKSHOP AND SUMMARIZING THE EXPERIENCE

Teach this game at the beginning of the week to the whole class, and then make it a fundamental part of your math workshop (for more on math workshops, see Chapter 5 in *From Reading to Math* by Maggie Siena). After students have had time to play many rounds, gather them together for a whole-class discussion. Roll a die six consecutive times. Have students discuss (and/or write about) how they would play the game using the numbers rolled, in the order rolled. Ask students to explain their reasoning: "Why did you decide to add? Multiply?"

ASSESSMENT
Sam's Game

If students work independently, consider having them do an assessment for adding, multiplying two-digit numbers by one-digit numbers, and probability. **REPRODUCIBLE 39** is provided for this purpose.

Roll for $1.00
Variation: Roll for 1

Overview

Roll for $1.00 reinforces the concept that ten ones (pennies) equal one ten (dime). Students take turns rolling a die, assigning the rolled number a value of penny or dime, and collecting that number of pennies or dimes. When students accumulate enough pennies to equate a dime, they exchange their pennies for a dime. The objective of the game is to form a collection of pennies and dimes totaling exactly or as close to one dollar as possible but not going over one dollar. A round of play is seven turns (rolls) for each player.

The game includes the variation, *Roll for 1,* which is suited for older students who are working with decimals. With this variation, students use tenths and hundredths in place of ones (pennies) and tens (dimes). Students add up their hundredths and tenths to see who is closer to (but not over!) the whole number 1. The variation provides practice adding decimals and helps develop an understanding that numbers decrease as they are placed to the right of the decimal point.

Materials

- die (labeled *1–6*), 1 per pair of students
- 30 pennies and 20 dimes per pair of students (the dimes and pennies can be real or play money)
- *Roll for $1.00* Game Board (REPRODUCIBLE 40), 1 per student
- *Roll for $1.00* Game Directions (REPRODUCIBLE G-27A), 1 per pair of students

Adapted from *Teaching Number Sense, Grade 2* by Susan Scharton (Math Solutions, 2005, 151).

Recommended Grades 2–5
Time Instruction: 30–45 minutes
Independent Play: 20–30 minutes

 TIME SAVER
Managing the Materials
For ease in managing the distribution of materials, place the required die, pennies, and dimes in quart-size sandwich bags (one bag for each pair of students playing the game). You may also just choose to place the coins in the bags and distribute the dice separately.

 TEACHING TIPS
Don't Have Enough Dice?
If you do not have enough dice for one per pair of students, use spinners sectioned 1–6.

Quiet Dice
Rolling dice can create lots of noise. To lessen the noise, use foam dice or pad students' workspaces with foam or fabric placemats.

Reusable Game Boards
Instead of making consumable copies of the *Roll for $1.00* Game Board, laminate a set or place copies in plastic sleeves and provide dry erase pens.

 See the Connections to the Common Core State Standards for Mathematics, page xv.

Related Games

Game 1: A "Mazing" 100

Game 7: Close to 100

Game 19: Making Moves on the Hundreds Chart

Key Questions

- How far away from one dollar are you after your _____ turn?

- What number would be helpful at this point in the game if you rolled it? Explain.

Teaching Directions

Part I: The Connection

Relate the game to students' ongoing work.

The Value of a Penny and a Dime

Ask students, "What do you know about the value of a penny and the value of a dime?" Have coins on hand for students to view or bring up coin images on an interactive whiteboard. Write the values on the board so students can see the placement of the zero and how it acts as a place-holder when used in the context of money. Write *.10* next to *Dime* and *.01* next to *Penny.* Highlight the zero in each.

Part II: The Teaching

Introduce and model the game to students.

1. Gather students around a table or demonstration area of your classroom. Tell students they will be playing the game *Roll for $1.00* in pairs. Explain that the goal of the game is to get on or as close to one dollar (but not over!) as possible by collecting pennies and dimes that correspond to each roll. Each player gets seven turns (rolls).

2. Roll the die. Ask a student, "Should the number rolled represent pennies or dimes?" Emphasize that a player may not choose a combination of both pennies and dimes on the same roll.

3. Have the student count out the corresponding number of coins. For example, if a 4 is rolled and the student assigns a value of pennies, the student counts out four pennies.

4. Introduce the *Roll for $1.00* Game Board (RE-PRODUCIBLE 40). Explain that this game board helps students keep track of their coins. Have the student place her four pennies in the first row of the Pennies column on the game board.

5. Roll the die again. This time, ask another student, "Should the number rolled be assigned a value in pennies or dimes?" Have the student count out the corresponding number of coins and place them on the game board in the appropriate column.

6. Continue modeling the game, repeating Step 5 until a student has ten pennies on the game board. At this point, introduce another rule of the game: When players have ten pennies, they must trade the ten pennies in for one dime. The dime can go anywhere on the game board, provided it is in the dimes column.

7. Play up to seven rounds (rolls). After the seventh round, as a class, total the pennies and dimes on the game board. How close are you to one dollar? Emphasize that players cannot go over one dollar; if they do, they are out of the game.

Part III: Active Engagement

Engage students to ensure they understand how to play the game.

8. Now give students an opportunity to explore the game in pairs. Explain that they will be competing with each other to get exactly or close to one dollar. Give each pair of students thirty pennies and twenty dimes (ideally in sandwich bags; if a die is included in the bags, have students keep the die in the bag for now). Also, distribute a copy of the *Roll for $1.00* Game Board (REPRODUCIBLE 40) to each student.

TEACHING TIP
Create Your Own Game Board
As an alternative to making copies of the game board (REPRODUCIBLE 40), students can make their own by drawing the chart and leaving plenty of space for the coins.

TECHNOLOGY TIP
Using an Interactive Whiteboard
Consider using an interactive whiteboard to model this game. To do so, create a notebook. On the first page, pull up an image of the front and back of both a penny and a dime. On the second page, place the image of both a penny and dime, but reduce the coin images so they are approximately the actual size of their real counterparts. Clone the two coins so that you have a sufficient number of coins to model the game. Leave space for the *Roll for $1.00* Game Board with columns for pennies and dimes.

TEACHING TIP
Pairing Students
When pairing students for this game, consider placing students of similar ability together. Like ability ensures mathematical engagement of both students. One student, for example, won't be making all the decisions for the game because of her strength in number sense and computation while the other becomes a bystander. However, after students have had experience in playing the game numerous times on numerous occasions, partnering them with someone who has different thinking provides students with an opportunity to grow in their mathematical understandings.

9. Repeat rolling the die and having students assign a value of pennies or dimes to the number, only this time, students take turns in pairs assigning the value and collecting the corresponding number of coins on their game board.

10. Stop after certain rolls and ask students, "How close are you to one dollar?"

11. After seven rolls, have students work together in pairs to total their coins and determine the winner. Refrain from discussing strategy at this point; focus on students' understanding of the procedures.

Part IV: The Link

Students play the game independently.

12. Set up students for independent practice of the game. In addition to the coins, make sure each pair of students has a die and two game boards (one per student). Also, distribute the game directions (REPRODUCIBLE G-27A).

13. This time, encourage students to write down their coin totals so that they get practice writing the cents symbol.

14. Give students time to play one game—meaning, seven turns (rolls) per student. Circulate to clarify misunderstandings. Remind students to trade their pennies for dimes when possible. Ask key questions such as:

- How far away from one dollar are you after your _____ turn?

- What number would be helpful at this point in the game if you rolled it? Explain.

TEACHING TIP
The Importance of Practice
Refrain from discussing skill or strategies during the active engagement part of the lesson. The purpose is to give students as much practice as possible first; they will then have the opportunity to come back later and discuss their experiences (see "Math Workshop and Summarizing the Experience").

TEACHING TIP
Providing Supportive Tools
If students struggle with determining the distance their number is from one dollar, provide them with tools such as a hundreds chart (REPRODUCIBLE A).

DIFFERENTIATING YOUR INSTRUCTION

There are several ways to modify the game according to the levels and needs of your students.

Roll for 0

Rather than adding up to one dollar, begin with one dollar and subtract to zero. Start with ten dimes and remove coins as you roll. Just as with *Roll for $1.00*, with each roll players must decide to choose dimes or pennies. Each player gets seven turns (rolls). If a player gets to zero before his seventh turn, he is out. If a player goes below zero at any time during the game, she is out.

Roll for a Quarter

During this version of the game, use nickels instead of dimes. When players have five pennies, they must trade the five pennies in for one nickel. The player who gets exactly or closest to twenty-five cents in seven turns (rolls) is the winner.

Roll for 100

Instead of rolling for one dollar, have students roll for one hundred dollars. Change the columns Dimes and Pennies on the game board to Tens and Ones. To vary the game even more, allow players to go over one hundred dollars but still be the winner if they are the closest to one hundred dollars.

Roll for $1,001

Try increasing the target number to 1,001 for students who are ready for practice adding even larger numbers.

Roll for 1

This variation of the game is suited for older students who are working with decimals. Students use tenths and hundredths in place of ones (pennies) and tens (dimes). The *Roll for 1* Recording Sheets **(REPRODUCIBLE 41)** and game directions **(REPRODUCIBLE G-27B)** are provided for this purpose. Students add up their hundredths and tenths to determine who is closer to (but not over!) the whole number 1. There is no "trading in of hundredths"; students just record their representation after each round.

To introduce students to this variation, write 1 where everyone can see it, then place a decimal point in front of the one so it reads one tenth. Ask students, "How does the decimal point change the value of the number one?" Write another *1* where everyone can see it. This time write a decimal point and a *0* to the left of the *1* so it reads .01. Ask students, "Which number is larger: one tenth or one hundredth?" Discuss the place values of both one tenth and one hundredth. Ask students, "Where have you seen numbers like these before?" Students' responses may include a scoreboard (seconds remaining in basketball, hockey, football, and so forth), at the grocery store, in an ad, or at a gas station.

MATH WORKSHOP AND SUMMARIZING THE EXPERIENCE

Teach this game at the beginning of the week to the whole class, and then make it a fundamental part of your math workshop (for more on math workshops, see Chapter 5 in *From Reading to Math* by Maggie Siena). After students have had time to play several games, gather them together for a whole-class discussion. Have them respond to the following prompts:

- I think the game is . . .
- The best way to play the game is . . .

Game 28

Spinning Sums and Differences

Recommended Grades 2–5
Time Instruction: 30–45 minutes
    Independent Play: 20–30 minutes

Overview

Spinning Sums and Differences builds understanding of the place value of numbers. The game offers two versions: one version emphasizes the importance of zero as a placeholder; the other offers students practice with place value of numbers less than one and supports the development of students' computation with decimals. To start the game, Player 1 rolls the die and spins the place value spinner. The spin determines the place value of the number rolled. Player 1 rolls and spins a second time, generating a second number. Player 2 does the same thing—rolls and spins, rolls and spins—creating two numbers. Using the numbers, players write two equations—one addition and one subtraction. Players solve both equations and check each other's sum and difference. The player with the larger sum earns 1 point. Likewise the player with the larger difference earns 1 point. Two points may be earned each round. The player with the highest score at the end of ten rounds is the winner.

Materials

- die (labeled *1–6*), 1 per pair of students
- Place Value Spinner (**REPRODUCIBLE 42** or **REPRODUCIBLE 43**), 1 per pair of students
- *Spinning Sums and Differences* Recording Sheet (**REPRODUCIBLE 44**), 1 per student
- paper clip, 1 per pair of students
- *Spinning Sums and Differences* Game Directions (**REPRODUCIBLE G-28**), 1 per pair of students
- paper and pencil

TIME SAVER
Managing the Materials
For ease in managing the distribution of materials, place a die, spinner, and paper clip in quart-size sandwich bags (one bag for each pair of students playing the game).

CCSS See the Connections to the Common Core State Standards for Mathematics, page xv.

Related Games

Game 7: Close to 100 (the variations Close to 0, Close to 1, and Close to 1,000)

Key Questions

- What has a greater value: one hundredth or one tenth? (Modify this question to fit the version of the game students are playing.)

- What spin are you hoping for: tenths, hundredths, or thousandths? (Modify this question to fit the version of the game students are playing.) Explain.

- What happens to the value of a number as it moves farther to the right of the decimal? (Again, change the question as needed to match the version of the game students are playing.)

Teaching Directions

Part I: The Connection

Relate the game to students' ongoing work.

Students need a foundation of place value to play this game and practice computation successfully. Review place value by doing the following: Write the number 2 where everyone can see it. Ask students to explain the value of this number. Then, write 0 to the right or left of the number, depending on the version of the game you intend to introduce:

- If introducing the game to second or third graders, add a zero to the left, so the number is 20. Ask students, "What is the value of the new number?" Discover what students know about place value.

- If introducing the game to fourth or fifth graders, add a zero to the right and place a decimal point in front of the zero so the number is .02. Ask students, "What is the value of the new number?" Explore their

TEACHING TIP
Arranging Students

For the modeling part of this game, have students make two concentric circles. In the first circle, students kneel or sit; in the second, students stand. This ensures that everyone can view the demonstration area.

TEACHING TIP
Choosing Place Value Spinners

For the purpose of this game, two place value spinners are provided.

Place Value Spinner 1 (REPRODUCIBLE 42)

The spinner is sectioned into ones, tens, and hundreds. It is recommended for use with students grade 2 and up who need practice and support with the Common Core State Standard in Number and Operations: *Understands place value and uses place value understanding and properties to add and subtract.*

Place Value Spinner 2 (REPRODUCIBLE 43)

The spinner is sectioned into tenths, hundredths, and thousandths. It is recommended for use with fifth graders or students needing support with the Common Core Standard in Number and Operations: *Perform operations with multidigit whole numbers and with decimals to hundredths.*

TECHNOLOGY TIP
Using an Interactive Whiteboard

If an interactive whiteboard is available, use the interactive spinner to model the game. The spinner should be divided into thirds and labeled either *Ones*, *Tens*, and *Hundreds* or *Tenths*, *Hundredths*, and *Thousandths*. Also, pull up an interactive die.

thinking with them; do they know the name of the new number?

Part II: The Teaching

Introduce and model the game to students.

1. Gather students around a table or demonstration area of your classroom. Explain to students they will be playing the game *Spinning Sums and Differences* in pairs. Indicate that the goal of the game is to score as many points as possible by building equations. Each game is ten rounds of play.

2. Introduce the place value spinner to students (see the Teaching Tip regarding spinner choices). Explain that students will be using a spinner and rolling a die to determine the numbers with which they will be working.

3. Explain that for the purpose of learning the game, the teacher will be Player 1 and the students will be Player 2. As Player 1, roll the die and spin the spinner.

4. Point out that the die determines the number; the spinner determines the place value of the number. For example, if a 3 is rolled and the spinner lands on Hundredths, the number is .03. Record the number where everyone can see it.

5. Repeat Steps 3 and 4 for Player 2 (the students). Ask one student to roll the die, another student to spin the spinner, and a third to record the number generated by the die and spinner.

6. Repeat this again for both Player 1 (the teacher) and Player 2 (the students). You should now have four numbers generated.

7. Introduce the computation part of the game. Explain to students that they will need to write two equations: an addition equation and a subtraction equation. The following

is an example of a round from a fifth-grade classroom using Place Value Spinner 2:

Player 1   Player 2

.03, .1   .002, .06

$.03 + .1 = .13$ $.002 + .06 = .062$

$.1 - .03 = .07$ $.6 - .002 = .598$

8. After the equations are recorded, ask the students, "Are the sums and differences correct?" Encourage discussion until all are in agreement. After the students agree that each player's sums and differences are correct, the round is over and it is now time to determine the score.

9. The score is determined by comparing both the sums and the differences. The student with the larger sum earns 1 point; likewise, the student with the largest difference earns 1 point. Sometimes a student will earn 2 points in a round or 0 points; often, each student earns 1 point each.

10. Tell students that in a full game, ten rounds are played. This means they will be writing ten addition equations and ten subtraction equations. Play as many rounds as needed for students to gain an understanding of place value, computation, and determination of larger and smaller numbers. Make sure students are sharing their thinking and methods of computation.

Part III: Active Engagement

Engage students to ensure they understand how to play the game.

11. Now give students an opportunity to explore the game either individually or in pairs. Let students determine whether they would like to work in a team of two or by themselves.

12. Make sure each student has a copy of the recording sheet (REPRODUCIBLE 44). Explain that, for this part of exploring the game, you will

TEACHING TIPS
Writing Subtraction Equations
Before writing the subtraction equation, explain that the larger number must come first. This ensures that negative numbers are not used in the game.

Focusing on Students' Thinking
As you model the game, encourage students to explain their way of adding and subtracting the numbers to their peers. The focus should be on students' thinking rather than on a specific computation procedure.

A CHILD'S MIND
Which Number Is Larger?
In the example provided here, students may have a discussion about why the sum .13 is larger than .062. Some students may focus on the numbers only and *not* their place value. On the other hand, more students may have an easier time identifying which difference is larger.

$.03 + .1 = .13$ $.002 + .06 = .062$

$.1 - .03 = .07$ $.6 - .002 = .598$

TEACHING TIP
Using Calculators
As the teacher, decide whether students may use calculators. One idea is to allow use of calculators only to support the settlement of disputes over the accuracy of sums and differences.

The Value of Choice
Giving students the opportunity to choose whether to work with a partner is one way of providing choice in the classroom. Typically, students know their capabilities and will choose to work with someone if they are uncertain about any part of the game.

continue to roll the die and spin the spinner; students are responsible for recording the numbers and creating the equations.

13. After each round, have students determine the scores. As everyone plays, clarify any misunderstandings and address misconceptions as a class. Continue playing rounds until you feel students are ready for independent play.

Part IV: The Link

Students play the game independently.

14. Set up students, this time all in pairs, for independent practice of the game. In addition to the recording sheet, be certain each pair of students has a die and a place value spinner (REPRODUCIBLE 42 or REPRODUCIBLE 43). Also, distribute the game directions (REPRODUCIBLE G-28).

15. Give students time to play ten rounds (a complete game). Circulate, continuing to clarify misunderstandings. Use this time to observe whether students are adding and subtracting correctly. Are they aligning the decimals if they are using column addition and subtraction? Ask key questions such as:

- What has a greater value: one hundredth or one tenth?

- What will result in a greater sum: adding tenths or adding thousandths? Explain.

- What spin are you hoping for: tenths, hundredths, or thousandths? Explain.

- What happens to the value of a number as it moves farther to the right of the decimal?

TEACHING TIP
The Importance of Asking Questions
Asking key questions assists you in understanding how or if students are developing strategies. Key questions also prompt students to hear each other's thinking and further develop their own understanding of the content.

MATH WORKSHOP AND SUMMARIZING THE EXPERIENCE

Teach this game at the beginning of the week to the whole class, and then make it a fundamental part of your math workshop (for more on math workshops, see Chapter 5 in *From Reading to Math* by Maggie Siena). After students have had time to play several games, hold a whole-class discussion. If students worked with the decimal version of the game, hold the discussion around the value of numbers to both the right and the left of the decimal point. Talk about the importance of zero as a placeholder. Write the problem .5 – .001 where everyone can see it. Ask students to turn and talk not about the answer but about how they would approach the problem. Have students share their ideas aloud. Some thinking might be to add zeros after the .5 so it reads .500 and then subtracting. Another common way of approaching the problem is to count back or think: What is one less than 500? Consider writing another sample problem where everyone can see it and have students turn and talk to share how they would approach the problem.

DIFFERENTIATING YOUR INSTRUCTION

Sam and Sally

Challenge students to discover sums and differences that split the score using the following scenario of Sam and Sally.

> Sam and Sally are playing the *Spinning Sums and Differences* game.
>
> Sam's two numbers are .3 and .1.
>
> Sally's numbers are .3 and .2.
>
> Sally's sum won, but Sam's difference won.

Figure out other numbers that would split the score. Do this for at least three rounds.

(Adapted from *Teaching Arithmetic: Lessons for Decimals and Percents, Grades 5–6* by Carrie De Francisco and Marilyn Burns [Math Solutions, 2001].)

ASSESSMENT

Writing Prompts

Have students respond in writing to one or both of the following scenarios:

Scenario 1: Sophie's Mistake

Sophie is playing *Spinning Sums and Differences*.

Her numbers are .5 and .03.

She got the sum of .8 and the difference of .2.

What is Sophie doing incorrectly? Help explain to Sophie why she is getting inaccurate answers.

Scenario 2: Devin's Mistake

Ana and Devin are playing *Spinning Sums and Differences*.

They have a disagreement over whose sum is greater.

Ana has a sum of .36 and Devin has a sum of .306.

Devin claims that his sum is larger because 306 is larger than 36.

Help Ana explain to Devin so that he understands the flaw in his thinking.

Take Five, Make Ten!

Recommended Grades 3–5

Time Instruction: 45–60 minutes
Independent Play: 20–30 minutes

TEACHING TIP
A Deck of Cards

For the purpose of this game, a deck of playing cards is four of each number Ace–9 (10s, face cards, and Jokers removed; an Ace represents the value of 1). Prepare decks of playing cards ahead of time, removing the appropriate cards. Alternatively, show students how to sort out cards from their deck and then replace them when finished.

TIME SAVERS
Coding Cards

Code each set of playing cards to keep it complete. Do this by placing a small symbol in the corner of each set's card; use a different symbol for each set so that, if sets become mixed up, you can sort them more easily.

Enlarged Numeral Cards

Instead of enlarging numeral cards, a quick and easy route for demonstration purposes is simply to write the five numbers on pieces of white paper. Use a thick black marker so the numbers can be seen clearly by everyone in the class.

Overview

This game gives students practice with all four operations and use of parentheses in equations. Students work individually or collaboratively in pairs. They draw five cards and use the numbers to construct five equations, each totaling ten. The equations may be built using all four operations—addition, subtraction, multiplication, and division. The game can end either after a predetermined amount of time (twenty minutes) or after students have used all the cards in the deck (about six rounds).

Materials

- playing cards (10s, face cards, and Jokers removed; Aces remain), 1 deck per student or pair of students

  or

- Numeral Cards 1–9 (REPRODUCIBLE B), 1 deck per student or pair of students

- Numeral Cards 1, 2, 3, 4, and 8 (REPRODUCIBLE B), enlarged for class use

- paper and pencil, 1 per student or pair of students

- *Take Five, Make Ten!* Game Directions (REPRODUCIBLE G-29), 1 per student or pair of students

 See the Connections to the Common Core State Standards for Mathematics, page xv.

Related Games

Game 7: Close to 100 (the variation Close to 20)

Game 12: Equation Building

Game 23: Oh No! 20!

Game 26: Roll 6 for 100

Key Questions

- What number combinations are helpful when making ten?

- If you draw a 2, what number would you also hope to draw in that round?

- If the equation you are building goes over ten, what operations could you use to make the answer less than ten?

Teaching Directions

Part I: The Connection

Relate the game to students' ongoing work.

Connect the lesson to previously taught lessons on operations and building equations. Categorize the four operations into increasing (growing) or decreasing (reducing) functions. Refer to the learning targets of the Common Core State Standards. Solve problems involving the four operations (Grade 3). Use the four operations with whole numbers to solve problems (Grade 4). Write and interpret numeric expressions (Grade 5).

Part II: The Teaching

Introduce and model the game to students.

1. Tell students they will be playing the game *Take Five, Make Ten!* individually or in pairs. Explain that the objective of the game is to use the operations addition, subtraction, multiplication, and division to build equations that total ten.

2. Explain to students that, during this game, they'll be using a deck of playing cards (or a deck of numeral cards 1–9, if you choose that

TECHNOLOGY TIP
Using an Interactive Whiteboard
If you are using an interactive whiteboard, prepare a notebook with the five cards as an alternative to enlarging numeral cards.

TEACHING TIPS
Using Parentheses and Order of Operations
More advanced students may also offer equations using parentheses and order of operations. For example:

$$(4 \times 1) + (2 \times 3)$$

Should students who have not been introduced to order of operations suggest equations such as this one, use it as a time to teach/introduce the idea of using parentheses (see the next tip). Those students who are ready for the more complex problems will grab on to the concept; those who aren't will typically stick with the less complex equations.

Teaching the Idea of Using Parentheses
Show students the following two equations to illustrate that parentheses in mathematics means you perform the operation within the parentheses first:

$$4 \times 1 + 2$$

$$4 \times (1 + 2)$$

In the first equation, work from left to right to solve the problem:

$$4 \times 1 + 2 = 6$$

Say, "Four times one is four, plus two is six."

In the second equation, solve what is in parentheses first, then work from left to right:

$$4 \times (1 + 2) = 12$$

Say, "One plus two is three. Four times three equals twelve."

option). The 10s, face cards, and Jokers are removed; all other cards are the value of the number on the card. Aces are equal to one. Students start each round with five cards.

3. Display the five enlarged numeral cards—1, 2, 3, 4, and 8—where everyone can see them. Ask students, "How might these numbers be combined to total ten?" Invite students to study the cards. Introduce the rules:

   - Addition, subtraction, multiplication, and division operations can be used.

   - A minimum of two and maximum of five of the numbers can be used.

   - Numbers cannot be repeated in the same equation unless there are two of the same number cards.

4. Solicit equation suggestions from the class. Record the equations as they are offered. Some possibilities for these cards are:

$$8 + 2$$

$$8 + 4 - 2$$

$$8 + 3 - 1$$

$$8 \times 1 + 2$$

$$2 \times 3 + 4$$

$$3 \times 4 - 2$$

$$8 - 3 \times 2$$

$$4 \times 2 + 3 - 1$$

$$1 + 2 + 3 + 4$$

Part III: Active Engagement

Engage students to ensure they understand how to play the game.

5. Now give students an opportunity to explore the game in pairs. Write (or draw) five more numbers (1–9) where everyone can see them.

6. Have pairs work together and use the five numbers to create five equations, each totaling

ten. Students should record their equations. Remind them of the rules:

- Addition, subtraction, multiplication, and division operations can be used.

- A minimum of two and maximum of five of the numbers can be used.

- Numbers cannot be repeated in the same equation unless there are two of the same number cards.

7. Circulate as students work. Help students to think about how the numbers might be combined. For example, if three of the numbers are 6, 1, and 3, offer suggestions such as, "What if you started with six? What number would you add to six to get ten?" It is likely that a student may quickly respond "Four!" but then realize that four is not one of the cards. Keep guiding; ask "What two numbers do you have that would equal four if you combined them?"

8. Have the game go on long enough so that each pair of students has had success in building equations with their cards that total ten.

Part IV: The Link

Students play the game independently.

9. Set up students for independent practice with the game. Give each pair a deck of playing cards or numeral cards, prepared according to the materials list. Also, distribute the game directions (REPRODUCIBLE G-29) as needed.

10. Instruct one partner to shuffle the deck and stack it neatly on the table or desk. The other partner should get a piece of paper and write the title of the game, *Take Five, Make Ten!* at the top of the piece of paper, then add their name and their partner's name below the title.

11. Each pair draws five cards from their deck. Pairs work together using the numbers they drew to create five equations, each totaling ten. Students should record their equations

TEACHING TIPS
Pairing Students
When pairing students for this game, place students of similar ability together. Although the game relies on the luck of the cards, computation skills and logical reasoning come in to play when students are determining which cards to play. Pairing students of similar ability increases mathematical engagement of all students while allowing students to explore the game at a rate that is both comfortable and meaningful to them. Students who are more fluent in their basic facts will likely move at a faster rate whereas those who are insecure in their facts will move more slowly and methodically.

Emphasize Collaboration
Explain that students will be playing in teams of two with their partner, not against him or her. The goal is for students to work together to understand how to play the game and the math involved. Students should come to an agreement on which numbers and operations to use, and the total of their equations.

TEACHING TIP
Shuffling Cards
Younger students are typically not able to shuffle the cards. If this is the case, demonstrate how to mix the cards with your hands, being careful to keep all the cards facing the same direction (either face down or face up).

TEACHING TIPS
Recording Your Thinking
Make sure students are recording their thinking and equations. It is important for students to be able to articulate how they solve each equation. It is equally valuable for other students to see how their partner is computing.

Unlucky Cards
There are times when players are unlucky with their cards and it is impossible to build five equations totaling ten. When students feel they have an unlucky round, have them draw another card (so six cards are in play) to help them move forward.

DIFFERENTIATING YOUR INSTRUCTION
There are several ways to modify the game according to the levels and needs of your students.

Offer Choice
Give students the choice to work in pairs or individually.

Take Six, Make Twenty!
During this version of the game, players draw six cards and use the six numbers to create five equations, each equation totaling twenty.

Ten Equations
Double the number of equations students must come up with from five to ten.

on their piece of paper. Remind them of the game rules.

12. Have students play three rounds of play (a round of play is drawing five cards and building five equations). As they play, circulate and continue to ask questions and clarify misunderstandings.

MATH WORKSHOP AND SUMMARIZING THE EXPERIENCE
Teach this game at the beginning of the week to the whole class, and then make it a fundamental part of your math workshop (for more on math workshops, see Chapter 5 in *From Reading to Math* by Maggie Siena). Build in time to observe students playing the game, noting student's individual skill level and computational fluency. Come together as a class later in the week. On chart paper, list the equations students have built that include a combination of operations. Use this chart as the foundation for revisiting the order of operations. Use one of the equations to model how placing parentheses makes an impact on the result. Also, discuss the order of the functions multiply, divide, add, and subtract. Invite students to choose one of the equations from the list and explore how they could change the answer with parentheses.

ASSESSMENT
Thinking About Equations
After students have had multiple experiences playing the game, distribute copies of the *Take Five, Make Ten!* Assessment **(REPRODUCIBLE 45)**. Use the assessment tool to measure students' potential and progress.

Target 300 (A Multiplication Game)

Overview

This two-player game emphasizes number sense, computation, and problem solving. Players take turns rolling a die and multiplying the number rolled by ten or multiples of ten. The goal is to be the player with a total sum of numbers exactly or closest to the target of 300 after five rolls. Although multiplication is the focus, computational practice using addition and subtraction also occurs. Number sense comes into play as students navigate the game and make choices about what numbers to use to reach the target number.

Materials

- die (labeled *1–6*), 1 per pair of students

- *Target 300 (A Multiplication Game)* Recording Sheet (REPRODUCIBLE 46), 1 per student

- *Target 300 (A Multiplication Game)* Game Directions (REPRODUCIBLE G-30), 1 per pair of students

Related Games

Game 16: Hit the Target (Mental Multiplication)

Game 25: Pathways (the variation Times Ten)

Key Questions

- How do you decide if a roll will be the value of one or ten?

- What strategies do you use when playing this game?

Recommended Grades 3–5

Time Instruction: 45–60 minutes
Independent Play: 20–30 minutes

 TEACHING TIPS

Don't Have Enough Dice?
If you do not have enough dice for one die per pair of students, use spinners sectioned 1–6.

Quiet Dice
Rolling dice can create lots of noise. To lessen the noise, use foam dice or pad students' workspaces with foam or fabric placemats.

 See the Connections to the Common Core State Standards for Mathematics, page xv.

Adapted from Lessons for Extending Multiplication: Grades 4–5 by Maryann Wickett and Marilyn Burns (Math Solutions, 2001, 92).

Teaching Directions

Part I: The Connection

Relate the game to students' ongoing work.

Connect this game to previous discoveries about the base ten number system and the powers of ten. Engage students by writing a basic multiplication fact such as *3 × 1 = 3*, then write the related multiple-of-ten fact: *3 × 10 = 30*. Show a few more basic facts and related multiple-of-ten facts. Solicit some from students.

Part II: The Teaching

Introduce and model the game to students.

1. Explain to students that they will be playing the game *Target 300 (A Multiplication Game)* with a partner. The objective of the game is to have a sum of numbers as close to 300 as possible after five rounds of play.

2. Replicate the chart on the *Target 300 (A Multiplication Game)* Recording Sheet (REPRODUCIBLE 46), making it large enough for the class to see. Let students know each of them will have their own recording sheet when they play the game.

ROUND	PLAYER I Name _____	PLAYER 2 Name _____
I		
2		
3		
4		
5		
TOTAL		

3. Explain that players take turns rolling a die. On his or her turn, the player must decide whether the number rolled is multiplied by

---

TEACHING TIP

Creating Your Own Recording Sheet
For this game, students may use the recording sheet available as **REPRODUCIBLE 46** or they may create their own. This can be done easily by folding a piece of notebook paper in half lengthwise to make a T-chart:

PLAYER I	PLAYER 2

10, 20, 30, 40, or 50. The number rolled is the multiplicand. Students determine the multiplier. List the multiplier options where everyone can see them:

Multiplier Options

× 10

× 20

× 30

× 40

× 50

4. *Every* player then records the equation and the product in the column on his or her chart. Stress that after an equation and a product are recorded, they may not be changed!

5. Emphasize the goal of the game is to be the closest to 300 after five rolls. After five rolls, players will add all their products to get a total sum. The player with the total sum exactly or closest to 300 is the winner. Provide students with an example, such as the following: If Player 1 has a total sum of 280 and Player 2 has a total sum of 310, Player 2 wins even though she went beyond the target number of 300, because she is closer to 300 than Player 1.

6. Play a round collectively as a class. Roll the die. Record the number rolled and think aloud—for example, "I rolled a two. The two becomes my multiplicand. If I multiply the two by ten I will have a total of twenty. I would still be two hundred eighty away from three hundred, and only four more rolls seems like too small of a product. What if I tried fifty, the largest number, as my multiplier? If I multiply two times fifty, that would be one hundred. One hundred is one-third of the way to three hundred; that seems like too large of a product for one round."

7. Ask students to turn to a partner and discuss their thinking about the question, "What

number would you choose as the multiplier? Ten, twenty, thirty, forty, or fifty?"

8. Give students a few minutes to share their thinking, then bring students back together as a class and have a few students share their ideas and reasoning with the whole class.

9. Determine a sensible multiplier, such as twenty or thirty and record the equation—for example, $2 \times 20 = 40$—in Player 1's column.

10. Repeat Steps 6–9 as needed until you feel students have a grasp of the procedures.

Part III: Active Engagement

Engage students to ensure they understand how to play the game.

11. Now give students an opportunity to explore the game further. Continue playing rounds, only this time tell students that they are, collectively, Player 2.

12. Ask one student to roll the die and share the number aloud. As before, have students discuss with each other what the multiplier should be.

13. Record the equation and the product that the students decide on in Player 2's column. Record another equation and product for Player 1.

14. Roll the die again. Continue having students discuss what the multiplier should be, and decide on an equation and product. Model your thinking as needed. For example, if the number 3 is rolled and you decide to multiply by forty, think aloud:

"Three times forty is the same as forty plus forty plus forty. Three time forty . . . hmmm. Well, three time four is twelve. I can add a zero to my partial product of twelve because of the power of ten. Three times forty must be one hundred twenty. That makes sense."

A CHILD'S MIND

Getting to 300 Fast!

Often, students want to multiply a roll of six times fifty to get to 300 quickly. Remind students they must play all five rounds (five rolls), then calculate the total sum of their products to determine who is closest to 300.

15. Be intentional in showing students how to keep a running sum of their products. The following is an example of what the chart might look like after five rounds of play:

ROUND	PLAYER 1	PLAYER 2
1	2 × 20 = 40	6 × 10 = 60
2	4 × 10 = 40 40 + 40 = 80	3 × 20 = 60 60 + 60 = 120
3	1 × 50 = 50 80 + 50 = 130	5 × 10 = 50 120 + 50 = 170
4	3 × 40 = 120 130 + 120 = 250	1 × 50 = 50 170 + 50 = 220
5	2 × 30 = 60 250 + 60 = 310	6 × 10 = 60 220 + 60 = 280
TOTAL	310	280

Player 1

310 is 10 away from 300.

Player 2

280 is 20 away from 300.

Figure 30.1 Sample completed student chart.

16. After you've played five rounds (five rolls) with students, have them calculate the sum of their products. Who is the winner—Player 1 (the teacher) or Player 2 (the students)?

Part IV: The Link

Students play the game independently.

17. Set up students for independent practice with the game. Each pair of students should have a die and one recording sheet (REPRODUCIBLE 46)

TEACHING TIP
Over and Under 300
When modeling the game, try to create a situation in which one player goes over 300 and the other goes under 300. In Figure 30.1, in the last round for Player 1, the teacher could have chosen to multiply two by twenty for a grand total of 290, which is still ten away from 300, but he wanted students to see how 300 is the target number. You can be over and still win the game. The goal is to get exactly or closest to the target of 300.

TEACHING TIP
Providing Choice in Student Pairs

For this game, allow students to choose their partners or use a random strategy (such as pulling sticks with student names on them). Regardless of the pairings, students of differing abilities will be able to access the mathematics required to play the game because students will use both estimation and computation skills.

TEACHING TIP
Supporting Students

Try to avoid the use of calculators during this game. To make the computation accessible for struggling students, provide a hundreds chart **(REPRODUCIBLE A)** or scratch paper to do repeated addition.

per player. Also, distribute the game directions (REPRODUCIBLE G-30) as needed.

18. Instruct students to determine who is Player 1 and who is Player 2. Player 1 rolls the die and decides a multiplier. Both players record the equation in Player 1's column on their recording sheets.

19. Next, Player 2 rolls the die, determines the multiplier, and both players record this equation in Player 2's column on their recording sheets. Remind students that the objective is to get exactly or the closest to 300 after five rounds of play.

20. After five rolls, students add their products and record the total sum. They then complete the statement at the bottom of the chart to determine the winner—the player closest to 300.

21. Monitor students. Look for those who are comfortable and moving fluently toward 300. Note those students who are hesitant. Try to gauge whether this is a result of strategizing or skill. This knowledge will help determine how to differentiate your instruction for your students. Some students may need more challenge, others more practice, and still others may need guided practice.

22. Give students time to play one game.

MATH WORKSHOP AND SUMMARIZING THE EXPERIENCE

Teach this game at the beginning of the week to the whole class, then make it a fundamental part of your math workshop (for more on math workshops, see Chapter 5 in From *Reading to Math* by Maggie Siena). Build in time to observe students playing the game, noting student's individual skill level and computational fluency. After students have had the opportunity to play several games, bring them together as a class and ask, "What is one strategy you used when playing this game?" Record students' strategies on a piece of chart paper titled, "Target 300 Strategies." Encourage students to add their strategies as they develop more expertise in playing *Target 300 (A Multiplication Game)*. Ask students, "What mathematic skills were used in playing the game *Target 300?*" Students will likely say multiplication, addition, subtraction (when determining how far away from 300), basic facts, and powers of ten. Have students turn in their recording sheets. This provides both a record of time on task and of the mathematics involved in the game. By reviewing students' individual work, you can diagnose problems with computation—both multiplication and addition—and logical reasoning.

DIFFERENTIATING YOUR INSTRUCTION

There are several ways to modify the game according to the levels and needs of your students.

Target 200

Change the target number to 200. This version of the game leads to more practice with multiplying by ten.

Target 500

Change the target number to 500. Increasing the target number leads to more practice with larger multiples of ten, because the target number of 500 still needs to be reached in five rounds.

Target 3,000

Students could even practice multiplying by one hundred and multiples of one hundred by changing the game to *Target 3,000*.

Target "Pick Your Sum"

Recommended Grades 1–3

Time Instruction: 30–45 minutes
Independent Play: 20–30 minutes

 TEACHING TIPS

Transparent Counters
When thinking of what to use for counters, use pieces that are transparent. In this way, the number is still visible on the game board when a counter is placed on it.

Reusable Game Boards
To make the *Target "Pick Your Sum"* game boards last longer than one use, laminate a set or place copies in plastic sleeves for use with dry erase markers.

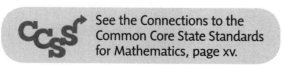

See the Connections to the Common Core State Standards for Mathematics, page xv.

Overview
During this game, students use mental math strategically when adding. To start, students decide on a target sum between twenty-five and fifty-five. During each turn, a player covers a number on the game board, adding it to the previously covered number. Players continue to add to the running total on every turn, attempting to be the first to get to the target sum. The first player to reach the target sum exactly is the winner.

Materials
- *Target "Pick Your Sum"* Game Board (REPRODUCIBLE 47), 1 per pair or group of students
- counters (discs, coins, beans, or tiles of any color), 20 per pair or group of students
- *Target "Pick Your Sum"* Game Directions (REPRODUCIBLE G-31), 1 per pair or group of students

Related Games
Game 7: Close to 100 (the variation Close to 20)

Game 13: Fifteen-Number Cross-Out

Game 27: Roll for $1.00

Key Questions
- How do you choose your next number?
- When you place a counter on the game board, how do you add the number on to the total?
- As you get closer to the target sum, does your strategy change? Explain.

Teaching Directions

Part I: The Connection

Relate the game to students' ongoing work.

Write a few number strings where everyone can see them and ask students to compute the sums mentally. Find volunteers to share how they combined the numbers. Typically, students work left to right, looking for combinations of ten within the number string or looking for doubles. When using the following number string, for example:

$3 + 5 + 7 + 5 + 2 + 3$

Possible strategies from students include:

- Some students will work left to right, accumulating a total as they go.

- Others will look for combinations of ten: $3 + 7$ and $5 + 5$, and then add $2 + 3$.

- And still others may combine doubles: $3 + 3$ and $5 + 5$ before adding $7 + 2$.

Conclude by pointing out to students that what they are practicing is called mental math. They are using their minds to compute.

Part II: The Teaching

Introduce and model the game to students.

1. Gather students around a table or demonstration area of your classroom. Explain to students that they will be playing the game *Target "Pick Your Sum"* in pairs or small groups. During this game, students will be practicing mental math with addition.

2. Show the *Target "Pick Your Sum"* Game Board (REPRODUCIBLE 47). Ask students, "What do you notice about this game board?" Likely responses are:

   - "There are five ones, five twos, five threes, five fours, and five fives."

   - "The numbers are in rows and columns."

   - "The numbers are on a grid."

TEACHING TIP
Arranging Students
For the modeling part of this game, have students make two concentric circles. In the first circle, students kneel or sit; in the second, students stand. This ensures that everyone can view the demonstration area.

TECHNOLOGY TIP
Using an Interactive Whiteboard
For the purpose of introducing the game board, scan it and display it on an interactive whiteboard or projector. Using a document camera to present the game board is also an option.

5	5	5	5	5
4	4	4	4	4
3	3	3	3	3
2	2	2	2	2
1	1	1	1	1

Target "Pick Your Sum" Game Board
(Reproducible 47)

3. Explain to students that, during this game, on each turn, a player covers a number on the game board and adds it to the previously covered number or numbers. Players continue to add to the running total on every turn, attempting to be the first to get to the target sum. The first player to reach the target sum exactly is the winner.

4. Model the game. To start, pick a number between twenty-five and fifty-five. For modeling purposes, start with the number 40. Tell students that this number is the target sum; remind them that the first player to reach this number is the winner.

TEACHING TIP
Color Counters
For this game, the color of the counters used does not matter because players' turns are combined to reach the target sum.

5. Ask a student to cover one of the numbers on the game board with a transparent counter, then place a second counter on another number. Add the two covered numbers together mentally and announce the sum. For example, if the student places a counter on the number 4 and you place your counter on the number 3, say, "Four plus three equals seven."

6. Now have the student place a third counter on yet another number on the game board. Ask the student to add that number to the running total of seven. If the student places her counter on the number 5, she should say,

"Seven plus five equals twelve." Alternatively, one can also add up all the covered numbers: "Four plus three plus five equals twelve."

7. Emphasize that each time a player places a counter on the game board, he or she must announce the new running total (sum). All players must agree on the answer. Explain that the goal is to be the first player to reach the target sum exactly. If a player goes over the target sum, he or she is out.

8. Point out that a square cannot be covered more than once on the game board.

9. Continue to model playing the game, taking turns with a student until the target sum is reached. Play enough sample games for students to experience two situations:

   • Situation 1: A player is forced to pick a number that pushes her over the target sum (and hence the player is out).

   • Situation 2: A player's remaining number choices on the game board are all too low—meaning, when added to the running total, it is impossible to hit the target sum exactly.

   Point out that the game involves strategy to win!

Part III: Active Engagement

Engage students to ensure they understand how to play the game.

10. Now give students an opportunity to explore the game in groups of four (one pair versus another pair). The group determines which pair is Player 1 and which is Player 2. Give each group a game board (REPRODUCIBLE 47) and twenty counters.

11. Announce a new target sum and write it where everyone can see it. Circulate as students play. Assist with misunderstandings in how the game is played as well as intervene in a game when miscalculations are being made.

TEACHING TIP
Recording the Numbers
Depending on students' skill levels, some will need to record the number string they are creating and refer back to it as the game progresses.

TEACHING TIP
The Importance of Practice
Refrain from discussing skill or strategies during the teaching or active engagement part of the lesson. The purpose, at this time, is to give students as much practice as possible first; they will then have the opportunity to come back later and discuss their experiences (see "Math Workshop and Summarizing the Experience").

TEACHING TIPS
Groups of Four
Having students work in groups of four supports everyone in their mental calculations. Twice as many brains at work leads to more correctness in running totals. However, this setup may increase classroom noise substantially, especially when students are trying to explain how they are adding the numbers mentally. Remember, classroom volume about mathematics is okay. Encourage students to share their thinking!

Using the Same Target Sum
By having all students play using the same target sum (consider a target sum such as twenty-five or fifty for starters), students will have a common experience that can then be referred to when summarizing (see "Math Workshop and Summarizing the Experience").

One way to do this is to ask, "How did you arrive at the latest sum?"

Part IV: The Link

Students play the game independently.

12. Set up students for independent practice with the game. This time, have students play in pairs instead of groups of four. Each pair should have a game board and twenty counters. Also, distribute the game directions (REPRODUCIBLE G-31) as needed.

13. Give students time to play at least one or two games. When observing and talking with students as they play, ask key questions such as:

    - What do you think about when selecting the number you are going to add?

    - When you place a counter on the game board, how do you add the number on to the total?

    - As you get closer to the target sum, does your strategy change? Explain.

TEACHING TIP
Pairing Students

For this game, pair students with someone of like ability. Pairing students with similar mathematical skills allows for the game to move at a comfortable rate for both players. It also encourages players who would benefit from recording the number string to do so, especially if they are paired with a peer who also needs to see the numbers being added. Likewise, students who are able to compute the number string mentally will be able to move at a faster rate and have more practice with mental math.

DIFFERENTIATING YOUR INSTRUCTION

There are several ways to modify the game according to the levels and needs of your students.

Providing Interlocking Cubes

Make interlocking cubes available to students who still need to represent addition with objects. Students can attach cubes in one long "string" as numbers accumulate on the game board.

Recording Your Work

Ask students to record their number strings to keep track of their moves/numbers in a linear manner. Students can then refer back to their recording as well as see the counters on the game board to assist in computation.

Teams

Have students continue to work in groups of four (pair versus pair). This is especially helpful for students who may be struggling.

Target "Pick Your Difference"

Instead of addition, play the game using subtraction. Select a target difference between twenty-five and fifty-five. Players cover numbers on the game board, subtracting from a running difference. The first person to reach zero is the winner.

MATH WORKSHOP AND SUMMARIZING THE EXPERIENCE

Teach this game at the beginning of the week to the whole class, then make it an integral part of your math workshop (for more on math workshops, see Chapter 5 in *From Reading to Math* by Maggie Siena). Build in time to observe students playing the game. Note their individual skill level and the strategies being used. Come together as a class later in the week and hold a discussion about the mathematics involved in the game. Refer to your notes during the discussion. Ask key questions such as:

- What are some of your strategies when playing *Target "Pick Your Sum"*?

- How does the strategy help you win?

- How does the strategy help you compute?

Ask students to share some of their number strings for the target sum of twenty-five or fifty. Record the number strings on chart paper. Post the chart paper so students can add more number strings as they continue to play more rounds of the game.

Tens Go Fish

Recommended Grades K–2
Time Instruction: 30–45 minutes
Independent Play: 20–30 minutes

TEACHING TIPS
A Deck of Cards

For this game, a deck of playing cards is four of each number Ace (1)–9 (10s, face cards, and Jokers removed). A deck of numeral cards is four of each number 0–10. Prepare decks of playing cards ahead of time by removing the appropriate cards. Alternatively, show students how to sort out cards from their deck and then replace them when finished.

TIME SAVER
Coding Cards

Code each set of playing cards to keep it complete. Do this by placing a small symbol in the corner of each set's card; use a different symbol for each set so that, if sets become mixed up, you can sort them more easily.

See the Connections to the Common Core State Standards for Mathematics, page xv.

Overview

Because our number system is based on ten, it is essential for students to become familiar with the ways ten can be made. This game gives students needed practice at constructing ten. *Tens Go Fish* is a version of the classic game Go Fish. In *Tens Go Fish*, players put aside pairs of cards that add up to ten. Then players take turns asking each other for a number card they need to make a pair that adds up to ten. Play continues until all the cards in the deck are used up or until one player goes out by having no remaining cards to play.

Materials

- playing cards (10s, face cards, and Jokers removed; Aces remain to represent a value of 1), 1 deck per pair of students
  or
- Numeral Cards 0–10 (REPRODUCIBLE B), 1 deck per pair of students
- *Tens Go Fish* Game Directions (REPRODUCIBLE G-32), 1 per pair of students

Related Games

Game 4: Anything but Ten!
Game 5: Build Ten
Game 10: Cross Out Sums

Key Questions

- If you are using Numeral Cards inquire, "What number will you 'go fishing' for if you are holding a [state any number 0–10]? Likewise, if students are using a deck of cards ask, "Which number will you request if looking for a match for [state any card (Ace) 1–9]?"

- How many combinations of ten can you make with the cards used in this game?

Teaching Directions

Part I: The Connection

Relate the game to students' ongoing work.

Ask students, "Have you gone fishing before?" Relate their experiences of going fishing to the game of *Tens Go Fish*. Tell students the "fishing pond" in the game is all the cards. They will be fishing for combinations of ten. If some students have played the classic game of Go Fish before, be sure to distinguish the two. In Go Fish, players look for pairs of cards that are matching numbers; in *Tens Go Fish*, players look for pairs of cards that, when added, equal ten.

Part II: The Teaching

Introduce and model the game to students.

1. Explain to students they will be playing the game *Tens Go Fish* in pairs. Gather students around a table or floor space.

2. Have a student help with the demonstration of the game. Pick a student who knows his or her combinations of ten well enough to play the game with ease. Deem that student as Player 1 and you as Player 2.

3. Deal out five cards to the student and five cards to yourself. Both of you may look at your cards; hold them in your hands in a fanned-out fashion.

4. Place the remaining cards face down between the two of you in a stack or a "pond," which means spreading the cards out so not just the top card is available for choosing.

5. Ask the student to look at her five cards and ask her if there are any pairs of cards that, when added, make ten. If so, tell the student to place those pairs near her on the table and

TEACHING TIP
Arranging Students
For the modeling part of this game, have students make two concentric circles. In the first circle, students kneel or sit; in the second, students stand. This ensures that everyone can view the demonstration area.

draw two cards to replace the cards played. Do the same with the cards in your hand. Make sure both the student and you read the cards out loud—for example, "Six plus four equals ten" (and place the 6 and 4 cards aside). Emphasize that this is the beginning move of every game; then the next step ensues.

6. Alternate turns. During her turn, Player 1 asks for a card that goes with a card in her hand to make ten. For example, if Player 1 is holding an 8, she might ask Player 2 for a 2. Two things can happen in this case (and on every turn):

   a. If Player 1 gets the card requested and that makes ten, Player 1 puts the pair of cards aside. Player 1's turn then continues; Player 1 asks for another card that makes a ten with any of the cards in her remaining hand.

   b. If Player 2 does not have the requested card that makes a ten, Player 1 takes the top card from the deck or chooses a card from the fishing pond. If the new card makes a ten with any of the cards in Player 1's hand, Player 1 sets that pair aside and continues to draw and pair cards. Player 1's turn is over when she no longer has a pair of cards in hand that makes ten.

7. Continue modeling turns of the game. As you play, say aloud the thought process. For example, "I have a three card, so I'm going to ask for a seven card because three plus seven make ten."

8. Model turns of the game until either the student or you match all the cards in your hand or there are no cards left to draw. At this point, introduce the two possibilities for winning the game:

   a. If a player pairs all his cards and has no cards left in his hand, he is the winner.

   b. If all the cards are played and no more pairs can be made, the player with the most pairs of ten is the winner.

Part III: Active Engagement

Engage students to ensure they understand how to play the game.

9. Now give students an opportunity to explore the game in groups of four divided into teams of two (Team 1 and Team 2). Give each group a deck of playing cards or numeral cards per the materials list.

10. As students play, circulate, supporting students with both the procedural side of the game and the mathematics. Ask procedural questions such as:

   - If you ask for a number card and your partner doesn't have it, what do they say/ what do you do?

   - When you get a pair, what do you do with the combination of ten?

   Also ask questions that prompt thinking about the mathematical concepts (note students' computational fluency with making ten):

   - If you are holding a [state any numeral, 1–9] card, what number will you go fishing for or ask for to make ten?

   - How many combinations of ten can you make with the cards used in this game?

Part IV: The Link

Students play the game independently.

11. Set up students in pairs for independent practice with the game. In addition to playing or numeral cards, make sure each pair has the game directions (REPRODUCIBLE G-32) as needed.

12. Instruct one partner to shuffle the deck and stack it neatly or create a fishing pond (spreading cards face down in a pool-like array) on their table or desk.

13. Have students play two games.

TEACHING TIP
The Importance of Asking Questions
Asking key questions assists you in understanding how or if students are developing strategies. Key questions also prompt students to hear each other's thinking and further develop their own understanding of the content.

TEACHING TIPS
Pairing Students
When pairing teams of students for this game, place students of similar ability together. If students are not yet ready to play this game in pairs, continuing teaming up two pairs to create a group of four to play. You can also vary the game depending on each pair's level (see "Differentiating Your Instruction" on the next page).

Shuffling Cards
Younger students are typically not able to shuffle the cards. If this is the case, demonstrate how to mix the cards with your hands, being careful to keep all the cards facing the same direction (either face down or face up).

DIFFERENTIATING YOUR INSTRUCTION

There are several ways to modify the game according to the levels and needs of your students.

Creating Card Variations

Some students may benefit from using cards that have both the number symbol and pictures representing the number on them (the illustrations on playing cards—diamonds, hearts, spades, clubs—work will for visual representations of the number). In this way, students can see, touch, and count up to ten. This option is recommended for primary grades. Other pairs (intermediate grades) may only require cards with just a number symbol on them (in this case, numeral cards may be preferred over playing cards).

Recording Your Equations

Have students record the equations they make during the game. As an extra challenge, have them add to their list any additional combinations that make ten. Collect students' list for use in the summarizing part of the game.

MATH WORKSHOP AND SUMMARIZING THE EXPERIENCE

Teach this game at the beginning of the week to the whole class, and then make it a fundamental part of your math workshop (for more on math workshops, see Chapter 5 in *From Reading to Math* by Maggie Siena). Build in time to observe students playing the game, noting student's individual skill level and computational fluency. Come together as a class later in the week and create a chart with combinations of ten. Use the cards to introduce the commutative property. For example:

$2 + 8 = 10$

$8 + 2 = 10$

Use the chart to present multiple ways of writing equations such as:

$10 = 2 + 8$

$10 = 8 + 2$

Wipeout (Fractional Relationships)

Overview

This game gives students practice in understanding fractional relationships such as whole to part and part to whole. The goal of the game is to be the first to discard all your pattern blocks. Both players begin with the same number (one, two, or three) of hexagons (considered the whole) as well as other pattern blocks (the parts): red trapezoids, blue rhombuses, and green triangles. Players roll a special die marked with fractions ($\frac{1}{2}, \frac{1}{3}, \frac{1}{3}, \frac{1}{3}, \frac{1}{6}, \frac{1}{6}$) and have three options of moves: (1) remove the pattern block represented by the fraction on the die, (2) exchange any of your blocks for equivalent blocks, or (3) do nothing.

Materials

- pattern blocks (6 yellow hexagons, 12 red trapezoids, 18 blue rhombuses, and 36 green triangles), 1 set per pair of students
- die (faces marked $\frac{1}{2}, \frac{1}{3}, \frac{1}{3}, \frac{1}{3}, \frac{1}{6}, \frac{1}{6}$), 1 per pair of students
- *Wipeout (Fractional Relationships)* Game Directions (REPRODUCIBLE G-33), 1 per pair of students

Related Games

Game 7: Close to 100 (the variation Close to 0)

Game 27: Roll for $1.00 (the variation Roll for 1)

Recommended Grades 4–5

Time Instruction: 45–60 minutes
Independent Play: 20–30 minutes

TEACHING TIPS
Don't Have Enough Pattern Blocks?
Although eighteen blue rhombuses and thirty-six green triangles allow for the most options when playing this game, if you have a limited supply of pattern blocks, twelve of each (rhombuses and triangles) should suffice.

Don't Have Dice?
If you do not have the dice required for this game, consider these options:

- Convert wooden cubes to dice by placing small, round, numbered stickers on each face of wooden cube.

- Use cards marked with the necessary fractions instead of dice. Instead of dice, players draw a card when it is their turn.

TIME SAVER
Managing the Materials
For ease in managing the distribution of materials, place the required die and pattern blocks in quart-size sandwich bags (one bag for each pair of students playing the game).

See the Connections to the Common Core State Standards for Mathematics, page xv.

Adapted from *Lessons for Introducing Fractions: Grades 4–5* by Marilyn Burns (Math Solutions, 2001, 153).

Key Questions

- How many trapezoids make a hexagon? In this game, what fractional part is a trapezoid?

- How many rhombuses make a hexagon? In this game, what fractional part is a rhombus?

- How many triangles make a hexagon? In this game, what fractional part is a triangle?

Teaching Directions

Part I: The Connection

Relate the game to students' ongoing work.

Connect the game to previous work with fractional parts. Discuss real-world fractions as they relate to students' lives. Many students participate in sports or enjoy watching them. Discuss how a basketball court has a centerline that creates two halves, as does an ice hockey rink or soccer field. Most playgrounds still have the game of Four-square painted on the blacktop. Connect the concept of the four smaller, equal-size squares that make one large square.

Part II: The Teaching

Introduce and model the game to students.

1. Explain to students that they will be playing the game *Wipeout* in pairs using pattern blocks. The winner is the first person to remove all of his or her pattern blocks. Gather students around a table or floor space.

2. Show students the specially marked die. Ask, "How are the faces labeled?" Have a few students examine the die and report to the group.

3. Place one yellow hexagon on the table. Tell students that the hexagon represents one whole.

4. Take the die and place face up the side of the die labeled $\frac{1}{2}$. With the red trapezoid, blue rhombus, and green triangle in the demonstration area, ask, "What pattern block would

TEACHING TIP
Arranging Students
For the modeling part of this game, have students make two concentric circles. In the first circle, students kneel or sit; in the second, students stand. This ensures that everyone can view the demonstration area.

TECHNOLOGY TIP
Using an Interactive Whiteboard
Consider using an interactive whiteboard to model this game. To do so, create a page with a hexagon, trapezoid, rhombus, and triangle. All these shapes are in the whiteboard tool kit. Clone the trapezoid, rhombus, and triangle as many times as needed for ease of exchanging pattern blocks. To rotate the blocks, simply touch the block and grab the rotation toggle. This action allows you to rotate the shapes in the way you wish.

be one half of the whole hexagon?" Discuss. Students should be able to discern that the trapezoid is half a hexagon. Place a trapezoid pattern block on the table.

5. Repeat Step 4 two more times, first with the $\frac{1}{3}$ side face up for everyone to see, then with the $\frac{1}{6}$ side face up for everyone to see. Encourage students to share their thinking as they determine that a third of a hexagon is a rhombus block and a sixth of a hexagon is a triangle block. Place these blocks on the table.

6. Review which pattern blocks beside the hexagon can be used in the game—red trapezoids, blue rhombuses, and green triangles. Say, "These are the pattern blocks used in *Wipeout*. We will not be using the narrow tan rhombus or the orange square." Point out that the red, blue, and green blocks represent the parts of the whole (the hexagon).

7. Ask a student sitting opposite you to be the opposing player. Begin by placing a yellow hexagon in front of the student and another yellow hexagon in front of you.

8. The game begins with each player exchanging the hexagon for equivalent fractional pattern block pieces. For modeling purposes, trade in your hexagon for one trapezoid, one rhombus, and one triangle:

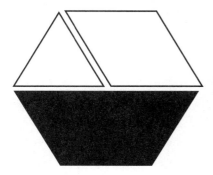

9. Next, explain the three moves listed on this page. Post these moves or have copies of the *Wipeout* Game Directions (REPRODUCIBLE G-33) available for all students.

 TEACHING TIP
Modeling the Game
Note the trade described in Step 9 ensures that, during the next roll, a pattern block can be removed. Do not divulge this to students; let them observe and make the discovery on their own.

 TEACHING TIP
Three Moves in the Game *Wipeout*
Roll the die and:

1. Remove the pattern block the fraction on the die represents,

2. Trade in any of your remaining pattern blocks for an equivalent portion, or

3. Do nothing.

Note that you can only choose one of these moves during each turn. You may not remove a pattern block (move 1) and trade in pattern blocks (move 2) in one turn.

TEACHING TIP
Equivalent Parts May Not Be Substituted
In the game *Wipeout*, equivalent parts may not be substituted. For example, two triangles (each having the value of one-sixth) may not be removed if a $\frac{1}{3}$ (represented by the rhombus) is rolled. Only a rhombus may be removed.

TEACHING TIP
The Importance of Practice
Refrain from discussing skill or strategies during the active engagement part of the lesson. The purpose at this time is to give students as much practice as possible first; they will then have the opportunity later to discuss their experiences (see "Math Workshop and Summarizing the Experience").

10. Now have the selected student roll the die and remove the fractional part shown. If the fractional part is not something he exchanged for, remind students of the other two moves (see "Three Moves in the Game *Wipeout*"). The winner of the game is the first player to discard all of his pattern blocks.

11. Continue modeling the game, alternating turns, until a player removes all the parts of the whole.

Part III: Active Engagement

Engage students to ensure they understand how to play the game.

12. Now give students an opportunity to explore the game in pairs. Make sure each pair has a set of pattern blocks per the materials list, as well as the special die. Set up students so that a yellow hexagon is in front of each player.

13. Circulate to observe whether the game is being played properly. Revisit the three game moves, making certain students understand how the game is played.

14. After students have played at least one round using a single hexagon to begin the game, bring them together to clarify the game moves. Be certain students understand that they may not exchange two one-sixths if a $\frac{1}{3}$ is rolled.

15. Last, introduce the fact that the game of *Wipeout* can actually begin with either one, two, or three hexagons, and that this is a decision players make at the beginning of the game. Emphasize that *both* players need to begin with the same number of hexagons (wholes). Play begins as before, players first exchanging *just one* of the hexagons for equivalent fractional pattern block pieces.

Part IV: The Link

Students play the game independently.

16. Set up students for independent practice of the game in pairs. In addition to the pattern blocks and die, distribute the game directions (REPRODUCIBLE G-33) as needed.

17. Students play for a certain amount of time, predetermined by you. Students beginning the game with just one hexagon (or whole) will most certainly finish their game more quickly than those students electing to begin with three hexagons (or wholes). Letting students know the amount of time remaining in this part of the lesson will help them determine whether they should start a new round with just one, two, or three hexagons.

TEACHING TIP
Pairing Students
The game of *Wipeout* involves skill, strategy, and luck; therefore, a random pairing of students will work. You might have students choose their partners or use a classroom management routine, such as pulling sticks labeled with students' names, to establish partners at random.

DIFFERENTIATING YOUR INSTRUCTION
For students who are ready for practice with equivalent fractions, eliminate the rule "equivalent portions may not be substituted."

MATH WORKSHOP AND SUMMARIZING THE EXPERIENCE

Teach this game at the beginning of the week to the whole class, and then make it a fundamental part of your math workshop (for more on math workshops, see Chapter 5 in *From Reading to Math* by Maggie Siena). Build in time to observe students playing the game, noting students' individual skill level and fluency with fractional relationships. Come together as a class later in the week and have students explain some of the fractional relationships they discovered when playing *Wipeout*. Students will likely be able to express that one-half is equivalent to three-sixths or one-third and one-sixth. Or that two-sixths is the same as one-third. Consider recording these understandings on chart paper, using both pictures of the pattern block relationships as well as the numerical representation of the concepts.

1 whole

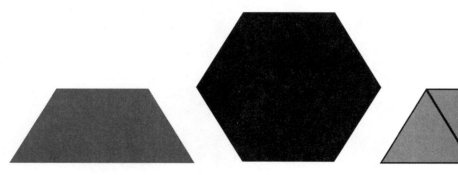

$$\frac{1}{2} = \frac{1}{6} + \frac{1}{6} + \frac{1}{6} \text{ or } \frac{1}{2} = \frac{3}{6}$$

one trapezoid is the same as three triangles

ASSESSMENT
Writing Prompt
Ask students to journal about the strategies they use when playing *Wipeout*.

Reproducibles

The following reproducibles are referenced and used with individual games. These reproducibles are also available in downloadable, printable format at www.mathsolutions.com/mathgamesreproducibles.

continued

Reproducibles Used with More Than One Game   236

The following reproducibles are referenced and used throughout the book; these tools are also easily adaptable for use in other games.

Game Directions   240

In addition to the above reproducibles, each game also has a reproducible condensed page of directions written for students. These reproducibles are numbered starting with the letter G.

ADDITION TABLE 0–5

Copy the game board as needed to play the game (one game board for each game).

+	0	1	2	3	4	5
0	0	1	2	3	4	5
1	1	2	3	4	5	6
2	2	3	4	5	6	7
3	3	4	5	6	7	8
4	4	5	6	7	8	9
5	5	6	7	8	9	10

ADDITION TABLE 0–10

Copy the game board as needed to play the game (one game board for each game).

+	0	1	2	3	4	5	6	7	8	9	10
0	0	1	2	3	4	5	6	7	8	9	10
1	1	2	3	4	5	6	7	8	9	10	11
2	2	3	4	5	6	7	8	9	10	11	12
3	3	4	5	6	7	8	9	10	11	12	13
4	4	5	6	7	8	9	10	11	12	13	14
5	5	6	7	8	9	10	11	12	13	14	15
6	6	7	8	9	10	11	12	13	14	15	16
7	7	8	9	10	11	12	13	14	15	16	17
8	8	9	10	11	12	13	14	15	16	17	18
9	9	10	11	12	13	14	15	16	17	18	19
10	10	11	12	13	14	15	16	17	18	19	20

MULTIPLICATION TABLE 1–6

Copy the game board as needed to play the game (one game board for each game).

✗	1	2	3	4	5	6
1	1	2	3	4	5	6
2	2	4	6	8	10	12
3	3	6	9	12	15	18
4	4	8	12	16	20	24
5	5	10	15	20	25	30
6	6	12	18	24	30	36

MULTIPLICATION TABLE 0–10

Copy the game board as needed to play the game (one game board for each game).

✕	0	1	2	3	4	5	6	7	8	9	10
0	0	0	0	0	0	0	0	0	0	0	0
1	0	1	2	3	4	5	6	7	8	9	10
2	0	2	4	6	8	10	12	14	16	18	20
3	0	3	6	9	12	15	18	21	24	27	30
4	0	4	8	12	16	20	24	28	32	36	40
5	0	5	10	15	20	25	30	35	40	45	50
6	0	6	12	18	24	30	36	42	48	54	60
7	0	7	14	21	28	35	42	49	56	63	70
8	0	8	16	24	32	40	48	56	64	72	80
9	0	9	18	27	36	45	54	63	72	81	90
10	0	10	20	30	40	50	60	70	80	90	100

ADDITION TIC-TAC-TOE
GAME BOARD, COMPLETED

Copy the game board as needed to play the game (one game board for each game).

2	3	4	5	6
7	8	9	10	11
12	13	14	15	16
17	18	19	20	21
22	23	24	25	26

1   2   3   4   5   6   7   8   9   10   11   12   13

ADDITION TIC-TAC-TOE
GAME BOARD, BLANK

Copy the game board as needed to play the game (one game board for each game).

CLOSE TO 0 RECORDING SHEETS

Copy the recording sheet as needed to play the game
(each player should have one sheet for five rounds of play).

NAME _____

SCORE

ROUND 1: _____ $^-$ _____ = _____   _____

ROUND 2: _____ $^-$ _____ = _____   _____

ROUND 3: _____ $^-$ _____ = _____   _____

ROUND 4: _____ $^-$ _____ = _____   _____

ROUND 5: _____ $^-$ _____ = _____   _____

TOTAL SCORE   _____

- -

NAME _____

SCORE

ROUND 1: _____ $^-$ _____ = _____   _____

ROUND 2: _____ $^-$ _____ = _____   _____

ROUND 3: _____ $^-$ _____ = _____   _____

ROUND 4: _____ $^-$ _____ = _____   _____

ROUND 5: _____ $^-$ _____ = _____   _____

TOTAL SCORE   _____

CLOSE TO 20 RECORDING SHEETS

Copy the recording sheet as needed to play the game
(each player should have one sheet for five rounds of play).

NAME _____

SCORE

ROUND 1: _____ + _____ + _____ = _____   _____

ROUND 2: _____ + _____ + _____ = _____   _____

ROUND 3: _____ + _____ + _____ = _____   _____

ROUND 4: _____ + _____ + _____ = _____   _____

ROUND 5: _____ + _____ + _____ = _____   _____

TOTAL SCORE   _____

- -

NAME _____

SCORE

ROUND 1: _____ + _____ + _____ = _____   _____

ROUND 2: _____ + _____ + _____ = _____   _____

ROUND 3: _____ + _____ + _____ = _____   _____

ROUND 4: _____ + _____ + _____ = _____   _____

ROUND 5: _____ + _____ + _____ = _____   _____

TOTAL SCORE   _____

CLOSE TO 100 RECORDING SHEET

Copy the recording sheet as needed to play the game
(each player should have one sheet for five rounds of play).

NAME _____   DATE _____

SCORE

ROUND 1: _____ _____ + _____ _____ = _____   _____

ROUND 2: _____ _____ + _____ _____ = _____   _____

ROUND 3: _____ _____ + _____ _____ = _____   _____

ROUND 4: _____ _____ + _____ _____ = _____   _____

ROUND 5: _____ _____ + _____ _____ = _____   _____

TOTAL SCORE   _____

Place a star by your best round. What was your strategy for this round?

_____

_____

_____

Was more skill or luck involved in this game? Explain.

_____

_____

_____

CLOSE TO 1,000 RECORDING SHEETS

Copy the recording sheet as needed to play the game
(each player should have one sheet for five rounds of play).

NAME _____

SCORE

ROUND 1: _____ + _____ = _____   _____

ROUND 2: _____ + _____ = _____   _____

ROUND 3: _____ + _____ = _____   _____

ROUND 4: _____ + _____ = _____   _____

ROUND 5: _____ + _____ = _____   _____

TOTAL SCORE   _____

- -

NAME _____

SCORE

ROUND 1: _____ + _____ = _____   _____

ROUND 2: _____ + _____ = _____   _____

ROUND 3: _____ + _____ = _____   _____

ROUND 4: _____ + _____ = _____   _____

ROUND 5: _____ + _____ = _____   _____

TOTAL SCORE   _____

CLOSE TO 100 ASSESSMENT: JOE'S GAME

NAME _____   DATE _____

While playing *Close to 100,* Joe had the following cards:

| 6 | 2 | 3 | 5 | 7 | 1 |

He followed these rules:

1. Use any four of the cards to make two numbers. For example, a 6 and a 5 could make either 65 or 56. Try to make numbers that, when added, give you a total that is close to 100.

2. Write the two numbers and their total. For example: *42 + 56 = 98.*

3. Find the score. The score is the difference between the total and 100. For example, if your total is 98, your score is 2. If your total is 105, your score is 5.

What are some of the possible number sentences Joe could have made? What would his score be? Come up with three different options.

SCORE

1. _____ _____ + _____ _____ = _____   _____

2. _____ _____ + _____ _____ = _____   _____

3. _____ _____ + _____ _____ = _____   _____

Which of the three options is the best? _____

Why?

_____

_____

*From *Math Games for Independent Practice: Games to Support Math Workshops and More, Grades K–5* by Jamee Petersen. © 2013 by Scholastic Inc. Permission granted to photocopy for nonprofit use in a classroom or similar place dedicated to face-to-face educational purposes. Downloadable at www.mathsolutions.com/mathgamesreproducibles.

COMPARE (SHAKE AND SPILL) CHART

Copy the chart as needed to play the game (one chart for each pair of players).

MORE RED	SAME	MORE YELLOW

CROSS OUT SINGLES GAME BOARDS
Version 1 (3-by-3 Array)

Copy the game boards as needed to play the game (each pair should have one sheet for three rounds of play).

NAME _____

NAME _____

Score for Each Round

1 _____ 2 _____ 3 _____

Total _____

Score for Each Round

1 _____ 2 _____ 3 _____

Total _____

CROSS OUT SINGLES GAME BOARDS

Version 2 (4-by-4 Array)

Copy the game boards as needed to play the game (each pair should have one sheet for three rounds of play).

NAME _____

NAME _____

Score for Each Round

1 _____ 2 _____ 3 _____

Total _____

Score for Each Round

1 _____ 2 _____ 3 _____

Total _____

CROSS OUT SUMS GAME BOARD
VERSION 1 (BLACKOUT)

Copy the game board as needed to play the game (one game board for each game).

2	3	4	5	6
7	8	9	9	10
10	10	11	11	11
12	12	13	14	15
16	17	18	19	20

CROSS OUT SUMS GAME BOARD
VERSION 2 (TIC-TAC-TOE)

Copy the game board as needed to play the game (one game board for each game).

2	4	6	8	10
13	10	14	10	15
18	12	20	12	19
11	16	11	17	11
3	5	7	9	9

DIGIT PLACE
(A SECRET NUMBER QUEST)
RECORDING SHEET

Copy the recording sheet as needed to play the game (one recording sheet per game).

Guess	Digit	Place

FIFTEEN-NUMBER CROSS-OUT RECORDING SHEET

Copy the recording sheet as needed to play the game (each pair should have one sheet for three games).

Player 1 / Game 1

5   5   5   5

Player 2 / Game 1

5   5   5   5

Player 1 / Game 2

5   5   5   5

Player 2 / Game 2

5   5   5   5

Player 1 / Game 3

5   5   5   5

Player 2 / Game 3

5   5   5   5

TWENTY-NUMBER CROSS-OUT
RECORDING SHEET

Copy the recording sheet as needed to play the game (each pair should have one sheet for three games).

Player 1 / Game 1

5 5 5 5 5 __ __ __ __ __ __ __ __ __ __ __ __ __ __ __

Player 1 / Game 2

5 5 5 5 5 __ __ __ __ __ __ __ __ __ __ __ __ __ __ __

Player 1 / Game 3

5 5 5 5 5 __ __ __ __ __ __ __ __ __ __ __ __ __ __ __

Player 2 / Game 1

5 5 5 5 5 __ __ __ __ __ __ __ __ __ __ __ __ __ __ __

Player 2 / Game 2

5 5 5 5 5 __ __ __ __ __ __ __ __ __ __ __ __ __ __ __

Player 2 / Game 3

5 5 5 5 5 __ __ __ __ __ __ __ __ __ __ __ __ __ __ __

FINDING FACTORS GAME BOARD
VERSION 1 (NUMBERS 1–30)

Copy the game board as needed to play the game (one game board for each game).

Player 1's Color _____

Player 2's Color _____

1	2	3	4	5
6	7	8	9	10
11	12	13	14	15
16	17	18	19	20
21	22	23	24	25
26	27	28	29	30

Player 1's Score _____

Player 2's Score _____

FINDING FACTORS GAME BOARD
VERSION 2 (NUMBERS 1–50)

Copy the game board as needed to play the game (one game board for each game).

Player 1's Color _____   Player 2's Color _____

1	2	3	4	5
6	7	8	9	10
11	12	13	14	15
16	17	18	19	20
21	22	23	24	25
26	27	28	29	30
31	32	33	34	35
36	37	38	39	40
41	42	43	44	45
46	47	48	49	50

Player 1's Score _____   Player 2's Score _____

GREATER THAN, LESS THAN, EQUAL TO
RECORDING SHEET Version 1 (Two Addends)

Copy the recording sheet as needed to play the game (one recording sheet per game).

	Player 1			Player 2

Round 1   _____ + _____   ☐   _____ + _____

Round 2   _____ + _____   ☐   _____ + _____

Round 3   _____ + _____   ☐   _____ + _____

Round 4   _____ + _____   ☐   _____ + _____

Round 5   _____ + _____   ☐   _____ + _____

Round 6   _____ + _____   ☐   _____ + _____

Round 7   _____ + _____   ☐   _____ + _____

Round 8   _____ + _____   ☐   _____ + _____

Round 9   _____ + _____   ☐   _____ + _____

Round 10   _____ + _____   ☐   _____ + _____

Together we had: _____ equalities and _____ inequalities.

_____ greater than (>).

_____ less than (<).

GREATER THAN, LESS THAN, EQUAL TO

RECORDING SHEET Version 2 (Three Addends)

Copy the recording sheet as needed to play the game (one recording sheet per game).

	Player 1				Player 2		

Round 1 ____ + ____ + ____ ☐ ____ + ____ + ____

Round 2 ____ + ____ + ____ ☐ ____ + ____ + ____

Round 3 ____ + ____ + ____ ☐ ____ + ____ + ____

Round 4 ____ + ____ + ____ ☐ ____ + ____ + ____

Round 5 ____ + ____ + ____ ☐ ____ + ____ + ____

Round 6 ____ + ____ + ____ ☐ ____ + ____ + ____

Round 7 ____ + ____ + ____ ☐ ____ + ____ + ____

Round 8 ____ + ____ + ____ ☐ ____ + ____ + ____

Round 9 ____ + ____ + ____ ☐ ____ + ____ + ____

Round 10 ____ + ____ + ____ ☐ ____ + ____ + ____

Together we had: _____ equalities and _____ inequalities.

_____ greater than (>).

_____ less than (<).

GREATER THAN, LESS THAN, EQUAL TO

RECORDING SHEET Version 3 (Subtraction)

Copy the recording sheet as needed to play the game (one recording sheet per game).

	Player 1			Player 2
Round 1	_____ — _____	☐	_____ — _____	
Round 2	_____ — _____	☐	_____ — _____	
Round 3	_____ — _____	☐	_____ — _____	
Round 4	_____ — _____	☐	_____ — _____	
Round 5	_____ — _____	☐	_____ — _____	
Round 6	_____ — _____	☐	_____ — _____	
Round 7	_____ — _____	☐	_____ — _____	
Round 8	_____ — _____	☐	_____ — _____	
Round 9	_____ — _____	☐	_____ — _____	
Round 10	_____ — _____	☐	_____ — _____	

Together we had: _____ equalities and _____ inequalities.

_____ greater than (>).

_____ less than (<).

GREATER THAN, LESS THAN, EQUAL TO RECORDING SHEET Version 4 (Multiplication)

Copy the recording sheet as needed to play the game (one recording sheet per game).

	Player 1		Player 2
Round 1	_____ ✕ _____	☐	_____ ✕ _____
Round 2	_____ ✕ _____	☐	_____ ✕ _____
Round 3	_____ ✕ _____	☐	_____ ✕ _____
Round 4	_____ ✕ _____	☐	_____ ✕ _____
Round 5	_____ ✕ _____	☐	_____ ✕ _____
Round 6	_____ ✕ _____	☐	_____ ✕ _____
Round 7	_____ ✕ _____	☐	_____ ✕ _____
Round 8	_____ ✕ _____	☐	_____ ✕ _____
Round 9	_____ ✕ _____	☐	_____ ✕ _____
Round 10	_____ ✕ _____	☐	_____ ✕ _____

Together we had: _____ equalities and _____ inequalities.

_____ greater than (>).

_____ less than (<).

HOW CLOSE TO 0? GAME BOARD   Reproducible 26

Copy the game board as needed to play the game (one game board per game for each pair of players).

	Player 1	Player 2
Round 1		
Round 2		
Round 3		
Round 4		
Round 5		
Round 6		
Round 7		

MORE! RECORDING SHEET

Copy this recording sheet as needed to play the game (each pair
of players should have one sheet for two games).

Player 1_____

Player 2_____

	Player 1 (total number of cubes)	Player 2 (total number of cubes)	Difference
Game 1			
Game 2			
TOTAL			

ORDER UP 21! RECORDING SHEET

Copy the recording sheet as needed to play ten rounds of the game. Each player or team of two should have a copy.

Round	Equation	Score
1.	_____	_____
2.	_____	_____
3.	_____	_____
4.	_____	_____
5.	_____	_____
6.	_____	_____
7.	_____	_____
8.	_____	_____
9.	_____	_____
10.	_____	_____

TOTAL _____

ORDER UP 21! ASSESSMENT

Name _____

Date _____

Blake and Jackson are playing the game *Order Up 21!* They drew the following cards:

| 4 | 5 | 2 | 3 |

Blake built this equation: $(4 \times 5) + 3 - 2$

Jackson built this equation: $4 + 2 + (5 \times 3)$

Both boys believe they have the best equation (the one that will yield them the lowest score—0 points) in the game of *Order Up 21!* Do you agree with Blake, Jackson, or both? Explain.

_____

_____

_____

If Blake and Jackson did not use parentheses in their equations, would it have affected their total? Explain.

_____

_____

_____

PATHWAYS GAME BOARD 1

Copy the game board as needed to play the game (one game board for each game).

81	54	63	36	72
28	18	32	81	24
48	64	21	16	56
12	9	42	49	27

3   4   6   7   8   9

PATHWAYS GAME BOARD 2

Copy the game board as needed to play the game (one game board for each game).

81	64	48	36	63
30	42	32	35	28
72	25	49	24	45
16	54	20	40	56

4   5   6   7   8   9

PATHWAYS GAME BOARD 3

Copy the game board as needed to play the game (one game board for each game).

54	28	42	72	63
77	36	16	99	64
49	32	44	81	121
56	48	66	88	24

4   6   7   8   9   11

PATHWAYS GAME BOARD 4

Copy the game board as needed to play the game (one game board for each game).

72	36	49	88	54
84	77	96	132	56
63	81	48	108	121
66	99	144	64	42

6   7   8   9   11   12

TIMES TEN GAME BOARD 1

Copy the game board as needed to play the game (one game board for each game).

90	450	300	810	200
180	630	540	350	250
240	150	210	270	360
420	280	160	490	120

3   4   5   6   7   9

TIMES TEN GAME BOARD 2

Copy the game board as needed to play the game (one game board for each game).

810	480	540	640	630
210	360	160	720	560
280	120	180	90	320
420	810	490	240	270

3   4   6   7   8   9

TIMES TEN GAME BOARD 3

Copy the game board as needed to play the game (one game board for each game).

560	400	200	640	160
720	250	490	240	450
300	420	320	350	280
810	640	480	360	630

4   5   6   7   8   9

TIMES TEN GAME BOARD 4

Copy the game board as needed to play the game (one game board for each game).

540	630	990	440	480
280	770	640	810	660
420	360	490	1210	880
720	160	320	560	240

4   6   7   8   9   11

ROLL 6 FOR 100 RECORDING SHEET

Copy the recording sheet as needed to play the game
(each player should have one sheet for four rounds of play).

Name _____

Equations: ROUND 1

Scoring

_____ had _____. _____ had _____.

_____ won because _____ is _____ closer to 100 than _____.

Equations: ROUND 2

Scoring

_____ had _____. _____ had _____.

_____ won because _____ is _____ closer to 100 than _____.

Equations: ROUND 3

Scoring

_____ had _____. _____ had _____.

_____ won because _____ is _____ closer to 100 than _____.

Equations: ROUND 4

Scoring

_____ had _____. _____ had _____.

_____ won because _____ is _____ closer to 100 than _____.

ROLL 6 FOR 100 ASSESSMENT

Name _____

Sam was playing a round of *Roll 6 for 100*. This is what he had recorded after five rounds:

$6 + 5 + 1 + 3 + 5$

When Sam rolls the die for a final time, what number should he hope for? Explain.

_____

_____

_____

_____

_____

- -

ROLL 6 FOR 100 ASSESSMENT

Name _____

Sam was playing a round of *Roll 6 for 100*. This is what he had recorded after five rounds:

$6 + 5 + 1 + 3 + 5$

When Sam rolls the die for a final time, what number should he hope for? Explain.

_____

_____

_____

_____

_____

ROLL FOR $1.00 GAME BOARD

Copy this game board as needed to play the game, one copy per player.

Name _____

Roll	Dimes	Pennies	Running Total
1			
2			
3			
4			
5			
6			
7			

_____ is _____ away from $1.00.

ROLL FOR 1 RECORDING SHEETS

Copy this recording sheet as needed to play the game, one recording sheet per player.

Name _____

Roll	Dimes (one-tenth of $1.00)	Pennies (one-hundredth of $1.00)	Running Total
1			
2			
3			
4			
5			
6			
7			

- -

Name _____

Roll	Dimes (one-tenth of $1.00)	Pennies (one-hundredth of $1.00)	Running Total
1			
2			
3			
4			
5			
6			
7			

SPINNING SUMS AND DIFFERENCES
PLACE VALUE SPINNER 1

Copy this spinner as needed to play the game, one spinner per pair of players.

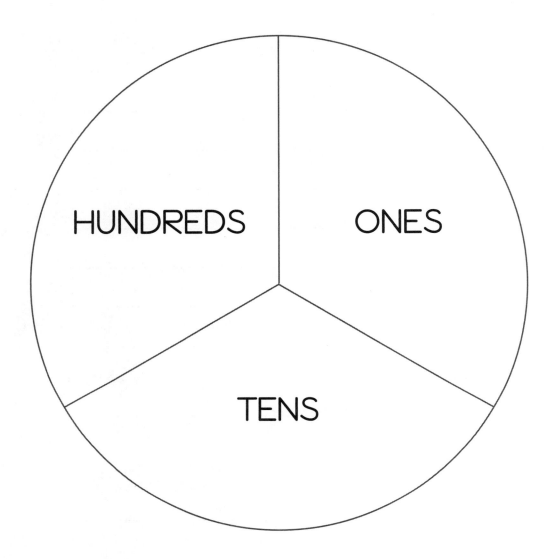

1. Pass out one large paper clip per pair of players.

2. Use the tip of a pencil to keep the paper clip on the spinner.

3. Spin the paper clip while holding the pencil or have a partner hold the pencil while you spin the paper clip.

SPINNING SUMS AND DIFFERENCES
PLACE VALUE SPINNER 2

Copy this spinner as needed to play the game, one spinner per pair of players.

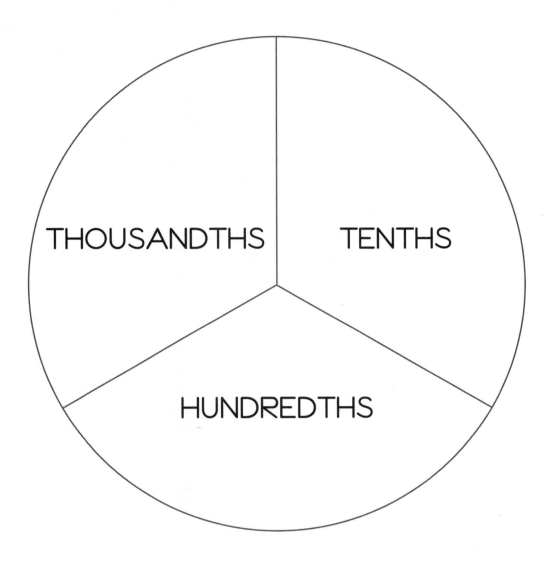

1. Pass out one large paper clip per pair of players.

2. Use the tip of a pencil to keep the paper clip on the spinner.

3. Spin the paper clip while holding the pencil or have a partner hold the pencil while you spin the paper clip.

SPINNING SUMS AND DIFFERENCES RECORDING SHEET

Copy this recording sheet as needed to play the game, one sheet per player.

Name _____

Player # _____

ROUND	NUMBERS GENERATED	ADDITION EQUATION	SUBTRACTION EQUATION	POINTS SCORED
1				
2				
3				
4				
5				
6				
7				
8				
9				
10				

TOTAL POINTS _____

TAKE FIVE, MAKE TEN! ASSESSMENT   Reproducible 45

Name _____   Date _____

Pretend you drew the following five cards for the game of *Take Five, Make Ten!*.
Build five equations. Use the back of this paper if you have more than five.

Equations

1. _____

2. _____

3. _____

4. _____

5. _____

Which equation do you think no one else in your class might have written?
Circle that equation and explain why you think it is original.

_____

_____

_____

_____

TARGET 300 (A MULTIPLICATION GAME)
RECORDING SHEET

Copy this recording sheet as needed to play the game, one sheet for each player for one game (five rounds).

ROUND	PLAYER 1 Name _____	PLAYER 2 Name _____
1		
2		
3		
4		
5		
TOTAL		

Multiplier Options

× 10

× 20

× 30

× 40

× 50

Player 1

_____ is _____ away from 300.

Player 2

_____ is _____ away from 300.

TARGET "PICK YOUR SUM"
GAME BOARD

Copy this game board as needed to play the game, one copy per game.

5	5	5	5	5
4	4	4	4	4
3	3	3	3	3
2	2	2	2	2
1	1	1	1	1

HUNDREDS CHART

1	2	3	4	5	6	7	8	9	10
11	12	13	14	15	16	17	18	19	20
21	22	23	24	25	26	27	28	29	30
31	32	33	34	35	36	37	38	39	40
41	42	43	44	45	46	47	48	49	50
51	52	53	54	55	56	57	58	59	60
61	62	63	64	65	66	67	68	69	70
71	72	73	74	75	76	77	78	79	80
81	82	83	84	85	86	87	88	89	90
91	92	93	94	95	96	97	98	99	100

NUMERAL CARDS

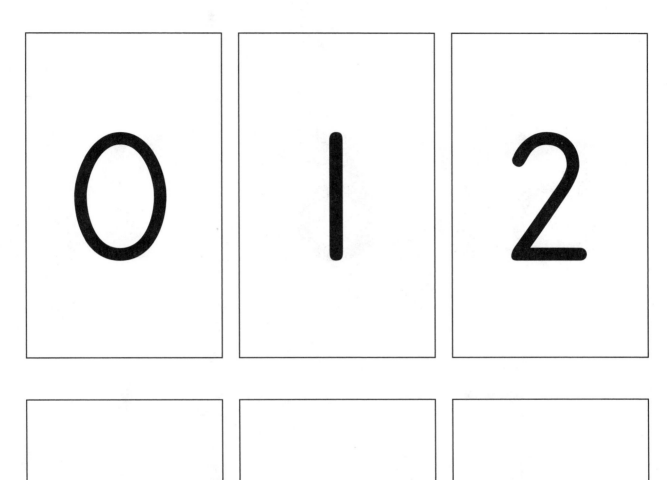

5 6 7

8 9 10

Game 1:
A "Mazing" 100

Objective

During this game, players create a maze from zero to one hundred by moving through the hundreds chart. Moves can be both horizontally (when adding ones) and vertically (when adding or counting by tens).

Materials

- Hundreds Chart (REPRODUCIBLE A), 1 per player or pair of players
- marker, crayon, or colored pencil, 1 per player or pair of players
- die (labeled *1–6*), 1 player or pair of players

Players

1 or 2
(players may play solo or as a team of two)

Directions

1. If playing in pairs, decide who is Player 1 and who is Player 2.

2. On the hundreds chart, write the word *Start* next to the square numbered 1. Write the word *End* next to the square numbered 100.

3. One player rolls the die. Move the corresponding number of squares (for the first roll, move in ones—this is only for the first roll), tracing your path with a marker, crayon, or colored pencil as you go.

4. The next player rolls the die. Both players decide if the number rolled will represent a 10 or a 1.

5. Move the corresponding number of squares, tracing your path as you go.

6. Repeat Steps 4 and 5 until you reach the end of the hundreds chart.

Game 2A:
Addition Table Trail

Objective

During this game, players take turns covering sums across or down the game board (the addition table) in an attempt to build a trail. The first player to complete his or her trail (from one side of the game board to the other) is considered the winner.

Materials

- Addition Table 0–5 or 0–10 (REPRODUCIBLES 1 and 2), 1 per pair of players
- counters (25 of each color), 50 per pair of players
- dice (2 labeled *0–5*, 2 labeled *5–10*), 4 per pair of players

Players

2

Directions

1. Each player chooses which color counter her or she will use (must be different).

2. Each player will be moving within the addition table in a different direction. Decide who will move horizontally and who will move vertically.

3. Take turns rolling the dice. Only two dice are rolled at a time. When it is the first player's turn, he or she selects two of the four dice to roll. Any combination of dice to roll can be chosen: both labeled *0–5*, both labeled *5–10*, or one of each. For example, a player might choose to roll both the *0–5* dice if he is trying to get a sum in the upper left quadrant of the board. Or, the player might roll both the *5–10* dice to get a sum in the lower right quadrant of the board. A player may also roll one of each.

4. The numbers that come up are the addends. Cover the sum that represents the roll on the addition table with one of that player's colored counters.

5. If the sum has already been covered, roll one of the dice again. If the sum of the new roll is covered, it is the other player's turn.

6. Take turns playing. The goal is to be the first player to make a trail across or down the addition table. The path may move up, down, forward, backward, and diagonally, as long as the path is continuous and connects the sides of the table in the player's designated direction (vertically or horizontally).

Game 2B:
Multiplication Table Trail

Objective

During this game, players take turns covering products across or down the game board (the multiplication table) in an attempt to build a trail. The first player to complete his or her trail (from one side of the game board to the other) is considered the winner.

Materials

- Multiplication Table 1–6 or 0–10 (REPRODUCIBLES 3 and 4), 1 per pair of players

- counters, 50 per pair of players (25 of each color)

- dice (2 labeled 0–5, 2 labeled 5–10), 4 per pair of players

Players

2

Directions

1. Each player chooses which color counter he or she will use (must be different).

2. Each player will be moving within the multiplication table in a different direction. Decide who will move horizontally and who will move vertically.

3. Take turns rolling the dice. Only two dice are rolled at a time. When it is a player's turn, select two of the four dice to roll. Any combination of dice to roll may be chosen: both labeled 0–5, both labeled 5–10, or one of each.

4. The numbers that come up are multiplied. Cover the product that represents the roll on the multiplication table with one of the player's colored counters.

5. If the product has already been covered, the player may roll one of the dice again. If the product of the new roll is covered, it is the other player's turn.

6. Take turns playing. The goal is to be the first player to make a trail across or down the multiplication table, from one side to the other. The path may move up, down, forward, backward, and diagonally, as long as the path is continuous and connects the sides of the table in the player's designated direction (vertically or horizontally).

Game 3: Addition Tic-Tac-Toe

Objective

During this game, players take turns marking the sum of two addends until one player has connected five sums in a row, column, or diagonal. This player is considered the winner.

Materials

- paper clips, 2 per pair of players
- tiles, 24 per pair of players (12 of each color)
- *Addition Tic-Tac-Toe* Game Board (REPRODUCIBLES 5 or 6), 1 per pair of players

Players

2

Directions

1. Decide who is Player 1 and Player 2 and which color of tiles each player will use.

2. Player 1 selects two numbers from those listed at the bottom of the game board and places a paper clip on each (if using Reproducible 6, players must first fill in the game board with numbers). These numbers become the addends. Player 1 covers the sum of the two addends on the game board with his color tile.

3. Player 2 moves *just one* of the paper clips to another number, adds the two addends, and covers the sum with her color tile.

4. Repeat Steps 2 and 3 until a winner is declared. The winner is the player who has connected five sums by placing five color tiles in either a row, column, or diagonal. Just as in the classic game of tic-tac-toe, some games will end in a tie.

Note: In some cases, both paper clips may be placed on the same number.

Game 4: Anything but Ten!

Objective

During this game, players take turns rolling dice until they reach 100 on the game board. The first player to reach 100 or beyond is the winner.

Materials

- Hundreds Chart (REPRODUCIBLE A), 1 per pair of players
- dice (1 labeled *0–5*, 1 labeled *5–10*), 2 per pair of players
- counters, each a different color, 2 per pair of players

Players

2

Directions

1. Each player chooses a counter and places it at 0, just before the square labeled *1* on the hundreds chart.

2. Players take turns rolling both dice:

   - If the number rolled is *not* a combination of ten, the player moves the total number of spaces. The player then has two choices: to end his or her turn or to roll again.

   - If the number rolled *is* a combination of ten, the player must remain at or go back to 0.

   - If a combination of ten is rolled at any point during the game, the player must go back to 0.

3. The winner is the first player to reach 100 or beyond on the game board (hundreds chart).

Game 5: Build Ten

Objective

During this game, players take turns rolling the die until they have built ten against their tens rod. The first player to build ten is the winner.

Materials

- die (labeled *1–6*), 1 per pair of players
- base ten rods, 2 per pair of players
- base ten cubes, 20 per pair of players

Players

2

Directions

1. Decide who is Player 1 and Player 2. Both players lay a tens rod on their workspace.

2. Player 1 rolls the die and collects the corresponding number of ones cubes. The player carefully places the ones cubes against the tens rod so that they are touching each other.

3. Player 2 rolls the die, collects the corresponding number of ones cubes, and places them against his tens rod.

4. Players continue to take turns rolling the die and placing the ones cubes against their tens rods. The first player to build ten wins.

Note: Players try to roll exactly ten; however, after three consecutive rolls they may go over ten to finish a round. For example, if a player has eight ones cubes, a roll of 2, 3, 4, 5, or 6 would complete the game.

Game 6: Circles and Stars

Objective

During this game, players roll a die and draw the corresponding number of circles and stars. Each player then records the two number sentences (addition and multiplication) that the model represents.

Materials

- die (labeled *1–6*), 1 per player or pair of players
- 12-by-18-inch sheet of white paper, 1 per player or pair of players
- pencil, 1 per player or pair of players

Players

1 or 2

Directions

1. Players fold the paper three times so that there are eight sections for recording:

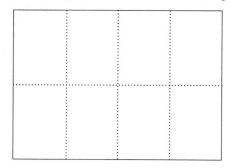

2. If there are two players, each player chooses a side and writes *Circles and Stars* and their name in the top left-hand box.

3. Roll the die. Draw the corresponding number of circles in the first section of the recording sheet. Make sure your circles are big enough to draw stars inside of them (at least the size of a quarter).

4. Roll the die again. Draw the corresponding number of stars in each circle.

5. Record the corresponding multiplication sentence.

6. Repeat Steps 3 through 6 until each player has played seven rounds and recorded their rounds in the corresponding sections of the paper.

Game 7A:
Close to 0

Objective

In this version of the game, each player is dealt eight numeral cards. Each player selects six of his or her cards to make two, three-digit numbers. The objective is to have the two, three-digit numbers, when subtracted, give a difference that is as close to 0 as possible.

Materials

- pencil, 1 per player
- Numeral Cards 0–9 (REPRODUCIBLE B) plus four blank cards with *Wild Card* written on each, 1 deck per player or group of players
- *Close to 0* Recording Sheets (REPRODUCIBLE 7), 1 per player

A Deck of Cards

For the purpose of this game, a deck of numeral cards is four copies of each numeral card listed in the materials, plus four wild cards (blank cards with *Wild Card* written on each).

Players

1, 2, or 3

Directions

1. Deal eight numeral cards to each player.

2. Each player selects any six of the cards in his or her hand to make two, three-digit numbers. For example, a 2, 6, and 5 could make 256, 265, 526, 562, 625, or 652. Wild cards can be used as any numeral. Try to make numbers that, when subtracted, give you a difference that is as close to 0 as possible.

3. Each player writes the two numbers and their difference on his or her copy of the *Close to 0* Recording Sheet. For example: $652 - 647 = 5$.

4. Each player figures out his or her score. The score for the round is the difference between the total and 0. In the example in Step 3, the score would be 5.

5. Put the cards that you used in a discard pile. Keep the two cards that you didn't use for the next round.

6. For the next round, deal six new cards to each player (players should add these cards to their hand of two cards for a total of eight).

7. Repeat Steps 2–5. When you run out of cards, shuffle the discard pile and use those cards again.

8. After five rounds, every player totals their score. The player with the score closest to 0 is the winner.

Game 7B:
Close to 20

Objective

In this version of the game, each player is dealt four numeral cards. Each player selects three of the numeral cards and adds the numbers. The objective is to have the three numbers be equal or close to 20.

Materials

- pencil, 1 per player
- Numeral Cards 0–9 (REPRODUCIBLE B) plus four blank cards with *Wild Card* written on each, 1 deck per pair or group of players
- *Close to 20* Recording Sheets (REPRODUCIBLE 8), 1 per player
- optional: counters

A Deck of Cards

For the purpose of this game, a deck of numeral cards is four copies of each numeral card listed in the materials, plus four wild cards (blank cards with *Wild Card* written on each).

Players

2 to 3

Directions

1. Deal five cards to each player.

2. Each player uses any three of the five cards in his or her hand to make a total as close to 20 as possible. For example, $8 + 7 + 3 = 18$. Wild cards can be used as any numeral.

3. Each player writes the three numbers and their total on his or her copy of the *Close to 20* Recording Sheet.

4. Each player figures out his or her score. The score for the round is the difference between the total and 20. For example, if you choose $8 + 7 + 3$, your total is 18 and your score for the round is 2.

5. After recording, each player takes the number of counters that equates to his or her score.

6. Put the cards that you used in a discard pile. Keep the two cards that you didn't use for the next round.

7. For the next round, deal three new cards to each player (players should add these cards to their hand of two cards for a total of five).

8. Repeat Steps 2–6. When you run out of cards, shuffle the discard pile and use those cards again.

9. After five rounds, every player totals their score and counts their counters. The two numbers should be the same. The player with the lowest score (and subsequently the fewest counters) is the winner.

Game 7C:
Close to 100

Objective

In this version of the game, players draw six numeral cards and select four to make two double-digit numbers. The objective is to have the two double-digit numbers, when added, equal a sum as close to 100 as possible.

Materials

- pencil, 1 per player
- Numeral Cards 0–9 (REPRODUCIBLE B) plus four blank cards with *Wild Card* written on each, 1 deck per player or group of players
- *Close to 100* Recording Sheet (REPRODUCIBLE 9), 1 per player

A Deck of Cards

For the purpose of this game, a deck of numeral cards is four copies of each numeral card listed in the materials, plus four wild cards (blank cards with *Wild Card* written on each).

Players

1, 2, or 3

Directions

1. Shuffle the cards and place them face down in a pile. Each player draws six cards and places the cards face up in a row in front of them.

2. Each player selects four cards from their six to construct two double-digit numbers that, when added, have a sum as close to 100 as possible. Wild cards can be used as any numeral.

3. Each player writes the equation on his or her copy of the *Close to 100* Recording Sheet. For example, *42 + 56 = 98* or *46 + 59 = 103*.

4. Each player figures out his or her score. The score for the round is the difference between the sum and 100. In the examples in Step 3, 42 + 56 = 98 would result in a score of 2 and 46 + 59 = 103 would be a score of 3.

5. Put the cards that you used in a discard pile. Keep the two cards that you didn't use for the next round.

6. For the next round, deal four new cards to each player (players should add these cards to their hand of two cards for a total of six).

7. Repeat Steps 2–5. When you run out of cards, shuffle the discard pile and use those cards again.

8. After five rounds, every player totals their score. The player with the lowest score is the winner.

Game 7D:
Close to 1,000

Objective

In this version of the game, players are dealt eight numeral cards. Each player selects six of his or her cards to make two, three-digit numbers. The objective is to have the two, three-digit numbers, when added, equal a sum that is as close to 1,000 as possible.

Materials

- pencil, 1 per player
- Numeral Cards 0–9 (REPRODUCIBLE B) plus four blank cards with *Wild Card* written on each, 1 deck per player or group of players
- *Close to 1,000* Recording Sheets (REPRODUCIBLE 10), 1 per player

A Deck of Cards

For the purpose of this game, a deck of numeral cards is four copies of each numeral card listed in the materials, plus four wild cards (blank cards with *Wild Card* written on each).

Players

1, 2, or 3

Directions

1. Deal eight numeral cards to each player.

2. Each player selects any six of their cards to make two, three-digit numbers. For example, a 2, 6, and 5 could make 256, 265, 526, 562, 625, or 652. Wild cards can be used as any numeral. Try to make numbers that, when added, give you a total that is close to 1,000.

3. Each player writes the two, three-digit numbers and the corresponding sum on his or her recording sheet. For example: *742 + 256 = 998.*

4. Each player figures out his or her score. The score for the round is the difference between the total and 1,000. For example, if your total is 998, your score is 2. If your total is 1,005, your score is 5.

5. Put the cards that you used in a discard pile. Keep the two cards that you didn't use for the next round.

6. For the next round, deal six new cards to each player (players should add these cards to their hand of two cards for a total of eight).

7. Repeat Steps 2–6. When you run out of cards, shuffle the discard pile and use those cards again.

8. After five rounds, every player totals their score. The player with the lowest score is the winner.

Game 8: Compare (Shake and Spill)

Objective

During this game, players take turns shaking and spilling a select group of two-color counters. Each time, players record whether there are more red counters, more yellow, or the same amount.

Materials

- two-color counters, 10 per player
- pencil, 1 per pair of players
- *Compare (Shake and Spill)* Chart (REPRODUCIBLE 12), 1 per pair of players

Players

2

Directions

1. With your partner, decide how many counters to use: six, seven, eight, nine, or ten. Also decide who is Player 1 and Player 2.

2. Player 1 shakes and spills the counters.

3. Player 2 records the results, placing a tally mark in the corresponding column of the chart.

4. Repeat Steps 3 and 4, alternating turns shaking/spilling and recording until you've collected twenty pieces of data (tally marks).

5. Extension: Record the addition sentences that describe the data.

Game 9: Cross Out Singles

Objective

During this game, players fill in the nine squares on their game boards with the numbers rolled. After all squares are filled in, players find the sums of the number strings (the rows, columns, and diagonal). They cross out any sums that appear only once, then total the remaining sums. This is their score. The objective is to be the player with the highest score out of three rounds.

Materials

- die (labeled *1–6*), 1 per player or group of players
- pencil, 1 per player
- *Cross Out Singles* Game Boards (REPRODUCIBLE 13), 1 per player

Players

1 or more

Directions

1. If playing with more than one player, decide who is Player 1.

2. Player 1 rolls the die. All players record the number in a square on the first array of their recording sheet. Remember, once a number is written it may not be changed.

3. Another player rolls the dice. All players record the number in a square on the first array of their recording sheet.

4. Repeat Step 3 until all nine squares on players' arrays have been filled.

5. Players then find the sums of the number strings (the rows, columns, and diagonal) and write the sums in the corresponding circles.

6. All players examine their sums. They cross out the sums that appear only once (in only one circle).

7. The total of the sums not crossed out is the player's score for that round. For example:

$$11 + 11 + 10 + 11 + 10 = 53$$

The player's score for the above example round is 53.

8. Repeat Steps 2–7. After three rounds are completed, players review their scores. The player with the highest score after three rounds is the winner.

Game 10: Cross Out Sums

Objective

During this game, players take turns drawing three cards from a deck. They form three different equations using the numbers on the cards, then cross off the equations' sums on their game board. The objective is to cross off all sums on the game board or reach a point at which no sums match those remaining on the game board.

Materials

- Numeral Cards 1–10 (REPRODUCIBLE B), 1 deck per pair of players

- *Cross Out Sums* Game Board, Version 1 (REPRODUCIBLE 15), 1 per pair of players

A Deck of Cards

For the purpose of this game, a deck of numeral cards is four copies of each numeral card listed in the materials.

Players

1, 2, or 4

Directions

1. Decide who is Player 1.

2. Player 1 draws three cards from the deck.

3. Players work together to create three different equations using the numbers on the cards.

4. Players then cross out the corresponding sums on the game board.

5. Players take turns drawing three cards and crossing out the sums of the equations on the game board.

6. Play continues until either all sums are crossed off the game board or there are no sums that match those remaining on the game board.

Game 11: Digit Place (A Secret Number Quest)

Objective

During this game players try to figure out a secret number through a series of guesses. After each guess, the player with the secret number reveals whether the number guessed shares a digit with the secret number. If it does, it's also noted whether the place value is correct. The objective of the game is to share and gain enough information to identify the secret number correctly.

Materials

- *Digit Place* Recording Sheet (REPRODUCIBLE 17), 1 per group of players
- pencil, 1 per player

Players

2 or 4

Directions

1. Decide who is Player 1.

2. Player 1 chooses a secret two-digit number. The two digits must be different.

3. The other player or players make a guess at the number. The guess is recorded in the first column of the recording sheet.

4. Player 1 records how many digits are correct in the Digits column and how many of those digits are in the correct place in the Place column.

5. Repeat Steps 3 and 4 until the number is guessed.

6. Switch roles so that a different player now chooses the secret two-digit number. Repeat Steps 3 and 4 until the number is guessed.

Game 12: Equation Building

Objective

During this game, players build equations based on numbers rolled with the dice. Players then turn those cards face down that share the same answer or answers as their equations. The objective of the game is to be the first player to turn all twenty cards of his or her color face down.

Materials

- dice (1 labeled *0–5*, 1 labeled *5–10*), 2 for each player
- playing cards (face cards and Jokers removed; Aces remain to represent the value of 1), 1 deck per pair of players
- paper and pencil, 1 per player

Players

2

Directions

1. Decide who is Player 1 and who is Player 2.

2. Players sort their deck of cards into red and black cards. Player 1 takes all the red cards and places them in numerical order (or an order that works for him), face up, on the table. Player 2 takes all the black cards and places them in numerical order (or an order that works for her), face up, on the table. Each player should have twenty cards.

3. Player 1 rolls the dice and creates equations with the numbers rolled. He may use any one of the four operations (addition, subtraction, multiplication, division) as long as the answer is a whole number. Player 1 records his equations for Player 2 to see.

4. Player 1 asks Player 2, "Do you agree with my equations and answers?" If the answer is no, Player 2 works with Player 1 until they come to an agreement.

5. Player 1 goes back to his line of red cards. He turns the cards face down that have the same numbers as the *answers* of the equations.

6. Alternate turns and repeat Steps 3–5.

7. Play continues; the first player to turn all twenty cards face down is the winner.

Game 13: Fifteen-Number Cross-Out

Objective

During this game, each player creates a list of numbers. Players then take turns rolling the dice. They add the numbers rolled and decompose the sum, then select either the sum or a combination of numbers in the decomposition to cross out on their lists. The objective of the game is to be the first player to cross out all the numbers on his or her list. Alternatively, both players might reach a point when they can no longer cross out numbers based on the sum; the winner is then the player with the fewest numbers remaining on his or her list.

Materials

- dice (labeled *1–6*), 2 per pair of players
- *Fifteen-Number Cross-Out* Recording Sheet (REPRODUCIBLE 18), 1 per pair of players

Players

2

Directions

1. Determine who is Player 1 and who is Player 2.

2. Using the recording sheet, each player makes a list of ten additional numbers. Use the three rules to guide your decisions.

Three Rules for Adding Ten More Numbers

1. The ten additional numbers may consist of any number 1–9, including more 5s.

2. Numbers may be repeated.

3. Not every number has to be used.

3. Player 1 rolls the dice and adds the two numbers rolled. The player announces the sum to her partner.

4. Both players now need to decompose the sum. Record your work in the space provided under the list on your recording sheet.

5. Now choose either the sum *or* one of the combinations and cross the chosen numbers off your lists. Both players cross off numbers; only one combination or sum can be crossed off on each list.

6. Player 2 rolls the dice and adds the two numbers rolled. The player announces the sum to his partner.

7. Repeat Steps 4–5. The game continues as long as a player is able to cross out a number or numbers on his or her list. If a player cannot make the sum with any numbers that remain on his or her list, that player waits until the next roll.

8. The game is won in two ways:

   a. The first player to cross out all the numbers on his or her list is the winner.

   or

   b. Both players reach a point when they can no longer cross out numbers; the winner is then the player with the fewest numbers remaining on his or her list.

Note: Reproducible 18 has space for three games to be played.

Game 14: Finding Factors

Objective

During this game, players take turns selecting numbers on the game board and identifying the number's factors. The first player selects and circles the number using her colored marker; the second player identifies and circles the number's factors using his colored marker. The objective of the game is to be the player with the highest score at the end. A player's score is the total of all the numbers circled in his or her color.

Materials

- markers or crayons, 2 per pair of players (each a different color)
- *Finding Factors* Game Board (REPRODUCIBLE 20 or 21), 1 per pair of players

Players

2

Directions

1. Decide who is Player 1 and who is Player 2. Each player chooses a different-color marker or crayon.

2. Player 1 chooses a number on the game board and circles it with her marker.

3. Player 2 finds all the factors for the number and circles those with his marker.

4. Player 2 chooses a number on the game board and circles it with his marker.

5. Player 1 finds all the factors for the number and circles those with her marker.

6. Players repeat Steps 2–5 until there are no factors left for the remaining numbers, alternating who circles the number first.

7. Players tally their scores by adding all the numbers of the same color together. Players show their work in the space below or next to the game board.

8. The player with the highest score is the winner.

GAME TIP
**Selecting Numbers with
No Factors Left: An Illegal Move**
Selecting a number with no factors remaining is an illegal move and that player loses his or her turn; the other player gets to play twice in a row (meaning, he or she gets to circle 2 numbers).

Game 15: Greater Than, Less Than, Equal To

Objective

During this game, players take turns drawing numeral cards and completing number sentences. Together, players determine which symbol (>, <, or =) goes with each sentence. The player with the greater sum keeps all four cards from the round. The objective of the game is to have the most cards at the end (ten rounds); this player is the winner.

Materials

- Numeral Cards 0–10 (REPRODUCIBLE B), 1 deck per pair of players
- *Greater Than, Less Than, Equal To* Recording Sheet (REPRODUCIBLES 22, 23, 24, or 25), 1 per pair of players

Players

2

Directions

1. Decide who is Player 1 and who is Player 2.

2. Player 1 draws two numeral cards from the stack and records the numbers in the blanks under Player 1 on the recording sheet.

3. Player 2 draws two more cards and records the numbers in the blanks under Player 2 on the recording sheet.

4. Together, compare the sides of the equation. Ask each other, "Which symbol will make the number sentence true?" Write the symbol in the box.

5. Compare sums. The player with the greater sum keeps all four cards from the round.

6. Repeat Steps 2–5 until all number sentences are complete on the recording sheet (ten rounds).

7. Together, complete the sentences on the bottom portion of the recording sheet.

8. Count your cards. The player with the most cards is the winner.

Symbols Key
= equal to
> greater than
< less than

Game 16: Hit the Target (Mental Multiplication)

Objective

During this game, players choose a target range and multiplicand. They then pick multipliers that they think, when multiplied by the multiplicand, will get a product between the target range numbers. The objective of the game is to hit the target (get a product between the target range numbers).

Materials

- paper and pencil, 1 per player

Players

2

Directions

1. Players decide who is Player 1 and who is Player 2.

2. Players choose a target range and write it on their paper.

Choosing a Target Range
There are three main ways a target range can be decided:

1. The range can be chosen by the class.

2. The range can be chosen by rolling a 1–6 die three times, then creating the largest number possible from the combination of three numbers, and adding 50 to get the range. For example, if a 4, 6, and 2 are rolled, the largest number is 642. Then, add 50 to the number to create the target range. In this case, the target range is 642–692.

3. The range can be chosen by selecting a target range from the target range charts posted around the classroom.

3. Player 1 picks a multiplicand—a number between 3 and 29. Player 1 writes the number on the paper.

4. Player 2 picks a multiplier—a number that he or she thinks, when multiplied by the multiplicand, will get a product between the target range numbers. Player 2 writes the number sentence on the paper.

5. Players work together to solve the number sentence. Compute mentally as much as possible. Player 2 writes the product on the paper.

6. Players discuss: Does the product hit the target? Why or why not? Players then proceed with one of the following, depending on the outcome:

   a. If the product does *not* hit the target, repeat Steps 4 and 5, with Player 2 picking another multiplier. Play continues until a product is reached that hits the target (lands within the range).

   b. If the product hits the target, players switch roles; Player 2 now picks a multiplicand and Player 1 picks the multiplier.

7. Players play ten rounds or for a predetermined amount of time like 20 minutes.

The Multiplicand and Multiplier
Remember, the multiplicand (the number first picked) remains the same until the target is hit; only the multiplier changes.

Game 17: How Close to 0?

Objective

During this game, players take turns rolling the die, assigning the number rolled a ones value or a tens value, and subtracting it from the number rolled previously. The objective is to get a number as close to 0 as possible by Round 7. If a player reaches or goes below 0 *before* Round 7, the other player wins.

Materials

- die (labeled *1–6*), 1 per pair of players
- pencil, 1 per pair of players
- *How Close to 0?* Game Board (REPRODUCIBLE 26), 1 per pair of players

Players

2

Directions

1. Decide who is Player 1 and who is Player 2.

2. Player 1 rolls the die and assigns a ones value or a tens value to the number rolled.

3. Player 1 subtracts the number from 100 and records her play on the game board in the Player 1, Round 1 box.

4. Player 2 repeats Steps 2 and 3, recording his computation in the Round 1, Player 2 box.

5. Player 1 now rolls the die a second time and assigns a ones value or a tens value to the number rolled.

6. Player 1 subtracts the number from the difference she calculated in Round 1 and records her play on the game board in the Player 1, Round 2 box.

7. Player 2 repeats Steps 5 and 6, recording his computation in the Player 2, Round 2 box.

8. Play continues for a total of 7 rounds. The difference in Round 2 becomes the starting number in Round 3, the difference in Round 3 becomes the starting number in Round 4, and so on.

9. The player closer to 0 after 7 rounds is the winner. If a player reaches or goes below 0 before Round 7, the game is over and the other player wins.

Game 18A: Leftovers with 15

Objective

Player 1 rolls the die and distributes the 15 tiles equally among the corresponding number of plates. Player 1 records the problem and keeps the tiles that are the remainder, and Player 2 starts off using only the tiles that were on the plates. Players take turns modeling and recording division problems. The game continues until no tiles are left to divide. The objective is to be the player at the end of the game with the highest sum of remainders (leftovers).

Materials

- color tiles, 15 per pair of players
- cup (to hold tiles), 1 per pair of players
- paper plates or coffee filters, 6 per pair of players
- die (labeled *1–6*), 1 per pair of players
- pencil and ruled paper

Players

2

Directions

1. Decide who is Player 1 and who is Player 2.

2. Player 1 rolls the die and lays out that number of paper plates.

3. Player 1 then takes the cup of tiles and divides the tiles equally onto the plates, keeping any leftover tiles aside.

4. Player 1 says and records the math equation that describes the plates and tiles. For example, "Fifteen divided into two groups is seven in each group, with a remainder of one." Player 1 records:

$$15 \div 2 = 7 \, R \, 1$$

5. Player 1 initials the equation and returns *only* the tiles that are on the plates to the cup for the next player's turn.

6. Player 2 repeats Steps 2–5. For example, Player 2 might roll 4, thus distributing the fourteen tiles among four plates and saying, "Fourteen divided into four groups is three with a remainder of two." Player 2 records:

$$14 \div 4 = 3 \, R \, 2$$

and returns the 12 tiles on the plates to the cup.

7. Player 1 now continues with the 12 tiles. Play alternates until all the tiles are gone.

8. Each player counts the number of tiles collected as remainders. The winner is the player with the most remainders—referred to as *leftovers*!

Game 18B: Leftovers with 100

Objective

During this version of *Leftovers,* players start by selecting and dividing a number 1–20 into the start number 100. The remainder becomes the first player's score. The second player subtracts the remainder from the start number to determine the next "new" start number. The game continues until the start number is 0. The objective is to be the player at the end with the highest sum of remainders (leftovers).

Materials

- pencil and ruled paper

Players

2

Directions

1. Decide who is Player 1 and who is Player 2.

2. Write the numbers *1–20* across the top of the paper and the words *Start number* near the margin. The start number is 100.

> 1 2 3 4 5 6 7 8 9 10 11 12 13 14 15 16 17 18 19 20
> Start number: 100

3. Player 1 chooses one of the numbers from 1–20 and crosses it out. Player 1 then divides the start number by that number. The remainder becomes Player 1's score. Player 1 marks the remainder with her initial.

4. Player 1 then subtracts the remainder from the start number to determine the next start number. An example of Steps 3 and 4 is shown here:

> 1 2 3 4 5 6 7 ✗ 9 10 11 12 13 14 15 16 17 18 19 20
> Start number: 100
> 100 ÷ 8 = 12 r 4 *B.P.*
> 96

5. Player 2 selects a different number from numbers 1–20 and crosses it out. Player 2 then divides the new start number by it. The remainder becomes Player 2's score. Player 2 marks the remainder with his initial.

6. Play continues until the start number is 0.

7. Players add their remainders. The player with the larger sum is the winner.

Game 19: Making Moves on the Hundreds Chart

Objective

During this game, players roll a specially labeled die to determine the corresponding number of spaces to move on a hundreds chart. The objective is to be the first player to land exactly on the square numbered 99.

Materials

- Hundreds Chart (REPRODUCIBLE A), 2 per pair of players

- game markers (counters or interlocking cubes of two different colors, for example), 2 per pair of players

- die (labeled *+10, +10, +10, −10, +1, −1*), 1 per pair of players

- paper and pencil, 1 per pair of players

Players

2

Directions

1. Decide who is Player 1 and who is Player 2.

2. Each player titles a piece of paper *Making Moves on the Hundreds Chart* to record their moves.

3. Each player places a game marker in the margin next to the 1 square on his or her hundreds chart.

4. Player 1 rolls the die and moves her marker the corresponding number of spaces.

5. Player 2 checks Player 1's accuracy. If the move is correct, Player 1 records the move as a number sentence.

6. Player 2 repeats Steps 3–5 using his hundreds chart.

7. The first player to land on square 99 exactly is the winner.

Impossible Moves

Sometimes a corresponding move on the hundreds chart will not be possible. For example, if a −1 is rolled as the first roll of the game, the player will not be able to move his game marker. Or, if the player is on square 98 and rolls a +10, the player will not be able to move his game marker. In the case of an impossible move, the player loses a turn.

Game 20: Missing Addend or Factor (Salute!)

Objective

During this game, two players start by each drawing a card and placing it on their forehead, number side facing out. The third player studies both cards and announces the sum of the two numbers. The other two players take turns figuring out the number they have on the card against their forehead. The first player to figure out his or her number wins both cards. The game continues until all the cards have been used. The objective is to be the player with the most cards at the end; the player with the most cards then plays the role of Player 3, the player who calls out the sums. This game can also be played as *Missing Factor,* using multiplication.

Missing Factor
To practice multiplication, the cards become factors and the third player calls out the product of the two numbers.

Materials

- Numeral Cards 0–10 (REPRODUCIBLE B), 1 deck per group of three players

  or

- playing cards, 1 deck per group of three players (face cards and Jokers removed; Aces remain to represent the value of 1)

Players
3

Directions

1. Shuffle the deck of cards and place the deck face down on a table or desk.

2. Decide who is Player 1, Player 2, and Player 3.

3. Players 1 and 2 each draw a card from the stack and quickly place the card to their forehead, number side facing out. Players 1 and 2 do *not* look at the number on their cards.

4. Player 3 calls out the sum of the two numbers.

5. The first player to name the addend he or she is holding to his or her forehead wins the round and collects both cards.

6. Repeat Steps 3 and 4 until all cards have been drawn.

7. The winner is the player with the most cards. Rotate roles; the player with the most cards now becomes Player 3 and calls the sums.

8. Shuffle the cards and play again.

A Deck of Cards
For the purpose of this game, a deck of numeral cards is four copies of each numeral card listed in the materials.

Game 21: More!

Objective

Players are dealt equally all the cards from a deck of playing cards. They each draw one card from their pile and compare the face value of the cards. The player with the greater value determines the difference between the two values and connects the corresponding number of interlocking cubes. As play continues, players continue to connect cubes; each player has a stick of cubes when all cards have been played. Players then compare the lengths, count their stick of cubes, and record the amount. The objective of the game is to build and compare visual representations of numbers.

Materials

- playing cards (Jokers removed; Aces are optional and represent the value of 1), 1 deck per pair of players
- interlocking cubes, approximately 150 per pair of players
- *More!* Recording Sheet (REPRODUCIBLE 27), 1 per pair of players
- pencil, 1 per pair of players

Players

2

Value of Face Cards

Ace = 1 (optional use)

Jack = 11

Queen = 12

King = 13

Directions

1. Decide who is Player 1 and who is Player 2.

2. Player 1 shuffles the deck of playing cards and deals all cards so each player has 26 cards.

3. Both players stack their cards in a pile neatly, face down, in front of them.

4. Both players take the top card from their pile and turn it over.

5. Players compare the face value of the cards. The player with the greater value represents the difference in values by using interlocking cubes. For example, if the difference is 3, the player with the greater value takes three interlocking cubes and snaps them together.

   (If the cards drawn happen to be the same value, set the cards aside, draw two new cards, and continue play.)

6. Repeat Steps 4 and 5, until all the cards are played. Players should always add on to their existing train of interlocking cubes so that, at the end of the game, each player has a stick of cubes.

7. When all cards have been played, compare the length of the interlocking cubes and record the total of each and the difference between them.

8. Play the game a second time.

9. After two games have been played, total your points for both games, record the sums in the TOTAL row, and again find the difference.

Game 22: Odd or Even?

Objective

Players work in pairs using a deck of playing cards. They start by taking the top two cards from the stack and placing the cards face side up, one overlapping the other. If the sum of the two cards is an even number, players "win" the cards and set them aside in their pile. Players then take two more cards from the deck. If the sum is odd, players take a third card from the deck and place it face up, once again overlapping it on the top card. Now if the top two cards are even, the players "win" these two cards and remove them from play. Play continues in this fashion, with players always looking at only the last two cards played. After all cards have been played, players count to see how many cards are in their pile versus in the pile formed by the deck. The winner (the players or the deck) is the one with the most cards. The goal of the game is to improve one's understanding of even and odd numbers while simultaneously "sparring" with a deck of cards.

Materials

- playing cards (face cards and Jokers removed; Aces remain to represent the value of 1), 1 deck per pair of players

  or

- Numeral Cards 1–10 (REPRODUCIBLE B), 1 deck per pair of players

Players

2

Directions

1. Shuffle the deck of playing cards and place them in a neat stack, face down.

2. Take the top two cards from the deck and turn them over. Place them face side up, overlapping, next to the deck.

3. Is the sum of the two numbers odd or even?

   a. If the sum is an even number, remove both cards from play and place them aside in a pile. You are playing against the deck and these are the cards you've won. Then, take two more cards from the deck and think: Is the sum of the two numbers odd or even? Continue play accordingly.

   The sum of these cards is the even number 8, so both would be removed from play.

   b. If the sum is an odd number, draw a third card from the deck and place it so that it overlaps the top card. If the two new top cards are even, you "win" them again; place them in your pile. Draw another card from the deck and place it so it overlaps the remaining card. The remaining card forms the beginning of the deck's pile of wins.

   The sum of the first two cards was an odd number 7, so a third card was drawn. The sum of the top two cards is now even (3 + 9 = 12), so these two cards are removed from play. The 4 card is placed in a separate deck.

4. Continue playing, repeating Step 3, until all the cards in the deck have been played.

5. To determine the winner, count the number of cards you and your partner have in your pile, then count the cards that remain with the deck. If you and your partner have more cards than the number of cards in the deck, you win!

Game 23: Oh No! 20!

Objective

During this game, two players (or two teams of two) play a hand of four cards each, adding or subtracting card values strategically until one player's (or team's) sum is or exceeds twenty. The objective of the game is not to be the first player (or team) to get to twenty or more.

Materials

- playing cards (6, 7, 8, 9, 10, and Jokers removed; face cards remain; Aces remain to represent the value of 1), 1 deck per pair of players

  or

- Numeral Cards 1–5 (REPRODUCIBLE B) plus four cards marked –5, four cards marked 0, and four wild cards, 1 deck per pair of players

---

Values of Face Cards

For the purpose of this game, a deck of playing cards is four of each number 2–5 (cards 6–10 removed) plus the face cards, which are assigned the following values:

Ace = 1

Jack = –5 (subtract 5)

Queen = 0

King: wild card (any number 1, 2, 3, 4, 5, –5, or 0)

Players

2 or two teams of 2

Directions

1. Decide who is Player 1 and who is Player 2. If playing in teams, decide who is on Team 1 and who is on Team 2.

2. Shuffle the deck of playing cards and deal four cards to each player or team.

3. Player or Team 1 starts by selecting a card from the hand of four cards and placing it in the middle of the playing area.

4. Player or Team 2 then selects a card from the hand of four cards, places it in the middle next to Player or Team 1's selected card, then announces the sum of the two cards.

5. Players or teams each draw one more card from the stack so they have four cards each.

6. Now Player or Team 1 selects a card from the hand of four cards, places it down, and announces the sum by adding the value to the existing sum.

7. Player or Team 1 then takes a new card from the stack to continue to have four cards in hand.

8. Player or Team 2 repeats Steps 6 and 7, building on Player or Team 1's new sum.

9. Play continues, alternating turns between the players or teams until one player's or team's sum is twenty or more.

   Remember: The objective of the game is *not* to be the first player or team to get twenty or more!

Game 24: Order Up 21!

Objective

After drawing four cards or rolling the four dice, players build an equation using all four numbers and applying the order of operations (parentheses, exponents, multiplication, division, addition, and subtraction). The objective is to build an equation that totals twenty-one. After each round, a player's or team's score is determined by how far away their total is from twenty-one. After ten rounds, the player or team with the lowest score is the winner.

Materials

- playing cards (face cards and Jokers removed; Aces remain and represent the value of 1), 1 deck per pair of players

  or

- Numeral Cards 0–10 (REPRODUCIBLE B), 1 deck per player, pair, or group of players

  or

- dice (2 labeled *0–5*, 2 labeled *5–10*), 2 of each per player, pair, or group of players

- *Order Up 21!* Recording Sheet (REPRODUCIBLE 28), 1 per player or pair of players

Players

1, 2, or 4

Directions

1. If playing in pairs, decide who is Player 1 and who is Player 2. If playing in teams, decide who is on Team 1 and who is on Team 2.

2. Roll all four dice or draw four cards.

3. Each player or team builds an equation using the four numbers and following the rules for building equations. Players write the equation on their recording sheet.

4. After each player or team has built an equation, determine the scores. The score for each round is how far away the total is from twenty-one. Players record their scores on the recording sheet.

5. Play ten rounds. After ten rounds, total your scores. The player or team with the lowest score is the winner.

A Deck of Cards

For the purpose of this game, a deck of cards is four of each number Ace (1)–10. If using a deck of playing cards, the 0 is not available.

Game Rules for Building Equations

- Players may use any combination of the four operations (addition, subtraction, multiplication, division).

- The numbers may be used in any order, but may only be used once. If a number is drawn/rolled twice, the number must be used twice in the equation.

- Remember to use parentheses.

- Numbers may be used as exponents.

- Numbers may also be used to form factions equivalent to whole numbers.

- Equations must be accurate mathematically.

Scoring

Points are determined by how far away the total of the equation is from 21. A score of 0 point means the player got exactly 21. A score of 1 point means the player got either 20 or 22. The goal is to have the lowest score.

Game 25A: Pathways (Products Tic-Tac-Toe)

Objective

Players select factors, multiply them, and cover the corresponding product on the game board. The objective of the game is to be the first player to complete a continuous pathway across the game board, from one side to the other.

Materials

- paper clips, 2 per pair of players
- game markers, 2 sets of 10 (each set a different color)
- *Pathways* Game Board
  (REPRODUCIBLES 30, 31, 32, or 33)

Players

2

Directions

1. Decide who is Player 1 and who is Player 2, and the color game marker each player will use.

2. Look at the factors listed at the bottom of the game board. Player 1 chooses two factors and places a paper clip over each.

3. Player 1 then multiplies the factors and covers the corresponding product on the game board with one of her game markers. *Remember:* Both paper clips may be placed on the same factor!

4. Player 2 moves just one of the paper clips to another factor, multiplies the two numbers, and places one of his game markers on the product.

5. Repeat Step 4, alternating turns. The winner is the first player to make a continuous pathway across the game board.

A Pathway
A pathway may include boxes that share a common side or common corner. Pathways move across the game board from left to right, not from top to bottom (although pathways will move up and down).

Game 25B: Times Ten

Objective

Players select factors, multiply them, and cover the corresponding product on the game board. The objective of the game is to be the first player to complete a continuous pathway across the game board, from one side to the other.

Materials

- paper clips, 2 per pair of players
- cubes, tiles, counters, or other game markers (2 sets of 10, each set a different color), 20 per pair of players
- *Times Ten* Game Board (REPRODUCIBLES 34, 35, 36, or 37), 1 per pair of players

Players

2

Directions

1. Decide who is Player 1 and who is Player 2, and the color game marker each player will use.

2. Look at the factors listed at the bottom of the game board. Player 1 chooses two factors and places a paper clip over each.

3. Player 1 multiplies the factors, determines the product, and then multiples the product by ten. Player 1 then covers the final product on the game board with one of her game markers. *Remember:* Both paper clips may be placed on the same factor!

4. Player 2 moves just one of the paper clips to another factor, multiplies the two numbers, and then multiples the product by ten. Player 2 places one of his game markers on the final product.

5. Repeat Step 4, alternating turns. The winner is the first player to make a continuous pathway across the game board.

A Pathway
A pathway may include boxes that share a common side or common corner. Pathways move across the game board from left to right, not from top to bottom (although pathways will move up and down).

Game 26: Roll 6 for 100

Objective

The objective of the game is to get to 100 or as close to 100 as possible (but not over!) through a combination of adding and multiplying the numbers rolled using a die. The die may be rolled up to six times. After each roll, players record an addition equation/number string. At any time up to six rolls, a player can decide to end her participation in the round by recording a multiplication equation. The other player may continue the round up to six rolls; the player closest to 100 is the winner.

Materials

- die (labeled *1–6*), 1 per pair of players
- *Roll 6 for 100* Recording Sheet (REPRODUCIBLE 38), 2 per pair of players
- pencil and ruled paper

Players

2

Directions

1. Decide who is Player 1 and who is Player 2.

2. Player 1 rolls the die and records the number on his recording sheet.

3. Player 1 rolls the die a second time, adding the number to the first and recording the equation.

4. Player 1 repeats Step 3 until he feels he has rolled a number that, when multiplied by the previous sum, will get him as close to 100 as possible. After the player multiplies, his round is done. The player has up to (but not more than!) six rolls. On the sixth roll, the player *must* multiply.

5. Player 2 repeats Steps 2–4, recording her equations/number string on her recording sheet.

6. After both players have completed a round, they determine the winner—the player with the total closest to but not more than 100. Players fill out the scoring sentence frames on their recording sheets.

7. Each player plays four more rounds of the game.

Game 27A: Roll for $1.00

Objective

Players take turns rolling a die, assigning the rolled number a value of penny or dime, and collecting that number of pennies or dimes. When players accumulate enough pennies to equate a dime, they must exchange their pennies for a dime. The objective of the game is to form a collection of pennies and dimes that totals exactly or as close to $1.00 as possible, but does not go over $1.00. A round consists of each player having seven turns (rolls).

Materials

- die (labeled *1–6*), 1 per pair of players
- 30 pennies and 20 dimes, per pair of players
- *Roll for $1.00* Game Boards (REPRODUCIBLE 40), 1 for each player

Players

2

Directions

1. Decide who is Player 1 and who is Player 2.

2. Player 1 rolls the die, decides whether the number rolled represents pennies or dimes, and places the corresponding number of coins in the appropriate space on his game board.

3. Player 2 rolls the die, decides whether the number rolled represents pennies or dimes, and places the corresponding number of coins in the appropriate space on her game board.

4. Players continue to take turns rolling the die and assigning a penny or dime value to the roll. When players have ten or more pennies, they must exchange their pennies for a dime. The dime can be placed in any space on the game board in the Dimes column.

5. The game is over after each player has taken seven rolls. Players total their coins. The winner is the player who has exactly or the closest to $1.00 (but not more!). Players who go over $1.00 are out.

Game 27B: Roll for 1

Objective

Players take turns rolling a die and assigning the rolled number a value of .1 or .01. At the end of seven turns (rolls) per player, players add up their hundredths and tenths to determine who is closer to (but not over!) the whole number one. The closest player is the winner.

Materials

- die (labeled *1–6*), 1 per pair of players
- *Roll for 1* Recording Sheets (REPRODUCIBLE 41), 1 per player
- calculators (optional)

Players

2

Directions

1. Decide who is Player 1 and who is Player 2.

2. Player 1 rolls the die and decides if the number rolled represents tenths or hundredths.

3. Player 1 records the play on her recording sheet.

4. Player 2 follows Steps 2 and 3.

5. Play alternates until each player has had seven turns (rolls).

6. The winner is the player who is the closest to (but not over!) one. Players who go over one are out.

Game 28: Spinning Sums and Differences

Objective

Player 1 rolls the die and spins the place value spinner. The die provides the number and the spin determines the place value of the number rolled. Player 1 rolls and spins a second time, generating a second number. Player 2 does the same thing—rolls and spins, rolls and spins—creating two numbers. Using the numbers, players write two equations—one addition equation and one subtraction equation. Players solve both equations and check each other's sum and difference. The largest sum and difference each earn 1 point; the player with the highest score at the end of ten rounds is the winner.

Materials

- die (labeled *1–6*), per pair of players
- Place Value Spinner (REPRODUCIBLE 42 or REPRODUCIBLE 43), 1 per pair of players
- paper clip, 1 per pair of players
- *Spinning Sums and Differences* Recording Sheet (REPRODUCIBLE 44), 1 per player
- paper and pencil

Players

2

Directions

1. Decide who is Player 1 and who is Player 2.

2. Player 1 rolls the die and spins the place value spinner. The die determines the number; the spinner determines the place value of the number. Player 1 records the number on her recording sheet.

3. Player 1 repeats Step 1 to create a second number.

4. Player 2 follows Steps 1 and 2 to generate his 2 numbers.

5. Each player uses the two numbers he or she generated to write 2 equations—1 addition equation and 1 subtraction equation.

6. Players solve both equations.

7. Players check each other's sum and difference; if there is disagreement, share your thinking.

8. Now determine the score of the round. The largest sum and difference each win 1 point.

9. Continue playing for ten rounds.

10. Total your scores using the recording sheet. The player with the highest total score is the winner.

Game 29: Take Five, Make Ten!

Objective

Players draw five cards and use the numbers to build five equations, each of which totals 10. The equations can involve addition, subtraction, multiplication, and division. Players keep track of their equations for each round. Each player earns 1 point for each equation built. Each round can be worth up to 5 points.

Materials

- playing cards (10s, face cards, and Jokers removed; Aces remain to represent a value of 1), 1 deck per player or pair of players

  or

- Numeral Cards 1–9 (REPRODUCIBLE B), 1 deck per player or pair of players

- paper and pencil

Players

1–2

Directions

1. Shuffle the deck of cards and draw five cards.

2. Using the numbers on the cards, build five equations, each totaling 10. Follow the game rules.

GAME RULES

- Addition, subtraction, multiplication, and division operations can be used.

- A minimum of two and maximum of five of the numbers can be used.

- Numbers cannot be repeated in the same equation unless there are two of the same number cards.

3. Record the five equations on paper.

4. The end of the game is determined when all cards have been played (typically six rounds).

5. The winner is the person with the most points (1 point per equation that equals 10).

EXAMPLE ROUND

If the cards Ace (1), 2, 3, 4, and 8 are drawn, possible equations are:

$8 + 2$

$8 + 4 - 2$

$8 + 3 - 1$

$8 \times 1 + 2$

$1 + 2 + 3 + 4$

Game 30: Target 300
(A Multiplication Game)

Objective

Players take turns rolling a die and multiplying the number rolled by ten or multiples of ten through fifty. The goal is to be the player with a total sum of exactly or closest to 300 after five rolls.

Materials

- die (labeled *1–6*), 1 per pair of players
- *Target 300 (A Multiplication Game)* Recording Sheets (REPRODUCIBLE 46), 1 per player

Players

2

Directions

1. Decide who is Player 1 and who is Player 2.

2. Player 1 rolls the die and decides whether to multiply the number rolled by 10, 20, 30, 40, or 50.

3. Both players record the multiplication sentence in the column Player 1 on their recording sheets. For example, if Player 1 rolls a 4 and decides to multiply it by 20, both players record:

ROUND	PLAYER I Name _____	PLAYER 2 Name _____
I	$4 \times 20 = 80$	

4. Player 2 repeats Steps 2 and 3, and both players record the mathematics in the column Player 2 on their recording sheets.

5. After each player has had five turns, both players add the products for all five rounds. The winner is the player closest to 300. Note that the total sum may go over 300.

Game 31: Target "Pick Your Sum"

Objective

To start, players decide on a target sum between 25 and 55. During each turn, a player covers a number on the game board and adds it to the previously covered number or numbers. Players or teams continue to add to the running total during every turn, attempting to be the first to get to the target sum. The first player or team to reach the target sum exactly is the winner.

Materials

- *Target "Pick Your Sum"* Game Board (REPRODUCIBLE 47), 1 per pair or group of players

- counters (discs, coins, beans, or tiles of any color), 20 per pair or group of players

Players

2–4

Directions

1. If playing in pairs, decide who is Player 1 and who is Player 2. If playing in teams, decide who is on Team 1 and who is on Team 2.

2. Choose a target sum between 25 and 55. Record it where all players can see it.

3. Player or Team 1 covers a number on the game board with his counter.

4. Player or Team 2 covers another number on the game board and adds that number to the first number covered. Player or Team 2 announces the sum aloud. For example, if Player or Team 1 places a counter on the number 4 and Player or Team 2 places a counter on the number 3, Player or Team 2 says, "Four plus three equals seven."

5. Player or Team 1 covers another number (for example, the number 5), adds that number to the running total, and states his thinking aloud. So, for our example, Player or Team 1 says, "Seven plus five equals twelve." Alternatively, Player or Team 1 can also add all the covered numbers, "Four plus three plus five equals twelve."

6. Repeat Step 5, with players or teams alternating turns. The first player or team to reach the target sum exactly is the winner. If a player or team goes over the target sum, they are out. If the remaining numbers on the game board are all too low to reach the target sum, players or teams must start the game over.

Reminder: Each square may only be covered once!

Game 32: Tens Go Fish

Objective

Players put aside pairs of cards that add up to ten. Then, players take turns asking each other for a number card they need to make a pair that adds up to ten. Play continues until all the cards in the deck are used up or until one player goes out by having no remaining cards to play.

Materials

- playing cards (10s, face cards, and Jokers removed; Aces remain to represent a value of 1), 1 deck per pair of players

  or

- Numeral Cards 0–10 (REPRODUCIBLE B), 1 deck per pair of players

Players

2–4

Directions

1. If playing in pairs, decide who is Player 1 and who is Player 2. If playing in teams, decide who is on Team 1 and who is on Team 2.

2. One player or team shuffles and deals the cards, five to each player. Place the remaining cards face down in the middle, either in a stack or a "fishing pond" (spreading cards face down in a pool-like array).

3. Players or teams examine their cards. Are there any pairs in their hand that, when added, make ten? If so, players or teams place those pairs near them on the table and draw two cards to replace the cards played.

4. Now players or teams alternate turns. During turns, players or teams ask for a card that will go with a card in their hand to make ten. For example, if Player or Team 1 is holding an 8 but not a 2, he might ask the other player or team for a 2. Two things can happen in this case (and on every turn):

   a. If Player or Team 1 gets the card requested to make ten, Player or Team 1 puts the pair of cards aside. Player or Team 1's turn then continues; Player or Team 1 asks for another card that makes a ten with any of the cards in his remaining hand.

   b. If Player or Team 2 does not have the requested card that makes a ten, Player or Team 1 takes the top card from the deck (or chooses a card from the fishing pond). If the new card makes a ten with any of the cards in Player or Team 1's hand, Player or Team 1 sets that pair aside and continues to draw and pair cards. Player or Team 1's turn is over when they no longer have a pair of cards in hand that makes ten.

5. A winner is determined in two ways:

   a. If a player or team has paired all their cards and has no cards left in their hand, they are the winner.

   b. If all the cards are played and no more pairs can be made, the player or team with the most pairs of ten is the winner.

Game 33: Wipeout
(Fractional Relationships)

Objective

Both players begin with the same number (1, 2, or 3) of hexagons (considered the "whole") as well as other pattern blocks (the "parts"): red trapezoids, blue rhombuses, and green triangles. Players roll a special die labeled with fractions ($\frac{1}{2}, \frac{1}{3}, \frac{1}{3}, \frac{1}{3}, \frac{1}{6}, \frac{1}{6}$) and have three options of moves: (1) remove the pattern block represented by the fraction on the die, (2) exchange any of your blocks for equivalent blocks, or (3) do nothing. The objective is to be the first player to discard all of your pattern blocks.

Materials

- pattern blocks (6 yellow hexagons, 12 red trapezoids, 18 blue rhombuses, and 36 green triangles), 1 set per pair of players
- die (faces labeled $\frac{1}{2}, \frac{1}{3}, \frac{1}{3}, \frac{1}{3}, \frac{1}{6}, \frac{1}{6}$), 1 per pair of players

Players

2

Pattern Blocks

Although 18 blue rhombuses and 36 green triangles allow for the most options when playing this game, if you have a limited supply of pattern blocks, 12 of each (rhombuses and triangles) should suffice.

Directions

1. Decide together how many yellow hexagons you want to play with—1, 2, or 3. Place the corresponding number of hexagons in front of each player.

2. Take turns rolling the die. On his or her turn the player has three options of moves to make (see "Three Moves in the Game").

3. The winner is the first player to discard all of his or her pattern blocks.

Reminder: Equivalent parts may not be substituted. In the game of Wipeout, equivalent parts may not be substituted. For example, two triangles (each having the value of $\frac{1}{6}$) may not be removed if a $\frac{1}{3}$ (represented by the rhombus) is rolled. Only a rhombus may be removed.

Three Moves in the Game
Roll the die and:

1. Remove the pattern block that the fraction on the die represents,

2. Trade in any of your remaining pattern blocks for an equivalent portion, or

3. Do nothing.

Note that you can only choose one of these moves on each turn. You may not remove a pattern block (move 1) and trade in pattern blocks (move 2) in one turn.